Research Series on Responsible Enterprise Ecosystems

This book series focuses on sustainability, governance, and diversity in SMEs, small businesses, and startups. The series aims to unlock the potential of sustainability, governance, and diversity within SMEs, fostering a new era of responsible and inclusive entrepreneurship.

Delving into the challenges and opportunities of sustainable practices and governance in these organizations, it provides a platform for scholars, researchers, and practitioners to share their valuable insights and experiences. The series encourages and features innovative approaches, best practices, and real-life case studies, showcasing successful integration of sustainability, governance, and diversity principles. This diverse collection of knowledge will resonate with readers from various backgrounds, including law, management, accounting, CSR practices, and more, encouraging a cross-disciplinary dialogue. From circular economy models to gender diversity initiatives, the books offer pragmatic solutions for sustainable corporate governance. As the world navigates socio-economic and environmental crises, the series also emphasizes the resilience of SMEs in regenerating societies. By championing ethical conduct and inclusiveness, the series envisions SMEs as powerful drivers of positive change.

With each volume maintaining a coherent pedagogy and content style, the series is a must-have resource for educators, managers, entrepreneurs, and scholars alike.

Yahaya Alhassan • Samuel Salia
Javed Hussain • Giuseppe Umberto Cantafio
Editors

Financial Innovation and Sustainable Enterprise in Developing and Emerging Economies

Modern FinTech Solutions to Ensure Inclusivity and Accessibility

Springer

Editors
Yahaya Alhassan
University of Sunderland in London
London, UK

Samuel Salia
Birmingham City University
Birmingham, UK

Javed Hussain
Birmingham City University
Birmingham, UK

Giuseppe Umberto Cantafio
American University of Bahrain
Riffa, Bahrain

ISSN 3004-8834 ISSN 3004-8842 (electronic)
Research Series on Responsible Enterprise Ecosystems
ISBN 978-3-032-04499-0 ISBN 978-3-032-04500-3 (eBook)
https://doi.org/10.1007/978-3-032-04500-3

This Springer imprint is published by the registered company Springer Nature Switzerland AG
The registered company address is: Gewerbestrasse 11, 6330 Cham, Switzerland

This book is dedicated to the cause of creating a deeper awareness of the intricate relationship between innovative financing technologies, the business environment, and entrepreneurship innovations to promote sustainable enterprises in developing and emerging economies as well as rethinking of the appropriate financing models for supporting the growth and sustainability of enterprises in these regions.

Foreword

In an era marked by mounting environmental challenges and rapid technological advancement, the intersection of financial innovation and sustainable enterprise has emerged as a critical frontier for economic transformation—particularly in developing and emerging economies. *Financial Innovation and Sustainable Enterprise in Developing and Emerging Economies* is a timely and insightful contribution to this evolving discipline, offering a multidimensional exploration of how innovative financial instruments, technologies, and strategies can engender sustainable development.

This book is configured around three pivotal themes. The first, *Green Finance and Sustainable Development*, delves into the transformative potential of green finance as a driver of inclusive growth. From the strategic deployment of diaspora bonds for climate resilience to the integration of eco-marketing and green finance in Uganda's hospitality sector, the chapters in this section illuminate how environmentally conscious financial mechanisms can empower local enterprises and foster long-term sustainability.

The second theme, *Financial Technologies and Sustainable Enterprise Development*, highlights the role of Fintech in reshaping access to capital and markets. Through case studies ranging from agritourism in Western Uganda to global analyses of institutional quality, the authors demonstrate how digital innovation, when aligned with sustainable marketing and governance, can unlock new pathways for enterprise development and economic inclusion.

The final section on *Sustainable Enterprise, Risk and Stock Markets* addresses the resilience of businesses and financial systems in the face of global disruptions such as the COVID-19 pandemic and climate change. These chapters offer critical insights into risk management, stock market behaviour, and adaptive strategies for financial institutions navigating an increasingly volatile world of business.

This book is not only a scholarly resource but also a practical guide for policymakers, entrepreneurs, and development practitioners seeking to harness the power of financial innovation for sustainable impact. It challenges conventional paradigms and presents a compelling case for reimagining finance as a tool for ecological stewardship, social equity, and economic resilience.

As the global community strives towards the Sustainable Development Goals, the insights presented here are both urgent and indispensable. I highly commend the authors for their rigorous research and visionary perspectives, and I invite readers to engage deeply with the ideas within these pages.

Buckinghamshire New University
Wycombe, UKWycombe, UK

Fred A. Yamoah

Preface

The link between financial innovation, enterprise, and sustainability presents a compelling narrative of sustainable business growth and transformation in the developing and emerging world. This book, *Financial Innovation and Sustainable Enterprise in Developing and Emerging Economies*, offers an interdisciplinary examination of how these variables interact to drive sustainable enterprise growth and economic development. We are excited as editors to present this insightful book, which has generated interest from various disciplines and contributors from Africa, Europe, and Asia.

Despite the scholarly attempt made to deepen our understanding of how technological innovation is helping to foster enterprise growth and sustainability across the world, evidence from existing literature suggests that there is a significant gap and lack of research on the intersection between financial innovation, the environment, and enterprise and how this promotes sustainable enterprise and economic growth in developing and emerging economies. For instance, although Woldie and Thomas (2017) shed light on the importance of financial innovation and entrepreneurship, their work broadens the focus on economic growth in emerging nations, making it more generic rather than specific. Similarly, the book edited by Islam et al. (2023) is insightful but fails to demonstrate how innovative financing technologies contribute to sustainable businesses; instead, it explores how innovation and technology, in general, enable emerging economies to achieve business sustainability, which is a significant limitation. The book is also narrow as it focuses only on emerging economies, omitting the intricate relationship between financial innovation and sustainable enterprise in developing economies. Equally, the book by Reyes-Mercado (2021) provides very insightful evidence of the link between entrepreneurship, finance, and technology, but does not explore how these critical concepts foster sustainable enterprise. The book is also generic rather than specific and lacks a clear context within emerging and developing economies. Finally, whilst a book edited by Kayizzi-Mugerwa and Ndulo (2018) is very stimulating and focuses on financial innovation, it fails to show how the financing innovations contribute to sustainable enterprise in developing and emerging economies; rather, it narrows its focus on financing innovation and sustainable development in the context of Africa, which is a significant limitation.

Therefore, it is in the above context that this book seeks to create deeper awareness of the intricate relationship between innovative financing technologies, the environment, entrepreneurship innovations, and sustainable enterprises in developing and emerging economies. This book aims to address this critical gap by examining the nexus between financial innovation, enterprise, and sustainable enterprise development in different regions of the world, particularly Africa, Asia, and Europe. Overall, this book is guided by the following three questions:

(a) How are firms in developing and emerging economies using green finance techniques to achieve sustainable growth and economic development?
(b) What is the link between financial technology and sustainable enterprise development?
(c) How can sustainable enterprises be built in the era of climate change and during and after pandemics?

Each chapter of this book addresses these questions using a thematic approach focusing on both theoretical and empirical analyses. Geographically, the contributors and scope of the book cover Africa, Europe, and Asia, providing a universal knowledge and understanding of the link between financial technology, enterprise, and sustainable firm growth.

Various critical issues are examined by contributors to this book. For instance, how can green finance be used as a catalyst for sustainable economic growth? How can financial innovations such as diaspora ponds be leveraged for climate projects in developing and emerging economies? What role do experiential marketing strategies and financial innovation play in agritourism sustainable enterprise outcomes? What is institutional quality's catalyst role in Fintech and economic development? How can innovative financing and sustainable marketing be integrated to boost sustainable agritourism enterprises? Addressing these critical questions provides an opportunity for the book to offer policy directions for practitioners, academics, and government organizations.

We are convinced that providing a wide-ranging perspective on the nexus between financial innovation and sustainable enterprise as well as exploring this phenomenon from the lenses of developing and emerging economies will provide a timely addition to prior research in this area as well as bring new ideas to the debate.

Below are five compelling reasons why this book stands out from other published competitive books:

(a) This is the first book that delves deep into the nexus between financial innovation and sustainable enterprise in developing and emerging economies.
(b) This book is wide-ranging as it triangulates innovative financing technologies and entrepreneurship innovations and shows how this fosters sustainable enterprise in developing and emerging economies.
(c) The book provides policy direction on how innovative financing technologies and entrepreneurship can be tailored to meet the unique challenges and opportunities of developing and emerging economies.

(d) The book helps the reader to understand how the business environment in the developing world can be optimized to encourage the inception and growth of sustainable enterprises.
(e) The book also provides directions on how to bridge the gap between traditional financial systems and modern Fintech solutions to ensure inclusiveness and accessibility for all entrepreneurs.

Overall, this book provides a wide-ranging examination of financial innovation and its transformative impact on sustainable enterprise and economic development in the context of developing and emerging countries. Each chapter of the book provides an interesting and unique perspective on the emerging evidence on the intersection between financial innovation, the environment, and enterprise and how this promotes sustainable enterprises in developing and emerging economies.

Chapter 1 explores how ecologically focused financial instruments and investments contribute to sustainable business practices and economic growth. It provides a deep examination of the evolution of green finance, how green finance operates, challenges and opportunities it provides, and its impact on sustainable business enterprises. The chapter highlights the importance of collaboration between public and private financial institutions in advancing green finance innovation and sustainable entrepreneurship and provides recommendations for developing and scaling up green finance initiatives.

Chapter 2 delves into the factors that motivate migrant participation in diaspora bonds issued to finance climate projects. The chapter employs a survey of 1265 migrants and interview responses from 17 diaspora investors and academic researchers in Europe to understand how diaspora bonds could be leveraged for climate projects in developing and emerging economies. The chapter highlights factors diaspora considers important when subscribing to diaspora bonds for climate projects.

Chapter 3 examines how eco-marketing strategies and green finance mechanisms can be synergized to promote the growth and sustainability of eco-hotels in Central Uganda. The aim is to address key barriers such as limited financial access, weak market visibility, and low consumer awareness of eco-friendly hospitality options. The chapter highlights the need for strategic partnerships with local communities and NGOs to enhance enterprises' eco-value proposition. To scale eco-tourism, the chapter suggests a coordinated approach linking eco-marketing with green finance is essential. The chapter also advocates for capacity-building for eco-hotel operators in green branding and financial literacy, as well as policy incentives to attract climate finance.

Chapter 4 explores the transformative relationship between financial technologies and sustainable enterprise development in developing economies. This chapter adopts a theoretical approach by taking a deep dive into how financial technology (Fintech) has revolutionized various aspects of enterprises in developing economies, transforming their operations, financial management, and product development. Using mainly secondary data, this contributor argues that Fintech has enabled enterprises to leverage emerging technologies such as artificial intelligence, data, edge computing, blockchain, and digital financial services to drive revenue, promote growth, and make products and services more accessible and efficient.

Chapter 5 investigates how experiential marketing strategies and financial innovation can improve sustainable agritourism enterprise outcomes in Western Uganda. With agritourism gaining recognition as a tool for sustainable rural development, this chapter explores how immersive marketing such as sensory appeal, emotional engagement, and educational interaction and emerging financial solutions like green microfinance and crowdfunding affect tourist satisfaction, brand loyalty to farms, and local economic empowerment. Through a robust mixed-methods design, the chapter demonstrates that integrating both experiential marketing and financial innovation into agritourism can support sustainable tourism and diversify rural economies.

Chapter 6 focuses on the intricate relationship between institutional quality, Fintech, and economic development. The chapter proposes that there is a significantly positive impact of Fintech inflows on economic development. Moreover, the economic impact of Fintech on GDP growth increases by almost four times anchored by institutional quality. The chapter, therefore, argues that institutional quality plays an anchoring role in determining the impact of Fintech on economic development.

Chapter 7 examines how the integration of sustainable marketing and innovative financing can drive the growth of agritourism in Western Uganda. The contributors argue that despite the region's potential in agritourism, entrepreneurs face challenges related to limited market access, weak branding, and inadequate financial resources. In this regard, the chapter proposes a synergistic framework that leverages green marketing and alternative financing models to enhance competitiveness and sustainability in agritourism enterprises. The chapter concludes that integrating sustainable marketing with innovative financing creates a powerful model for inclusive and resilient agritourism enterprise development. To enhance the marketing-finance-enterprise linkage in rural agritourism, the chapter recommends the development of tailored microfinance products and expanding financial inclusion through mobile-based tools.

Chapter 8 investigates how a fully integrated local strategy for promoting sustainable university roadside businesses and enterprises amidst the COVID-19 pandemic in Uganda using baseline information. The practical implication of the outcomes of the research work outlined in this chapter is that it can be used to protect entrepreneurs against other pandemics which can affect this business sustainability.

Progressing the debate on the effects of the COVID-19 pandemic, Chap. 9 highlights for the first time the effects of the pandemic and lockdown on the stock returns of companies that can easily move online and for those that find it difficult to do so. The chapter proposes that a firm's flexibility in adopting to or changing situations with regard to an efficient product and services delivery in response to changing demand is the key for any firm to survive unusual global changes, in general, and particularly the effects of pandemics. As much as the ease to move online may be a part of the process of being flexible and adapting to global economic and social changes, it may not be very useful in promoting the firms' value if the final product or service that is moved online is not consistent with what is in demand and is driven by the global economic and social change.

Chapter 10 concludes the book by providing empirical evidence on the relationship between climate risk management and bank performance. The chapter offers actionable insights for bank managers on effective climate risk management strategies and evidence-based recommendations for policymakers and regulators. The chapter underscores the growing importance of climate risk management in the banking sector and its potential implications for financial performance, systemic stability, and the transition to a low-carbon economy.

The conceptualization and philosophy for this book emerged from the recognition that whilst scholarly attempts have been made to deepen our understanding of how technological innovation is helping to foster enterprise growth and sustainability across the world, evidence from existing literature suggests that there is a significant gap and lack of research on the intersection between financial innovation, the environment, and enterprise and how this promotes sustainable enterprises in developing and emerging economies. By bringing together diverse perspectives and case studies, we hope to advance the discourse on these critical issues and inspire further research and practice.

Our sincere gratitude goes to the contributors whose valuable insights have enriched this book, and to the reviewers whose insights have enhanced its quality. We are also very grateful to the University of Sunderland in London, Birmingham City University, and the American University of Bahrain for their support in bringing this book project to fruition. Furthermore, we acknowledge the invaluable role of finance professionals and business enterprises whose experiences and innovations are espoused in this interesting book.

We invite the reader to meticulously engage with the ideas and insights presented in this book, and to join us in discovering how technological innovation is helping to foster enterprise growth and sustainability across the world. It is our hope that this book will contribute significantly to meaningful progress in addressing some of the most pressing challenges facing developing and emerging economies.

London, UK
Birmingham, UK
Birmingham, UK
Riffa, Bahrain
July 2025

Yahaya Alhassan
Samuel Salia
Javed Hussain
Giuseppe Umberto Cantafio

Financial Innovation and Sustainable Enterprise in Developing and Emerging Economies: An Introduction

Finance is not just a tool; it's the lifeblood that powers enterprises, driving economic and social cohesion across the globe. In the heart of this dynamic is the concept of financial embeddedness, which acts as a catalyst for forward-thinking enterprises. Whilst developed economies have long enjoyed robust financial infrastructures, developing and emerging economies often grapple with financial constraints. These limitations not only stifle enterprise growth and sustainability but also curtail job creation, a critical component for socioeconomic stability. Yet, there's a silver lining; the dawn of technological innovation has ushered in transformative changes, especially in the financial landscapes of developing and emerging nations. Whilst many nations have hopped onto the Fintech bandwagon, its impact has been profound in developing economies, levelling the playing field, and allowing them to stand toe to toe with their global counterparts.

However, despite the scholarly attempt made to deepen our understanding of how technological innovation is helping to foster enterprise growth and sustainability across the world, evidence from existing literature suggests that there is a significant gap and lack of research on the intersection between financial innovation, the environment, and enterprise and how this promotes sustainable enterprises in developing and emerging economies. This is the book's focus, which aims to not only fill this gap but also provide a timely addition to prior research on the emerging evidence of the intricate relationship between innovative financing technologies, the business environment, entrepreneurship innovations, and sustainable enterprises in developing and emerging economies. The book also aims to provide a wide-ranging perspective on the nexus between financial innovation and sustainable enterprise as well as makes an effort to explore the phenomenon from the lenses of developing and emerging economies to give the reader a deeper and broad understanding of issues.

Central to this book's conceptualization and philosophy is that it takes a new, nuanced, and comprehensive look at how sustainable enterprises in developing and emerging economies are being promoted through innovative financing technologies and entrepreneurship innovations from the perspectives of experts, academics, and practitioners from developing and emerging economies. Also, given that enterprise is a key enabler of economic growth and the prominent role played by emerging and developing economies in shaping global GDP, entrepreneurship, and business investing, it is critically imperative to explore this phenomenon for business sustainability and to achieve the ideals of the Sustainable Development Goals (SDGs) for a more sustainable future.

Accordingly, it is plausible to argue that creating a deeper awareness of the intricate relationship between innovative financing technologies, the business environment, and entrepreneurship innovations to promote sustainable enterprises in developing and emerging economies would not only enhance our understanding but would provoke debate as well as a rethinking of the appropriate financing models and tools for supporting the growth and sustainability of enterprises in these regions.

Whilst most finance and enterprise books are narrow in scope and orientation as they often focus on developed economies, this book is wide-ranging and broad in scope as well as makes an effort to explore issues from the lenses of developing and emerging economies to give the reader a deeper and broad understanding of issues.

This book generated interests from various contributors from Africa, Europe, and Asia. The contributors examined various issues consistent with the theme of the book in ten chapters that make up the book. This explains why the book has been divided into three parts and ten chapters.

Part I explores Green Finance and Sustainable Development in three chapters.

Part II looks at Financial Technologies and Sustainable Enterprise Development in four chapters.

Part III, the final part of the book, looks at Sustainable Enterprise, Risk, and Stocks Markets in three chapters.

The remainder of this introductory chapter looks at what each of the contributors says about how the theme of the book is espoused in each of the countries where the authors are based or where the research was conducted.

The very first chapter by Yahaya Alhassan explores how ecologically focused financial instruments and investments contribute to sustainable business practices and economic growth globally. It provides a deep examination of the evolution of green finance, how green finance operates, challenges and opportunities it provides, and its impact on sustainable business enterprises. The chapter is quite interesting as it highlights the importance of collaboration between public and private financial institutions in advancing green finance innovation and sustainable entrepreneurship.

The second chapter by Samuel Salia, Eugene Bempong Nyantakyi, Javed Hussain, Eric Ofosu-Hene, and Yahaya Alhassan, whose expertise is grounded in finance and enterprise, adopts a mixed-methods approach in shedding light on the use of diaspora bonds for climate projects in developing and emerging economies. Central to the proposition demonstrated in this chapter is that a climate emergency requires investment in mitigation and adaptation projects. It highlights factors the diaspora considers important when subscribing to diaspora bonds for climate projects. It further argued that impact investing diaspora bonds has the potential to partially bridge the climate finance gap in developing and emerging economies.

In the third chapter, Florence Prescah Muheebwa, Faith Ahabyoona Mugisha, and Milly Kwagala Oudi unpack how eco-marketing strategies and green finance mechanisms can be synergized to promote the growth and sustainability of eco-hotels in Central Uganda. Using the convergent parallel design, this intellectual stimulating chapter reveals that whilst eco-hotels in Central Uganda adopt some sustainable practices, many lack structured marketing strategies and access to tailored green financing. The authors argued that to scale eco-tourism, a coordinated approach linking eco-marketing with green finance is essential.

Part II begins with Chap. 4 written by Joseph Asare, which focuses on the relationship between financial technologies and sustainable enterprise development in developing economies. This chapter adopts a theoretical approach by taking a deep dive into how financial technology (Fintech) has revolutionized various aspects of enterprises in developing economies, transforming their operations, financial management, and product development. Using mainly secondary data, this contributor argues that Fintech has enabled enterprises to leverage emerging technologies such as artificial intelligence, data, edge computing, blockchain, and digital financial services to drive revenue, promote growth, and make products and services more accessible and efficient.

In Chap. 5, Florence Prescah Muheebwa investigates how experiential marketing strategies and financial innovation can improve sustainable agritourism enterprise outcomes in Western Uganda. With agritourism gaining recognition as a tool for sustainable rural development, this contributor explores how immersive marketing such as sensory appeal, emotional engagement, and educational interaction and emerging financial solutions like green microfinance and crowdfunding affect tourist satisfaction, brand loyalty to farms, and local economic empowerment. The chapter concludes that integrating both experiential marketing and financial innovation into agritourism can support sustainable tourism and diversify rural economies.

Incorporating institutional quality dimension to the debate is the sixth chapter written by John Agyekum Addae, Sheraz Ahmed, Mikael Collan, Mara Madaleno, and Gilbert Zana Naab using panel data from 45 countries. The contributors examined the intricate relationship between institutional quality, Fintech, and economic development in a global context. The chapter concludes that there is a significantly positive impact of Fintech inflows on economic development. Moreover, the economic impact of Fintech on GDP growth increases by almost four times anchored by institutional quality. This shows that institutional quality plays an anchoring role in determining the impact of Fintech on economic development.

Chapter 7, which is the last chapter of Part II written by Florence Prescah Muheebwa, Milly Kwagala Oudi, and Faith Ahabyoona Mugisha, takes an insightful approach to understanding how the integration of sustainable marketing and innovative financing can drive the growth of agritourism in Western Uganda. The contributors argue that integrating sustainable marketing with innovative financing creates a powerful model for inclusive and resilient agritourism enterprise development.

Part III of the book begins with Chap. 8, which is well researched and written by David Katamba, Tom Tamale, Maureen Basuuta, and Veronica Mukyala. These contributors used baseline information to create a fully integrated local strategy for promoting sustainable university roadside businesses and enterprises amidst the

COVID-19 pandemic. The practical implication of this research work is that it can be used to protect entrepreneurs against other pandemics which can affect this business sustainability.

The second chapter of Part III is Chap. 9, which is written by Samuel Salia, Amin Karimu, Yahaya Alhassan, and Meney Orlyne Ahochi. Similar to the insights elaborated in Chap. 8 about the effects of the COVID-19 pandemic, these contributors highlight for the first time the effects of the pandemic and lockdown on the stock returns of companies that can easily move online and for those that find it difficult to do so. The authors argue that, as a whole, a firm's flexibility in adapting to or changing situations with regard to an efficient product and services delivery in response to changing demand is the key for any firm to survive unusual global changes, in general, and, in particular, the effects of pandemics. As much as the ease to move online may be a part of the process of being flexible and adapting to global economic and social changes, it may not be very useful in promoting the firms' value if the final product or service that is moved online is not consistent with what is in demand and is driven by the global economic and social change.

The final chapter (Chap. 10) by Vasco Victor offers insights on how global systemically important banks (G-SIBs) are managing financial risks associated with climate change, focusing on adaptation and mitigation strategies. This research contributes to the academic literature by providing empirical evidence on the relationship between climate risk management and bank performance. It offers actionable insights for bank managers on effective climate risk management strategies and evidence-based recommendations for policymakers and regulators. The findings underscore the growing importance of climate risk management in the banking sector and its potential implications for financial performance, systemic stability, and the transition to a low-carbon economy.

University of Sunderland
London, UK
Yahaya Alhassan

Birmingham City University
Birmingham, UK
Samuel Salia

Birmingham City University
Birmingham, UK
Javed Hussain

American University of Bahrain
Riffa, Bahrain
Giuseppe Umberto Cantafio

Acknowledgments

We wish to express our sincere gratitude to all the contributors whose valuable insights have enriched this book, and to the reviewers whose insights have enhanced the quality of the volume. Without their dedication, commitment, and hard work, this book would not have been possible. We thus sincerely express our appreciation and gratitude to all these great individuals who have contributed to the success of this book. The four editors are very grateful to those of you who contributed to this project with their impressive chapters in this book. Many of you despite your busy schedules felt obliged to help in putting together this very fascinating addition to the literature on the intersection between financial innovation, the environment, and enterprise and how this promotes sustainable enterprises in developing and emerging economies.

We would like to thank our publishing team at Springer, particularly, Sneha Arunagiri (Production Editor, Books), Christian Rauscher (Editorial Director), Barbara Bethke (Associate Editor), and other members of the publishing team who have supported this project and other projects.

We thus dedicate this book to the cause of creating deeper awareness of the intricate relationship between innovative financing technologies, the business environment, and entrepreneurship innovations to promote sustainable enterprises in developing and emerging economies as well as rethinking of the appropriate financing models for supporting the growth and sustainability of enterprises in these regions.

We apologize for any errors or omissions that may appear anywhere in the book; please be assured that no harm was intended to anybody. Finally, our profound gratitude goes to our families for the time granted us to write this book.

Contents

About the Editors

Yahaya Alhassan is the Head of Academic Operations at the University of Sunderland in London. Dr. Alhassan is responsible for leading the integration and execution of the University of Sunderland's strategic and operational priorities across all academic programmes at the London campus (UoSiL). He also oversees the development and implementation of the Academic Programme Offer, as well as the integration of the University's Research and Innovation Strategy. Alongside his leadership role, Dr. Alhassan maintains an active research profile. His current research explores investment in financial technology (Fintech) and firm growth, with several of his papers published in high-ranking ABS 3* journals. He has co-edited books, has authored multiple book chapters in finance and enterprise, and frequently presents at academic conferences, contributing meaningfully to the field of finance since 2019. Dr. Alhassan has over 20 years' experience in teaching, academic leadership, and management, gained through his roles at the University of Sunderland in London as well as previous positions in the higher education and consultancy sectors. He holds a PhD in Business Management (Finance) from Anglia Ruskin University, an MBA in Finance and a Master of Education from the University of Sunderland, and a BA (Hons) in Business Management from Arden University. He is also Senior Fellow of the Higher Education Academy (HEA).

Samuel Salia is Associate Professor of Finance at Birmingham City University (UK) where he currently leads research and teaches finance. He holds a PhD in Finance from Birmingham City University. He is a member of the UK Institute of Consulting and has consulted for international organizations including the African Union and GIZ. Before joining BCU, Samuel was Senior Lecturer in Finance and Faculty Head of Doctoral Training (Business and Law) at De Montfort University. Before this, he was Lecturer in International Finance and Programme Director for MSc International Banking and Finance at the University of Wolverhampton. He has worked as Management Consultant with the Ghana Ministry of Employment (MDPI) and as Managing Director of SAS Capital Money Lending Limited and has also held academic appointments abroad. He has had over 11 years of banking and consultancy experience in the SME sector, specializing in entrepreneurial finance.

The findings of Samuel's research have influenced the practice of ethnic minority businesses in the UK, financial institutions, and the policy of regional bodies in Africa. For example, he recently worked on a BAL HEIF-funded project that provided training and support to Afro-Caribbean-owned businesses in the Midlands (UK) in response to COVID-19 challenges. He has also worked on projects such as evaluating the impact of services of Opportunity International Savings and Loans-Ghana and Village Savings and Loans Associations. As Technical Advisor, he developed a policy booklet for the African Heads of State and Governments on the AU 2021 theme of the year. He has served as a keynote speaker at national and international conferences. His focus has recently been on exploring issues of diaspora (migrant) remittance, Fintech, and investment in developing countries. Samuel has published extensively on issues relating to access to finance, green finance, SME innovation, and entrepreneurial training. His work has been published in the *International Journal of Finance and Economics* (ABS ranking 3*), *International Journal of Entrepreneurial Behaviour and Research* (ABS ranking 3*), *IEEE Transactions on Engineering Management* (ABS ranking 3*), and *Journal of Small Business and Enterprise Development* (ABS ranking 2*), among others. Samuel has examined and supervised PhD students, and on the strength of his research, he has received research funding totaling £26,000. He has served as a reviewer for highly ranked academic journals including the *International Journal of Entrepreneurial Behaviour and Research* and the *Journal of Small Business and Enterprise Development*, among others.

Javed Hussain is Professor of Entrepreneurial Finance at Birmingham City University where he currently leads the Accounting and Finance Group. Professor Hussain completed his PhD (1996) and M. Soc. Sci (1987) in Money, Banking, and Finance from the University of Birmingham and a first degree in Economics, BA (Hons) from Birmingham Polytechnic (1985). Currently, Professor Hussain supervises several PhD students in the areas of corporate, micro, and small business finance. He also takes postgraduate courses on Research Methods and International Financial Strategy. Before joining Birmingham City University, Professor Hussain held posts in finance within public and private sector organizations. He was a financial analyst with the Forward Trust Group (now a subsidiary of HSBC bank), and before that, he worked for Birmingham City Council. He has collaborated on several research projects funded by public sector clients. He has published extensively on issues of bank finance for SMEs with a particular focus on ethnic firms and has co-authored papers and chapters in several journals and books. He is currently co-editing *Reading in Entrepreneurial Finance* book with Dr. Jonathan Scott. Furthermore, he is conducting collaborative research on differences in entrepreneurship and SME financing between developed and developing countries, in particular, considering the issues of SMEs within the Malaysian context. Professor Hussain regularly presents papers at national and international conferences and engages in research with colleagues from several other UK institutions, Professor Paul Mosley on microfinance, Dr. Paul Stuart, University of West of Scotland, on the presence of venture capital among ethnic minorities, and Dr. Jonathan Scott,

Teesside University, on entrepreneurship. He is a peer referee for several international journal publications. You may contact Professor Javed Hussain informally to explore your research interests or possible collaborative projects within his specialist area of interest.

Giuseppe Umberto Cantafio is Associate Professor at the American University of Bahrain. Prior to his current role, he worked as Senior Lecturer in Business Management at the University of Sunderland in London. Dr. Cantafio holds a PhD in Urban Regeneration and Economic Development from Università Mediterranea of Reggio Calabria, Italy, and MSc Civil and Environmental Engineering and BSc Civil and Environmental Engineering from the University of Calabria, Italy. He is also Senior Fellow of the Higher Education Academy (HEA). Prior to joining the University of Sunderland in London, he worked as a lecturer and researcher on the impacts and scenarios evaluation of Autonomous and Connected Transport at the University of Greenwich. Dr. Cantafio held posts at Northeastern University in Boston, San Diego State University, and the Universita Mediterranea of Reggio in Calabria, Italy, where he was a researcher for the MAPS-LED Project, exploring multidisciplinary approaches to plan smart specialization strategies for local Economic Development. Dr. Cantafio is also a freelance consultant with clients in both the UK and Italy and guest editor for SAGE journals, Power, and IGI Publishing.

Part I
Green Finance and Sustainable Development

Chapter 1
Green Finance and Enterprise: A Catalyst for Sustainable Economic Growth

Yahaya Alhassan

1.1 Introduction

The growing climate risks and regulatory shifts have deepened the need for sustainable development around the world. The environmental impacts of the activities of firms have often been overlooked by traditional financial systems (Cunha et al., 2021.). However, recent development in finance involving the integration of environmental concerns into investment decision making, generally known as green finance, has emerged as a pivotal response. Evidence from various studies (Fu et al., 2023; Wang et al., 2022) suggests that green finance promotes investments activities that yield positive environmental outcomes and sustainable development. Given that business organisations do not only create economic activities and drive innovation but also influence resource consumption and emissions, aligning enterprise behaviour with green financial frameworks is central to achieving long-term environmental and economic goals.

Evidence from IPCC (2018) suggests that reducing global warming to about 1.5 °C needs swift and radical change in energy and industrial systems, which will require huge investments in green technologies. The need for substantial investments in green technologies has also been highlighted by the United Nations Environment Programme (UNEP). For instance, the organisation in the year 2021 estimated that the annual global investments in climate solutions must increase significantly to about $4.1 trillion by 2030 to achieve sustainability goals (UNEP, 2021). In light of this, green finance plays a pivotal role in mobilising and channelling funds towards low-carbon, climate-resilient, and inclusive economic activities.

Y. Alhassan (✉)
University of Sunderland in London, London, UK
e-mail: yahaya.alhassan@sunderland.ac.uk

Y. Alhassan et al. (eds.), *Financial Innovation and Sustainable Enterprise in Developing and Emerging Economies*, Research Series on Responsible Enterprise Ecosystems, https://doi.org/10.1007/978-3-032-04500-3_1

The growing relevance of green finance in achieving long-term environmental and economic goals is supported by various studies. For instance, Banga (2019) examines the relationship between green bonds, climate finance, infrastructure development and sustainable enterprise in emerging markets. Campiglio et al. (2018) also argues that there is the need for realignment of financial systems with sustainability objectives to address systemic risks and foster green innovation. The need for global policy framework and public-private partnership in scaling up green finance has also been proposed by various studies (Singh, 2022; Morgado & Lasfargues, 2017).

There is also evidence that suggests that the enterprise sector is undergoing a paradigm shift as environmental, social and governance (ESG) considerations gain prominence in investment decisions. For example, evidence from Morningstar (2022) suggests that global sustainable fund assets increased to about $2.7 trillion, which demonstrates the desire and increased investor confidence in ESG-aligned enterprises. This evolution reflects a broader transition toward sustainable capitalism, where financial performance is increasingly linked to environmental and social impact.

Given the rising prominence of green finance in achieving long-term environmental and economic goals., this study aims to achieve the following objectives:

- Examine the foundations and evolution of green finance
- Analyse key green financial instruments and mechanisms
- Explore the interaction between green finance and enterprise development
- Evaluate challenges of green finance initiatives

The rest of the chapter is structured as follows: Review of existing literature relevant to green finance and enterprise presented next (Sect. 1.2). Section 1.3 provides the methodology employed. Section 1.4 discusses green finance case studies and empirical evidence. Whilst Sect. 1.5 evaluates the challenges and barriers to green finance and enterprise. Section 1.6 provides the conclusion and recommendations.

1.2 Related Literature

1.2.1 Green Finance and Its Evolution

Green finance can be described as business financing activities designed specifically to support environmentally sustainable development (Belova et al., 2023; Lee, 2020). Behera and Nanda (2025) have shown that the term green finance covers a range of financial instruments and investment activities such as green bonds, ESG investing and sustainability practices linked loans. In theory, the concept of green finance begun and gained prominence in the 1990s and the early part of 2000s. The increased importance was because of greater global awareness of the dangers of climate change and the need for sustainable development.

The foundational principles of green finance are deeply rooted in the idea that financial markets can play a transformative role in addressing environmental challenges by allocating capital toward projects and enterprises that promote environmental stewardship. Green finance essentially, integrates ecological risk assessment into the core of financial decision-making and seeks to internalize the environmental externalities that have historically been ignored in conventional financial systems (Azam et al., 2024).

Over the past two decades, green finance as an investment strategy has evolved significantly. At the early stages, green finance was used to fund renewable energy and environmental protection projects through a mix of public sector and international development finance initiatives. However, green finance has rapidly expanded into conventional financial markets, partly due to growing climate risks and regulatory shifts (Dupir, 2024). For instance, evidence from Climate Bonds Initiative (2022) suggests that green bonds issuance globally increased from about $1 billion in the year 2008 to over $500 billion annually in the last few years. Several events have contributed to the development of green finance. For instance, the establishment of environment and social risk management standards for financial institutions under the Equator Principles has been found to contribute to the evolution of green finance (Nedopil et al., 2021). Nanayakkara and Colombage (2022) have also shown that the International Capital Market Association played a significant role in the development of green finance through the introduction of the Green Bond Principles in 2014. Besides, Chua et al. (2022) have demonstrated that the recommendations made by the Climate-related Finance Task Force further played a role in the evolution of green finance. These initiatives have without doubt contributed positively to the scaling up of green finance across the world.

The concept of green finance is intricately linked to climate finance, which is widely described as financing or investment activities directed at climate mitigation and adaptation (Zhao & Li, 2024). While climate finance is typically associated with public funding and multilateral commitments, green finance includes broader market-driven instruments that support sustainability goals beyond climate, such as biodiversity conservation, circular economy, and pollution reduction (Nasir & Ahmed, 2024).

Various studies (Hussain et al., 2025; Weber & Saravade, 2019) have highlighted the importance and necessity for financial sector reforms to incorporate green finance due to its potential positive impact on risk adjusted investment returns. The link between corporate sustainability goals and green finance has also been identified by some scholars (Khalid et al., 2025; Cai & Song, 2024). The evolution of green finance also reflects increasing consumer demand and regulatory pressures (Liu, 2024). Consequently, financial institutions are now expected to not only deliver returns but also demonstrate environmental accountability. Besides, regulatory bodies, such as the European Central Bank and the U.S. Securities and Exchange Commission, have introduced disclosure mandates and climate stress-testing, underscoring the systemic importance of environmental risks (Gualandri et al., 2024).

1.2.2 Green Finance Instruments

The green finance consists of various financial instruments designed to provide capital to support sustainable projects (Fu et al., 2023). The aim of this is to encourage environmentally responsible behaviour by individuals and firms to achieve sustainable development across the world. The main instruments of green finance are discussed below:

1.2.2.1 Green Bonds

Evidence from Bhutta et al. (2022) suggests that green bonds are debt financial instruments designed to raise capital to support projects that have positive environmental outcomes. Projects likely to attract this type of funding include climate adaptation, renewal energy and energy efficiency. This is consistent with Ye and Rasoulinezhad (2023) who have demonstrated that green bonds have the potential to contribute positively to reducing climate change risk and renewable energy expansion. The green bond market has grown significantly reaching over $2 trillion globally since it was first issued in 2008 by the World Bank (Debrah et al., 2024). The issuance of these bonds often follows strict guidelines such as meeting the requirements of the Green Bond Principles, use of the money raised for environmentally friendly projects and impact reporting (Shishlov et al., 2016). Due to rising demand for green bonds, they are often oversubscribed when issued, since they are attractive to investors seeking stable returns aligned with ESG values (Joshi et al., 2024).

1.2.2.2 Sustainability Linked Loans

Sustainability linked loans are debt financial instruments which have specific requirements for the beneficiary to achieve sustainability performance targets. Quite often the terms of the loan particularly the interest rates are determined by sustainability outcomes achieved by the borrower (Du et al., 2023). Sule et al. (2024) have shown that Sustainability linked loans are designed to provide greater financial benefit for the borrower to meet environmental goals including reducing carbon emission and energy efficiency. Similarly, evidence from Auzepy et al. (2023) suggests that Sustainability linked loans been proven to be very effective in motivating business enterprises to incorporate sustainability in their business practices and overall strategy. In view of the growing popularity of these loans, the Loan Market Association has formulated Sustainability Linked Loan Principles to regulate the market.

1.2.2.3 Green Investment Funds

Green Investment Funds are designed to raise substantial amount of money to invest in firms or development that have positive environmental outcomes or linked to green innovation (Zhang et al., 2023; Falcone, 2020). Notable examples include mutual funds, exchange-traded funds, and private equity funds that integrate ESG criteria into portfolio selection. These financial instruments are designed to help investors diversify their portfolio and achieve environmental objectives (Li, 2023). Sundaram (2023) have demonstrated that ESG fund assets globally have grown considerably, confirming the rising interest in sustainability aligned financial instruments.

1.2.2.4 Carbon and Emission Pricing

Carbon and emission pricing systems are designed in a way that provide financial incentives for investors and business enterprises based on achieving emission reduction targets (Narassimhan et al., 2018). In this regard, Digitemie and Ekemezie (2024) have shown that carbon and emission pricing systems provide opportunities for firms to foster cost-effective decarbonisation by trading surplus emission allowances received. Perhaps, it is in this context that Khurshid et al. (2023) concludes that carbon pricing is an effective and viable short-term tool for enterprises to achieve the SDGs. The two most effective carbon and emission pricing systems are the emission trading system operated by European Union and Chinese emission trading system (Zhang et al., 2017). Overall, studies (Digitemie & Ekemezie, 2024; Zhu et al., 2022) have shown that carbon and emission pricing does not only promote positive corporate sustainability practices but also helps to attract green investments.

1.2.2.5 Green Banks

Green banks are financial institutions that provide capital for investments in green or climate mitigation projects (Nix et al., 2025; Schub, 2015). These banks use various mechanisms including loan guarantees and partnership investment schemes to mitigate against risks associated with sustainable projects and attract funding from the private sector (David & Venkatachalam, 2019). Studies (Ozili, 2022; Fu et al., 2023) have shown that other organisations such as Development Finance Institutions have played a pivotal role in securing funding for green infrastructure projects in the developing world. The Green Climate Fund and the International Finance Corporation are examples of the institutions who contributed positively to scaling capital investments climate related projects (Amighini et al., 2022).

1.2.3 The Role of Enterprises in Green Finance

Business enterprises are not only contributors to climate change but key players in fostering innovative and sustainable solutions in achieving sustainable development (Westman et al., 2019). Perhaps, it in this context that Arunachalam (2024) argues that enterprise's role in green finance includes mobilisation of funds for sustainable business ventures and sustainability initiatives or practices aimed at addressing environmental issues.

Various studies (Matriano, 2024; Siegrist et al., 2020) have examined the role of enterprises in green finance. For instance, Bagh and Iftikhar (2024) have demonstrated that business enterprises received and use green finance instruments such as sustainability linked loans, green bonds and equity investments linked to ESG. Maybe, it is on this basis that Siegrist et al. (2020) concluded that enterprises can lower their cost of capital by embedding sustainability goals in their operational and long-term plans. Firms in the manufacturing sector, for instance, can access low-interest loans to acquire environmentally friendly technologies or upgrade existing ones (Ghisetti et al., 2017). Enterprises can also embed ESG principles in their operations to attract sustainability focused investors (Mukonzo & Dzingirai, 2025).

There is also evidence that some firms are adopting green financial strategies thereby playing a major role in promoting green finance and contributing to sustainable development globally. For example, Fu et al. (2023) have demonstrated that enterprises contribute to green finance by embedding environmental objectives into financial planning, budgeting, and risk management aimed at attracting green capital. Other practices of firms that are aimed at improving access to green investments include publication of ESG reports and participating in voluntary disclosure schemes (Yeoh, 2021).

Enterprises also drive green innovation by developing and deploying sustainable technologies, products, and business models (Islam, 2023). The link between enterprise and green finance can be found through the development of clean technology, renewable energy and participation in environmental projects by business startups and SMEs. In this regard, Tian (2018) concludes that investments in such business enterprises have increased significantly due to their positive to low-carbon transition. The role of enterprises in fostering sustainable supply chains have also been reported. For instance, evidence from Vachon and Klassen (2006) suggests that firms have redesigned their procurement and supply chain practices to influence their upstream and downstream partners to adhere to environmental standards. Doing this not only reinforces corporate sustainability but also expands the reach of green finance throughout value chains.

1.3 Research Methodology

The research employed a mixed-methods approach combining both qualitative and quantitative techniques to ensure a comprehensive understanding of the relationship between green finance and sustainable enterprise development. The first stage of the research involved a systematic review of existing literature aimed at gathering theoretical and empirical insights into green finance and sustainable enterprises. The existing literature used includes peer reviewed journal articles, policy papers and reports. The sources used were selected based on ranking of the Journal or reputation of the institution, relevance of the content and frequency of citation. To gain quantitative insights into green finance and sustainable enterprises, quantitative data was extracted from national and international financial databases and analysed. The data sets largely comprise of statistics on green investments, financial performance of enterprises, ESG investments, and green bonds issue from the databases maintained by the IMF, World Bank, UNEP and OECD.

Consistent with the mixed methods approach adopted by the study, case study analysis was also employed to evaluate real-world use of green finance or climate related investments and their impact on five sustainable enterprises across the world. The case study enterprises were selected using purposive sampling strategy. The business enterprises chosen were from different industries and regions of the world. Analysis of the case studies helped the researcher to identify key success factors common to the enterprises studied, common challenges, and modes of green finance integration into firm growth strategies.

In addition to the above, green regulatory documents, green frameworks and sustainability standards from various institutions were analysed using content analysis. The documents analysed were from the European Commission, The International Financial Reporting Standards Foundation (IFRS) and the Task Force on Climate-related Financial Disclosures (TCFD). Analysis of these documents was done to provide an understanding of policy coherence and institutional readiness. Overall, the use of both qualitative and quantitative evidence and techniques provides a balanced and rigorous examination of the relationship between green finance and sustainable enterprise development.

1.4 Empirical Case Studies

To gain a deeper understanding of the impact of green finance on the development of enterprises, this section of the chapter discusses several case studies drawn from various regions of the world and sectors of the global economy. These empirical case studies provide evidence of how green finance initiatives have contributed positively to the firms studied transition to sustainability and measurable positive environmental outcomes. The case studies also outline the key factors for success and the difficulties of implementing green finance initiatives.

1.4.1 Ørsted: Transformation Via Green Bonds

Ørsted, initially set up as a fossil-fuel energy company is a very good example of how an enterprise transformed itself using green financial instruments by shifting its primary activities towards renewable energy (Voldsgaard & Rüdiger, 2021). The transformation of the company was achieved through green bonds and significant investments in green infrastructure (Rendtorff, 2023). Specifically, from 2017 to 2022 the company raised over €3 billion by issuing green bonds and used this to develop renewable energy infrastructure across Europe (Srivastava, 2021). The Green Bond Principles also played a pivotal role in Ørsted's transformation as the company followed these guidelines which ensured investor confidence and transparency in the use of proceeds from the green bonds (Svirskyi, 2025). Certainly, the use of green bonds contributed positively to the initial transformation and continued revolution of Ørsted as the company has now divested its fossil fuel assets entirely. The firm now pride itself to be "a renewable energy company with a clear vision: to create a world that runs entirely on green energy" (Ørsted, 2025).

Therefore, Ørsted transformation from a fossil-fuel energy company to a renewable energy firm provides empirical evidence of how green finance can be a catalyst for sustainable enterprise development. This is consistent with Ye and Rasoulinezhad (2023) who argues that the use of green finance instruments such as green bonds is a viable strategy for achieving sustainable firm growth and positive environmental outcomes. This view is not rare as Ghisetti et al. (2017) have shown that embedding sustainability practices to upgrade operational processes using green finance can yield positive environmental outcomes and enterprise growth.

1.4.2 Tata Power: Acceleration of Renewable Energy Portfolio through Green Finance

Another company that has used green finance to accelerate its renewable energy portfolio is Tata Power. The company in the year 2022, raised a significant amount of $320 million using sustainability linked loans to expand its solar and wind operations (Das, 2022). The use of green finance by the company to expand its renewable energy portfolio created a pathway for achieving its sustainability goals of achieving net-zero emission and increasing its renewable energy capacity three-fold by the year 2045 and 2030 respectively. The terms of the loans Tata Power received were tied to key performance indicators (KPIs) like the green bond principles and emission pricing system. The loan terms specifically included sustainability targets tied to margins and aligning financial incentives with environmental outcomes.

This case study provides evidence of how Tata Power used green finance to increase its renewable energy capacity and diversify its energy mix aimed at mitigating regulatory and reputational risks. The financing model adopted by Tata Power also demonstrates how green finance can be used as a catalyst for enterprises transition strategies for sustainable economic growth and achieving positive environmental outcomes (Marín-Rodríguez et al., 2024). This is supported by Hussain et al. (2024) who found that "green finance act as a catalyst for sustainability performance by providing the necessary financial resources and incentives for enterprises to invest in sustainable technologies and practices". The successful use of green finance to drive the transition of Tatah Power to a renewable energy company is also consistent with Auzepy et al. (2023) who have confirmed that sustainability linked loans are a viable strategy for motivating business enterprises to incorporate sustainability in their business practices and overall strategy.

1.4.3 Tesla Use of Equity and ESG Investment in Green Innovation

A further case study example of the practical application of green finance to enterprise investment strategies to achieve sustainability goals is Tesla Inc. The company is known for using private capital and ESG investment as a catalyst for fostering green innovation (Leong, 2024). For instance, between 2003 and 2009 the company was financed by private capital from the founders including Elon Musk. Tesla in 2010 went public through IPO targeting green focused investors (Liu, 2024). While Tesla is not known to have used green bonds or sustainability linked loans, its operations and business model focusing on electric vehicles, domestic and commercial solar energy aligns with green finance objectives. Perhaps, the organisation's attractiveness to green focused investors is partly due to its ESG alignment, particularly in the decarbonization of the transport and energy sectors (Kandpal et al., 2024). It is therefore not surprising that the company is listed as a top holding in many ESG-focused funds, reflecting investor confidence in its green growth potential.

This Tesla example of attracting green focused investors by adopting a business model aligned with green finance objectives demonstrates that business enterprises can achieve high market capitalization and financial returns while advancing sustainability goals. This is in line with the outcome of Yu et al. (2023) who concludes that green finance can significantly enhance the financial performance of green enterprises through capital aggregation. The Tesla case study also provides evidence of how ESG aligned investment instruments can foster firm early innovation and subsequent growth. Another important implication of the Tesla case study is the influence of government policy, particularly incentives for green business models such as EV subsidies which contributed positively Tesla's profitability and growth.

1.4.4 Brazilian Development Bank: Green Credit for SMEs

The Brazilian Development Bank was set up in 1952 to provide long-term financing for business activities that contribute to the development of the Brazilian economy. The bank in recent years has developed sustainability linked loans products for small and medium size enterprises involved in renewable energy and sustainable agriculture (Ferraz & Ferraz, 2022). Using tailor made financial schemes such as the Climate Fund and Finem, Banco provided credit facilities at low interest rates to enterprises with positive environmental outcomes (Bartelega & Mendonça, 2024). For instance, the bank has been reported to have financed more than one hundred small firms involved in solar energy production, helping the enterprises to reduce their environmental footprints (Isah et al., 2023). This is a confirmation of the Brazilian Development Bank's involvement in green finance and contribution to sustainable economic development of Brazil.

A key message from the Brazilian Development Bank case study is that financial institutions can contribute to the sustainable economic growth by de-risking green investments for small businesses. Another key insight from the case study is that providing access to green credit lines to small local enterprises can be a viable strategy for achieving sustainable enterprises development and positive environmental outcomes. This is consistent with Hussain et al. (2024) who have demonstrated that "green finance can act as a catalyst for sustainability performance by providing the necessary financial resources for enterprises to invest in sustainable business practices".

1.4.5 The Green Investment Group

The Green Investment Group was founded in 2012 by the UK government to mobilise private investment for green energy infrastructure. Operating as a green bank, the company mobilised over £5 billion for green projects between 2012 and 2020 (Geels et al., 2022). Major green projects financed by the Green Investment Group include wind farms, energy storage systems, and low-carbon transport infrastructure. Utilizing various financing models such as loan guarantees and equity stakes, the company was able to attract major institutional investors and mitigate against project risks.

This case study example provides evidence of how green financial institutions can mobilise significant amount of capital for green projects, thereby contributing to sustainable economic development. The case study also illustrates how public-private partnership arrangements can provide appropriate investments for capital intensive green projects. This is consistent with David and Venkatachalam (2019) who have shown that banks can use partnership investment schemes to mitigate against risks associated with sustainable projects.

1.5 Green Finance and Enterprise Challenges

Green finance has proven to be very useful financial instrument for supporting projects that have positive environmental outcomes. However, various studies have identified several challenges affecting its effectiveness and scalability. Perhaps, it is in this context that Khan et al. (2022) argues that the full potential of green finance could be achieved if the challenges inhibiting its effectiveness are addressed. Some of the key challenges to green finance and enterprises are discussed below.

1.5.1 Lack of Data

One of the major challenges to the effectiveness of green finance is the lack of appropriate and reliable environmental data for decision making by investors, lenders and even regulators. The lack of reliable information has been shown to affect the risk assessment of green projects, which leads to capital been allocated to other ventures instead of green projects (Karamoozian et al., 2022). Besides, evidence from Jonsdottir et al. (2022) suggests that most small firms fail to disclose ESG data due to lack of resources, which affects their ability to attract green investments. Other studies have identified lack of appropriate reporting framework to be another issue which results to information asymmetry and affecting investor confidence in green projects and thereby restricting capital for sustainability projects. In this regard, developing a reporting framework that align with international agreements could provide a consistent approach and reduce information asymmetry which could improve investor confidence and increase funding for green projects (Johnson et al., 2019).

1.5.2 Inconsistent Policy and Regulatory Framework

Evidence from Nerlich et al. (2025) suggests that lack of consistent policy and regulatory framework is a major obstacle to green investment. This is due to the existence of different regulations and policies in different countries which create significant burden on firms as they must meet diverse national requirements. The lack of consistent policy or regulatory framework have been shown to erode investor confidence and discourage green finance mobilisation (Del Sarto, 2025). Perhaps, it is in this context that Okeke et al. (2024) argues that green finance regulatory and policy frameworks in most developing and emerging economies are significantly underdeveloped or very weak. The outcome of Chen et al. (2024) suggest that the prevalence of weak regulations and policies have negatively impacted on the uptake of green finance instruments in the emerging markets. Developing a unified policy and regulatory framework for green investments could facilitate international capital flows which could increase investor confidence and rationalise regulations of green finance.

1.5.3 Perceived High Risk

Various studies (Abba et al., 2022; Spasenic et al., 2022; Hwang et al., 2015) have shown that green projects are often perceived to be high risk investments due to lack of appropriate regulatory framework and long payback periods. The lack of consistent regulatory framework creates uncertainty and affects investor confidence, which limits the supply of green capital and increases cost of borrowing for business enterprises. Inadequate feasibility studies for green projects, particularly, climate adaptation and clean infrastructure have also been reported to negatively affect availability of green finance (Ozili, 2022). There is also evidence that banks lack the capacity to adequately assess the risks and returns associated with green finance projects, which affect capital flow to such projects (Akomea-Frimpong et al., 2022). In this regard, Clark et al. (2018) have demonstrated that without appropriate risk evaluation and mitigation mechanisms, green projects will continue to struggle to attract private funding. Dikau and Volz (2019) provides evidence of the mechanisms that regulators and financial institutions such as central banks can employ to assess and mitigate against environmental risk to foster green finance and sustainable development.

1.5.4 Inadequate Knowledge of Green Finance

There is evidence that most entrepreneurs have very little knowledge and understanding pf the concept of green finance and how sustainability issues are reported by firms. For instance, Luo and Cheng (2023) have shown that small and medium size firms fail to align their business practices with sustainability objectives such as the SDGs and access green finance because of lack of financial knowledge. Lack of sustainable financial literacy initiatives, particularly in the developing and emerging economies account for this limited financial literacy (Kyeyune & Ntayi, 2025). This constrained financial literacy has been shown to reduce the flow of funding for green projects (Siddik et al., 2023). The outcome of Luo and Cheng (2023) suggests that improving the financial literacy of enterprises could contribute positively to the development of sustainable business model and access to green finance. This is consistent with Babajide et al. (2023) who have also shown that developing financial competences could help enterprises achieve positive sustainability outcomes.

1.5.5 Lack of Product Innovation and Market

Analysis of existing literature suggests that lack of product innovation, particularly financial products linked to sustainability is a major challenge affecting green finance. For instance, evidence from Banga (2019) suggests that whilst financial products such as green insurance and sustainability linked loans exist in the developed world, this is not the case in most developing countries. This creates regional disparities, which affect the global effort to drive sustainable growth through green finance. Lack of market for green finance products such as green bonds, green insurance and sustainability linked loans have also been shown to hamper market development for green finance (Bhutta et al., 2022). Perhaps, it is this reason that Kwilinski et al. (2025) argues that investors, governments and banks have a major role to play in developing green finance markets which could contribute positively to sustainable development.

Studies (Gao et al., 2024; Gilchrist et al., 2021) have also shown that the high transaction costs associated with finance products appears to affect the supply of funds for green projects. Clearly, there is the need for policy makers to create a conducive environment for the creation of an efficient green finance market which could foster product innovation and reduce transaction costs. This recommendation is consistent with Fu et al. (2023) who concludes that a collaborative effort and homogeneous policy measures are required to advance green finance which has the potential to promote sustainable economic growth.

1.5.6 Unequal Access and Benefits

Various studies have raised concerns about the benefits of green finance, which have been found to appear to disproportionally accrue to large business organisations and rich western nations. This suggests that poorer communities that often suffer more from climate related disasters may be excluded, prompting other studies (Van Niekerk, 2024; Desalegn & Tangl, 2022) to conclude that green finance deployment does not support inclusive growth. Designing green finance products that align with gender and local rights issues could address this challenge and foster inclusive growth. One approach that has been proposed is a policy framework that encourages the flow of green capital to poorer communities and projects that support vulnerable groups. In this regard, Nasir and Ahmed (2024) have demonstrated that green finance can foster social inclusiveness if appropriately designed and deployed.

1.5.7 Lack of Trust and Misleading Claims

There are concerns that projects that attract green finance are often presented as environmentally friendly but some of these projects have been proven to yield negative environmental outcomes (Ozili, 2022). This misrepresentation has created a trust deficit which has affected investor confidence in supporting green projects. Perhaps, it in this context that Bo and Battisti (2024) contends that greenwashing is a major challenge facing the green finance market. Lack of appropriate regulatory framework and pressures from key stakeholders have been shown to contribute to greenwashing (Alaudhli, 2024). Creating a global mechanism for enforcing and verifying the environmental benefits of green finance initiatives could foster trust and prevent greenwashing (Buttigieg & Pulis, 2024). Similarly, Fu et al. (2023) have demonstrated that the development of equitable monitoring and reporting systems could improve the reliability of green fiancé activities.

1.6 Conclusion and Recommendations

Green finance is certainly a potent strategy for transforming the global economy to a more sustainable future. The growing threat of climate change requires innovative financial instruments that integrate modern financial systems with sustainability requirements. In this respect, this chapter has outlined how green finance has evolved to date, the role played by business enterprise and the key challenges. Developing a unified policy and regulatory framework for green investments could facilitate international capital flows which could increase investor confidence and rationalise regulations of green finance. Besides, improving the financial literacy of enterprises could contribute positively to the development of sustainable business model and access to green finance. Moreso, developing a reporting framework that align with international agreements could provide a consistent approach and reduce information asymmetry which could improve investor confidence and increase funding for green projects. Investors, governments and banks have a major role to play in developing green finance markets which could contribute positively to sustainable development.

References

Abba, Z. Y. I., Balta-Ozkan, N., & Hart, P. (2022). A holistic risk management framework for renewable energy investments. *Renewable and Sustainable Energy Reviews, 160*, 112305.

Akomea-Frimpong, I., Adeabah, D., Ofosu, D., & Tenakwah, E. J. (2022). A review of studies on green finance of banks, research gaps and future directions. *Journal of Sustainable Finance & Investment, 12*(4), 1241–1264.

Alaudhli, R. J. (2024). Greenwashing risk and its mitigation for sustainable finance. *Ajrsp, 6*(61), 05–33.

Amighini, A., Giudici, P., & Ruet, J. (2022). Green finance: An empirical analysis of the Green Climate Fund portfolio structure. *Journal of Cleaner Production, 350*, 131383.

Arunachalam, M. (2024). Analysis of stakeholders interests in green finance. In *The Palgrave handbook of green finance for sustainable development* (pp. 89–119). Springer International Publishing.

Auzepy, A., Bannier, C. E., & Martin, F. (2023). Are sustainability-linked loans designed to effectively incentivize corporate sustainability? A framework for review. *Financial Management, 52*(4), 643–675.

Azam, M., Haroon, M., Rahman, S. U., Ali, H., & Chani, M. I. (2024). The theoretical perspective of green finance. In *The Palgrave handbook of green finance for sustainable development* (pp. 19–47). Springer International Publishing.

Babajide, A., Osabuohien, E., Tunji-Olayeni, P., Falola, H., Amodu, L., Olokoyo, F., Adegboye, F., & Ehikioya, B. (2023). Financial literacy, financial capabilities, and sustainable business model practice among small business owners in Nigeria. *Journal of Sustainable Finance & Investment, 13*(4), 1670–1692.

Bagh, T., & Iftikhar, K. (2024). Understanding the theoretical context of green finance. In *The Palgrave handbook of green finance for sustainable development* (pp. 49–87). Springer International Publishing.

Banga, J. (2019). The green bond market: A potential source of climate finance for developing countries. *Journal of Sustainable Finance & Investment, 9*(1), 17–32.

Bartelega, C. F., & Mendonça, A. R. R. D. (2024). The BNDES'ROLE in the green economy: Institutional framework, disbursements and resource mobilisation (2010-2021). *Brazilian Journal of Political Economy, 44*(4), e243614.

Behera, I., & Nanda, P. (2025). Green finance strategies: Driving sustainable business models through innovative financing solutions. In *Sustainable financing—A contemporary guide for green finance, crowdfunding and digital currencies: Sustainable financing* (pp. 79–96). Springer Nature.

Belova, N., Posadneva, E., Plaksa, J., Tesalovsky, A., & Volkodavova, E. (2023). Opportunities of green lending to finance environmental projects to achieve the principles of sustainable development. *Journal of Law and Sustainable Development, 11*(1), e0268–e0268.

Bhutta, U. S., Tariq, A., Farrukh, M., Raza, A., & Iqbal, M. K. (2022). Green bonds for sustainable development: Review of literature on development and impact of green bonds. *Technological Forecasting and Social Change, 175*, 121378.

Bo, S., & Battisti, E. (2024). Green finance and greenwashing: Charting a sustainable path forward. *Qualitative Research in Financial Markets*, 1–20.

Buttigieg, C. P., & Pulis, S. (2024). Strategic initiatives to address greenwashing. In *ERA Forum* (pp. 1–11). Springer.

Campiglio, E., Dafermos, Y., Monnin, P., Ryan-Collins, J., Schotten, G., & Tanaka, M. (2018). Climate change challenges for central banks and financial regulators. *Nature Climate Change, 8*(6), 462–468.

Cai, X., & Song, X. (2024). Towards sustainable environment: Unleashing the mechanism between green finance and corporate social responsibility. *Energy & Environment, 35*(2), 986–1003.

Chen, J. M., Umair, M., & Hu, J. (2024). Green finance and renewable energy growth in developing nations: A GMM analysis. *Heliyon, 10*(13), e33879.

Chua, W. F., James, R., King, A., Lee, E., & Soderstrom, N. (2022). Task force on climate-related financial disclosures (TCFD) implementation: An overview and insights from the Australian accounting standards board dialogue series. *Australian Accounting Review, 32*(3), 396–405.

Clark, R., Reed, J., & Sunderland, T. (2018). Bridging funding gaps for climate and sustainable development: Pitfalls, progress and potential of private finance. *Land Use Policy, 71*, 335–346.

Climate Bonds Initiative. (2022). *Green Bond Market Summary*. [online]. Accessed June 6, 2025, from https://www.climatebonds.net

Cunha, F. A. F. D. S., Meira, E., & Orsato, R. J. (2021). Sustainable finance and investment: Review and research agenda. *Business Strategy and the Environment, 30*(8), 3821–3838.
David, D., & Venkatachalam, A. (2019). A comparative study on the role of public–private partnerships and green investment banks in boosting low-carbon investments. In *Handbook of green finance* (pp. 1–28). Springer.
Das, S. (2022). Tata power raising $320 m in sustainability-linked loans. *The Economic Times*.
Debrah, C., Chan, A. P., Darko, A., Owusu-Manu, D. G., & Ohene, E. (2024). *Green 13 finance*. Rethinking Pathways to a Sustainable Built Environment (p. 277).
Del Sarto, N. (2025). The European regulatory framework: Policies and regulations for sustainable finance. In *ESG factors and financial outcomes in banks: Quantitative insights into the ESG-cost of debt relationship* (pp. 61–94). Springer Nature.
Desalegn, G., & Tangl, A. (2022). Enhancing green finance for inclusive green growth: A systematic approach. *Sustainability, 14*(12), 7416.
Digitemie, W. N., & Ekemezie, I. O. (2024). Assessing the role of carbon pricing in global climate change mitigation strategies. *Magna Scientia Advanced Research and Reviews, 10*(2), 022–031.
Dikau, S., & Volz, U. (2019). Central banking, climate change, and green finance. In *Handbook of green finance* (pp. 81–102). Springer.
Du, K., Harford, J., & Shin, D. D. (2023). *Who benefits from sustainability-linked loans?*. European Corporate Governance Institute–Finance Working Paper (917).
Dupir, M. (2024). The evolution of green finance: Systemic risk, investment strategies, and regulatory implications in sustainable capital markets. *Young Economists Journal/Revista Tinerilor Economisti, 21*(43).
Falcone, P. M. (2020). Environmental regulation and green investments: The role of green finance. *International Journal of Green Economics, 14*(2), 159–173.
Ferraz, J. D. M., & Ferraz, D. L. D. S. (2022). Do espírito do capitalismo ao espírito empreendedor: a consolidação das ideias acerca da prática empreendedora numa abordagem histórico-materialista. *Cadernos EBAPE. BR, 20*(1), 105–117.
Fu, C., Lu, L., & Pirabi, M. (2023). Advancing green finance: A review of sustainable development. *Digital Economy and Sustainable Development, 1*(1), 20.
Gao, J., Hua, G., & Huo, B. (2024). Green finance policies, financing constraints and corporate ESG performance: Insights from supply chain management. *Operations Management Research, 17*, 1–15.
Geels, F. W., Pereira, G. I., & Pinkse, J. (2022). Moving beyond opportunity narratives in COVID-19 green recoveries: A comparative analysis of public investment plans in France, Germany, and the United Kingdom. *Energy Research & Social Science, 84*, 102368.
Ghisetti, C., Mancinelli, S., Mazzanti, M., & Zoli, M. (2017). Financial barriers and environmental innovations: Evidence from EU manufacturing firms. *Climate Policy, 17*(sup1), S131–S147.
Gilchrist, D., Yu, J., & Zhong, R. (2021). The limits of green finance: A survey of literature in the context of green bonds and green loans. *Sustainability, 13*(2), 478.
Gualandri, E., Bongini, P., Pierigè, M., & Di Janni, M. (2024). *Climate risk and financial intermediaries: Regulatory framework, transmission channels, governance and disclosure*. Springer Nature.
Hussain, M., Jaweed, M., Murtaza, M., & Ali, M. (2025). Green bonds and sustainable investment strategies: Evaluating risk-return profiles, market growth, and the role of climate-conscious portfolios in sustainable finance. *Advance Journal of Econometrics and Finance, 3*(2), 39–53.
Hussain, S., Rasheed, A., & Rehman, S. U. (2024). Driving sustainable growth: Exploring the link between financial innovation, green finance and sustainability performance: Banking evidence. *Kybernetes, 53*(11), 4678–4696.
Hwang, B. G., Zhao, X., See, Y. L., & Zhong, Y. (2015). Addressing risks in green retrofit projects: The case of Singapore. *Project Management Journal, 46*(4), 76–89.
IPCC 2018. Special Report: Global Warming 1.5°C. October. https://www.ipcc.ch/sr15/

Isah, A., Dioha, M. O., Debnath, R., Abraham-Dukuma, M. C., & Butu, H. M. (2023). Financing renewable energy: Policy insights from Brazil and Nigeria. *Energy, Sustainability and Society, 13*(1), 2.

Islam, M. T. (2023). Newly developed green technology innovations in business: Paving the way toward sustainability. *Technological Sustainability, 2*(3), 295–319.

Joshi, D., Paul, S., Singh, P., Mane, N. S., & Yadav, M. (2024). Sustainable finance: The role of green bonds in driving ESG investments. *Library of Progress-Library Science, Information Technology & Computer, 44*(3).

Jonsdottir, B., Sigurjonsson, T. O., Johannsdottir, L., & Wendt, S. (2022). Barriers to using ESG data for investment decisions. *Sustainability, 14*(9), 5157.

Johnson, L., Sachs, L., & Lobel, N. (2019). Aligning international investment agreements with the sustainable development goals. *Columbia Journal of Transnational Law, 58*, 58.

Kandpal, V., Jaswal, A., Santibanez Gonzalez, E. D., & Agarwal, N. (2024). Sustainable energy transition, circular economy, and ESG practices. In *Sustainable energy transition: Circular economy and sustainable financing for environmental, social and governance (ESG) practices* (pp. 1–51). Springer Nature Switzerland.

Karamoozian, A., Wu, D., Lambert, J. H., & Luo, C. (2022). Risk assessment of renewable energy projects using uncertain information. *International Journal of Energy Research, 46*(13), 18079–18099.

Khalid, F., Su, C. Y., Weiwei, K., Voinea, C. L., & Srivastava, M. (2025). Financial mechanism for sustainability: The case of China's green financial system and corporate green investment. *China Finance Review International, 15*(1), 93–116.

Khan, K. I., Mata, M. N., Martins, J., Nasir, A., Dantas, R. M., Correia, A. B., & Saghir, U. S. (2022). Impediments of green finance adoption system: Linking economy and environment. *Impediments of green finance adoption system: Linking economy and environment., 2*, 217–237.

Khurshid, A., Rauf, A., Qayyum, S., Calin, A. C., & Duan, W. (2023). Green innovation and carbon emissions: The role of carbon pricing and environmental policies in attaining sustainable development targets of carbon mitigation—Evidence from Central-Eastern Europe. *Environment, Development and Sustainability, 25*(8), 8777–8798.

Kwilinski, A., Lyulyov, O., & Pimonenko, T. (2025). The role of innovation development in advancing green finance. *Journal of Risk and Financial Management, 18*(3), 140.

Kyeyune, G. N., & Ntayi, J. M. (2025). Empowering rural communities: The role of financial literacy and management in sustainable development. *Frontiers in Human Dynamics, 6*, 1424126.

Lee, J. W. (2020). Green finance and sustainable development goals: The case of China. *Journal of Asian Finance Economics and Business, 7*(7), 577–586.

Leong, W. Y. (2024). *ESG and green sustainable technology: Catalysts for the next production revolution*. ESG Innovation for Sustainable Manufacturing Technology: Applications, Designs and Standards (p. 75).

Li, B. (2023). The role of financial markets in the energy transition: An analysis of investment trends and opportunities in renewable energy and clean technology. *Environmental Science and Pollution Research, 30*(43), 97948–97964.

Liu, B. (2024). Development history and enlightenment of electric vehicles based on Tesla's financial perspective. *Advances in Economics, Management and Political Sciences, 114*, 185–194.

Liu, X., Cifuentes-Faura, J., Wang, C. A., & Wang, L. (2024). Can green finance policy reduce corporate carbon emissions? Evidence from a quasi-natural experiment in China. *The British Accounting Review*, 101540.

Luo, W., & Cheng, J. (2023). Transition to sustainable business models for green economic recovery: Role of financial literacy, innovation and environmental sustainability. *Economic Change and Restructuring, 56*(6), 3787–3810.

Marín-Rodríguez, N. J., González-Ruiz, J. D., & Botero, S. (2024). Evolution of green finance: Mapping its role as a catalyst for economic growth and innovation. *Journal of Risk and Financial Management, 17*(11), 507.

Matriano, M. T. (2024). Green finance and how sustainability is shaping the investment strategies. *Global Scientific Journals, 12*(12), 447–458.
Morgado, N. C., & Lasfargues, B. (2017). Engaging the private sector for green growth and climate action: An overview of development co-operation efforts.
Morningstar. (2022). *Global Sustainable Fund Flows: Q4 2022 in Review*. [online] Accessed June 6, 2025, from https://www.morningstar.com/lp/sustainable-funds-landscape
Mukonzo, B., & Dzingirai, M. (2025). *15 green leadership and ESG*. Financial Inclusion and Sustainable Development in Sub-Saharan Africa (p. 231).
Nanayakkara, M., & Colombage, S. (2022). Does compliance to green bond principles matter? Global evidence. *Australasian Accounting, Business and Finance Journal, 16*(3).
Nasir, N., & Ahmed, W. (2024). Green finance initiatives and their potential to drive sustainable development. In *Climate change and finance: Navigating the challenges and opportunities in capital markets* (pp. 3–29). Springer Nature Switzerland.
Narassimhan, E., Gallagher, K. S., Koester, S., & Alejo, J. R. (2018). Carbon pricing in practice: A review of existing emissions trading systems. *Climate Policy, 18*(8), 967–991.
Nedopil, C., Dordi, T., & Weber, O. (2021). The nature of global green finance standards—Evolution, differences, and three models. *Sustainability, 13*(7), 3723.
Nerlich, C., Köhler-Ulbrich, P., Andersson, M., Pasqua, C., Abraham, L., Bańkowski, K., Emambakhsh, T., Ferrando, A., Grynberg, C., Groß, J., & Hoendervangers, L. (2025). *Investing in Europe's green future: Green investment needs, outlook and obstacles to funding the gap* (No. 367). ECB Occasional Paper.
Nix, P., Goldstein, A., & Oppenheimer, M. (2025). Quasi-governmental organization under pressure: The Connecticut Green Bank's response to a budget shock. *Environmental Policy and Governance, 35*, 647–661.
Okeke, N. I., Bakare, O. A., & Achumie, G. O. (2024). Integrating policy incentives and risk management for effective green finance in emerging markets. *International Journal of Frontiers in Science and Technology Research, 7*(1), 76–88.
Ørsted. (2025). *Who we are* [online] Accessed June 22, 2025, from https://orsted.com/en/who-we-are
Ozili, P. K. (2022). Green finance research around the world: A review of literature. *International Journal of Green Economics, 16*(1), 56–75.
Rendtorff, J. D. (2023). Sustainable solutions to the global climate problem: The case of the renewable and green energy company Ørsted. In *Value creation for a sustainable world: Innovating for ecological regeneration and human flourishing* (pp. 63–80). Springer International Publishing.
Schub, J. (2015). Green banks: Growing clean energy markets by leveraging private investment with public financing. *Journal of Structured Finance, 21*(3), 26–35.
Shishlov, I., Morel, R., & Cochran, I. (2016). Beyond transparency: Unlocking the full potential of green bonds. *Institute for Climate Economics, 2016*, 1–28.
Siddik, A. B., Rahman, M. N., & Yong, L. (2023). Do fintech adoption and financial literacy improve corporate sustainability performance? The mediating role of access to finance. *Journal of Cleaner Production, 421*, 137658.
Siegrist, M., Bowman, G., Mervine, E., & Southam, C. (2020). Embedding environment and sustainability into corporate financial decision-making. *Accounting & Finance, 60*(1), 129–147.
Singh, V. K. (2022). Regulatory and legal framework for promoting green digital finance. In *Green digital finance and sustainable development goals* (pp. 3–27). Springer Nature Singapore.
Spasenic, Z., Makajic-Nikolic, D., & Benkovic, S. (2022). Risk assessment of financing renewable energy projects: A case study of financing a small hydropower plant project in Serbia. *Energy Reports, 8*, 8437–8450.
Srivastava, S. (2021). *From dong to orsted: A leading utility's green energy transition*. Institute for Energy Economics and Financial Analysis.

Sule, A. K., Eyo-Udo, N. L., Onukwulu, E. C., Agho, M. O., & Azubuike, C. (2024). Green finance solutions for banking to combat climate change and promote sustainability. *Gulf Journal of Advance Business Research, 2*(6), 376–410.

Sundaram, A. K. (2023). ESG investing. In *Handbook of business and climate change* (pp. 503–524).

Svirskyi, V. (2025). Green bonds as a driver towards a climate-neutral economy in Europe. In *Innovation in capitalist economies: Crises, challenges and opportunities* (p. 109).

Tian, H. (2018). Role of capital market to accelerate the transition to low-carbon energy system. In *Financing for low-carbon energy transition: Unlocking the potential of private capital* (pp. 211–238).

UNEP. (2021). Emissions gap report 2021. October 2021. https://www.unep.org/resources/emissions-gap-report-2021

Van Niekerk, A. J. (2024). Economic inclusion: Green finance and the SDGs. *Sustainability, 16*(3), 1128.

Vachon, S., & Klassen, R. D. (2006). Extending green practices across the supply chain: The impact of upstream and downstream integration. *International Journal of Operations & Production Management, 26*(7), 795–821.

Voldsgaard, A., & Rüdiger, M. (2021). Innovative enterprise, industrial ecosystems and sustainable transition: The case of transforming DONG energy to Ørsted. In *Handbook of climate change mitigation and adaptation* (pp. 1–52). Springer.

Wang, K. H., Zhao, Y. X., Jiang, C. F., & Li, Z. Z. (2022). Does green finance inspire sustainable development? Evidence from a global perspective. *Economic Analysis and Policy, 75*, 412–426.

Weber, O., & Saravade, V. (2019). Green finance and the transition to a low-carbon economy. *Journal of Sustainable Finance & Investment, 9*(3), 233–251.

Westman, L., Luederitz, C., Kundurpi, A., Mercado, A. J., Weber, O., & Burch, S. L. (2019). Conceptualizing businesses as social actors: A framework for understanding sustainability actions in small-and medium-sized enterprises. *Business Strategy and the Environment, 28*(2), 388–402.

Ye, X., & Rasoulinezhad, E. (2023). Assessment of impacts of green bonds on renewable energy utilization efficiency. *Renewable Energy, 202*, 626–633.

Yeoh, P. (2021). The sustainability of environmental, social and governance (ESG) reporting in the US and the UK. *Business Law Review, 42*(6), 272–281.

Yu, B., Liu, L., & Chen, H. (2023). Can green finance improve the financial performance of green enterprises in China? *International Review of Economics & Finance, 88*, 1287–1300.

Zhang, M., Liu, Y., & Su, Y. (2017). Comparison of carbon emission trading schemes in the European Union and China. *Climate, 5*(3), 70.

Zhang, X., Song, Y., & Zhang, M. (2023). Exploring the relationship of green investment and green innovation: Evidence from Chinese corporate performance. *Journal of Cleaner Production, 412*, 137444.

Zhao, X., & Li, X. (2024). The role of green finance in mitigating climate change risks: A quantitative analysis of sustainable investments. *Environmental Science and Pollution Research, 31*(5), 7569–7585.

Zhu, B., Xu, C., Wang, P., & Zhang, L. (2022). How does internal carbon pricing affect corporate environmental performance? *Journal of Business Research, 145*, 65–77.

Dr. Yahaya Alhassan is the Head of Academic Operations at the University of Sunderland in London. Dr. Alhassan is responsible for leading the integration and execution of the University of Sunderland's strategic and operational priorities across all academic programmes at the London campus (UoSiL). He also oversees the development and implementation of the Academic Programme Offer, as well as the integration of the University's Research and Innovation Strategy. Alongside his leadership role, Dr. Alhassan maintains an active research profile. His current research explores investment in financial technology (FinTech) and firm growth, with several of his papers published in high-ranking ABS 3* journals. He has co-edited books, authored multiple book chapters in finance and enterprise, and frequently presents at academic conferences, contributing meaningfully to the field of finance since 2019. Dr. Alhassan has over 20 experience in teaching, academic leadership, and management, gained through his roles at the University of Sunderland in London as well as previous positions in the higher education and consultancy sectors. He holds a PhD in Business Management (Finance) from Anglia Ruskin University, an MBA in Finance and a Master of Education from the University of Sunderland, and a BA (Hons) in Business Management from Arden University. He is also a Senior Fellow of the Higher Education Academy (HEA).

Chapter 2
Leveraging Diaspora Bonds for Climate Projects in Developing and Emerging Economies

Samuel Salia, Eugene Bempong Nyantakyi, Javed Hussain, Eric Ofosu-Hene, and Yahaya Alhassan

2.1 Introduction

Diaspora finance is essential in financing climate projects in order to reduce carbon emission and its negative health impacts, develop climate resilient infrastructure for developing and emerging economies and ensure environmental sustainability (Salia & Bempong Nyantakyi, 2022; Taghizadeh-Hesary & Yoshino, 2019). This shows that diaspora finance could be used to address climate change challenges in developing and emerging countries by pooling finance from diasporans (people who permanently reside as minorities in one or several countries) and supporting climate mitigation and adaptation projects (Chirambo, 2017). In particular, diaspora bonds stand out as a far more viable option to finance climate change projects in developing economies than any other financing arrangement because the diasporan is motivated to support such projects in the home economy to demonstrate empathy and to preserve a "personal haven" (Lapshyna, 2019).

S. Salia · J. Hussain
Birmingham City University, Birmingham, UK
e-mail: samuel.salia@bcu.ac.uk; javed.hussain@bcu.ac.uk

E. B. Nyantakyi
African Development Bank, Abidjan, Côte d'Ivoire
e-mail: e.bempongnyantakyi@afdb.org

E. Ofosu-Hene
De Montfort University, Leicester, UK
e-mail: eric.ofosu-hene@dmu.ac.uk

Y. Alhassan (✉)
University of Sunderland in London, London, UK
e-mail: yahaya.alhassan@sunderland.ac.uk

Y. Alhassan et al. (eds.), *Financial Innovation and Sustainable Enterprise in Developing and Emerging Economies*, Research Series on Responsible Enterprise Ecosystems, https://doi.org/10.1007/978-3-032-04500-3_2

In the last decade, developing countries and some emerging economies have gained significant awareness of climate degradation. However, they face a climate finance gap that has been exacerbated by the recent Covid-19 pandemic. Key studies (Sangiorgi & Schopohl, 2021; Graham, 2020; Chowdhury & Jomo, 2022) have acknowledged that multi-stakeholder participation is required to address this climate finance gap. However, the literature on climate finance has placed little emphasis on the role of diaspora (migrants) as a key stakeholder (Salia & Bempong Nyantakyi, 2022). This study aims to bridge the gap.

The literature (Du & Takeuchi, 2019; Akanle et al., 2022; Welde et al., 2022) suggests that diaspora remittances are vital for poor countries' household consumption (Maara et al., 2019); government balance of payment (Rizvi et al., 2019); and international foreign reserves (Das et al., 2021). The diaspora makes considerable economic and social contributions to their countries of origin. This study examines migrant's motivation to invest in diaspora bonds (i.e., a sovereign bond issued to overseas residents of a country) for climate projects.

The world has failed to meet its own target of US$100 billion of investment in climate projects every year (Chowdhury & Jomo, 2022). Developed countries do not implement climate targets due to economic and political risk (Monasterolo, 2020). In contrast, developing and some emerging countries' low climate project investment is due to unattractive returns and risk for international financial markets (Banga, 2019). The low GDP and large informal economies of poor countries results in low revenue, hence, low climate investment (Mpofu, 2022). Stern (2022) argues that to overcome the funding gap for climate projects there is a need for alternative financing.

The general evidence suggests that at the time of climate related natural disasters such as, hurricanes Grace and Ida, diaspora remittance increased to Latin America and the Caribbean, resulting in a growth of 21.6% in 2021 alone (Nnyanzi et al., 2022). The diaspora is motivated to support the home economy to demonstrate empathy and to preserve a "personal haven" (Lapshyna, 2019). This shows strong psychological ties of the diaspora to their home country (Nyame-Asiamah et al., 2020). Whilst prior studies evidence diaspora's connection to the home country is the driver to assist at the time of natural disasters. However, there is limited evidence that explores diaspora financing for preventive climate projects. This study seeks to explore whether diaspora will invest in bonds issued to finance climate mitigation and adaptation projects.

Indeed, rudiments of bond behaviour globally have largely remained driven by economic and governance structure (Mikutowski et al., 2019; Capelle-Blancard et al., 2019). Nevertheless, various evaluations of developing and some emerging countries bond issuers have begun to question this common view (Bhutta et al., 2022). These countries bond issuers pay higher-than-normal coupon rates on bonds but observed risk measures like agency ratings and debt to gross domestic product (GDP) ratios do not explain the deviation from the norm (Olabisi & Stein, 2015). Also, primary spreads for the average bond issuer in developing and some emerging countries are higher than other regions (Presbitero et al., 2016). Thus, this makes these countries have little control over their market borrowing costs (Senga et al., 2018).

The above outcomes coupled with the spillover effects of global market uncertainty, widens the gap on access to international finance for developing and some countries (Mecagni et al., 2014). Bearing in mind the most recent World Bank (2019) data shows that developing countries need to spend 4.5% of their GDP to achieve its infrastructure-related sustainable development goals. A major shift is that mobilizing finance through the diaspora has gained traction within the World Bank, as a strategy to bridge this financing gap in developing and some emerging countries. The diaspora is defined as a transnational community whose members (or their ancestors) emigrated or were dispersed from their original homeland but remain oriented to it and preserve a group identity (Grossman, 2019). This study focuses on bilateral diaspora stock, rather than the whole transnational community.

Amid the greatest recession in 2008, diaspora workers transferred US$336 billion to their countries of origin (Ratha et al., 2010). According to the World Bank this is almost three times the amount of official aid flows from Organization for Economic Corporation and Development (OECD) member states. The World Bank (2019) estimates most recent remittance incomes have reached US$689 billion, representing annual growth rates that are well above 10%, and equivalent to about 2.5% of the gross national income of the developing world (Ranjan et al., 2023). As such, the diaspora can drive the activities of debt markets and contribute to financial deepening of their countries of origin by serving as investors with their savings. This, however, depends on the home country's financial innovativeness and capacity to build trust to mobilize the resources of diaspora through special investment vehicles. The importance of diaspora bonds as an investment proposition is viewed from this perspective. A diaspora bond in this context is broadly defined as a debt instrument issued by a country—or potentially, a sub-sovereign entity or a private corporation—to raise finance from its overseas diaspora (Moyo, 2021).

Over half a century Markowitz (1952) and Miller et al. (1961) asset selection and return predictability theory have motivated investment in bond markets. Against this backdrop, the concept of investor rationality governs utility function: causing rational investors to prefer to be better off than worse off, thus demanding higher returns in the process where they perceive high risk. In the case of diaspora bond investment, return expectations are somewhat moderate. While economic theories assume rational behaviour on the part of investors, consistent with behavioural finance issues of psychology and emotion may enter the investment equation. In fact, it is contended that altruist emotions significantly and positively affect diaspora investment interest in their home country (Gillespie et al., 1999). Thus, altruism alters the action of diaspora investors and can lead to decisions such as investing in non-rated diaspora bonds as a show of patriotism to their country of origin. For example, Nielsen and Riddle (2010) document a strong motivation for diaspora to invest in post-conflict nations mainly because of the daunting state of the economies to attract foreign investors. However, there is limited evidence that explores diaspora financing for preventive climate projects. This study seeks to explore whether diaspora will invest in bonds issued to finance climate mitigation and adaptation projects.

To fill this knowledge void, we surveyed 1265 migrants and interviewed 17 diaspora investors and academic researchers in Europe during 2021 and 2022. Our results show the willingness of the diaspora to invest in bonds for climate projects is conditional on a number of factors. The migrant's connection to the home country is positively correlated with participation in the bonds; as supported by earlier literature (Nyame-Asiamah et al., 2020). Bonds with frequent coupon payments and longer maturity are more attractive to high-income earners.

This study makes two important contributions. It is the first empirical study that examines factors that attract the diaspora to invest in bonds for climate projects. Secondly, the study considers the salient features of the diaspora bond. The rest of the paper is arranged as follows: (2) Background and hypothesis development, (3) Methodology, (4) Results and Discussion, and (5) Conclusions.

2.2 Background and Hypothesis Development

2.2.1 Motivational Dynamics of Diaspora Investment in Bonds

Various migration studies over the past five decades have examined the relevance of the diaspora (Alexander, 2017; Cohen et al., 2018). However, the question of who a diaspora is remains, to a large extent, unanswered. Nearly two decades after (Brubaker, 2005) criticism of the "'let-a-thousand-diasporas-bloom' approach," there is still a lack of agreement on the meaning of the concept. Different studies are fine describing the diaspora as; temporary and permanent migrants, dispersed groups and native peoples, linguistic communities, global religions, and even such categories as "liberal," "queer," or "digital". According to Grossman (2019) this conceptual stretching negates the clear boundaries that a concept must possess to be applicable for empirical and comparative research and threatens to void "diaspora" of any meaning. Concepts emboldens theory, harnesses interdisciplinary studies (Podsakoff et al., 2016) and explains the importance of an entity (Goertz, 2006). Thus, to conduct empirical research about diasporas or to compare, analyse, and theorize about different diasporas, we must define them clearly. According to (Sheffer, 2006, 122), a diaspora is perceived as:

> A social-political formation, created as a result of either forced or voluntary migration, whose members regard themselves as of the same ethnonational origin and who permanently reside as minorities in one or several countries. Members of such entities [or "diasporans"] maintain regular or occasional contacts with what they regard as their homelands and with individuals and groups of the same background residing in other host countries.

Over half a century Markowitz (1952) and Miller et al. (1961) asset selection and return predictability theory have motivated investment in bond markets. Various structural approaches have drawn upon these works to generate styled facts about asset return predictability and recursive utility function (Peavy, 1990; Hong et al., 2017). According to Peavy (1990) the potential to improve the net worth of a portfolio is a critical driver in the investment decision making process. Implicitly, bond securities promising better future cash flows are preferred in investment decision making. Furthermore, Hong et al. (2017) suggest that the concept of investor rationality is drawn upon to contextualise utility function: rationality drives individual investors to prefer to be better off than worse off, causing them to manage risk and return expectations actively, and in the process demand higher returns to compensate for taking additional risk (Nielsen & Riddle, 2010). One empirical implication of this theory is that in a cross section, investors prefer high returns over higher risk.

In the case of diaspora bond investment, return expectations are somewhat moderate (Lainer-Vos, 2013). While economic theories assume rational behaviour on the part of investors, consistent with behavioural finance issues of psychology and emotion may influence the investment model. These factors alter the action of investors and can lead to decisions such as investing in non-rated diaspora bonds as a show of patriotism to the diaspora investor's country of origin (Licuanan et al., 2015). The first systematic review of diaspora investment motivation by Aharoni (1966), for example, find that American Jews invested sizeable amounts of money in Israel even though they consider it high risk. Aharoni concluded that strong psychological ties of the Jews to their homeland accounted for this behaviour. The study also finds that the motivation too: (a) assist in the building of the Israeli economy (b) preserve a personal haven, and (c) gain prominence in the Jewish community; further deepened these behaviours. Gillespie et al. (1999) who later explored the diaspora and home country investment relationship find that altruist emotions and positive investments performance expectations derived interest in investing in their countries of origin. Nielsen and Riddle (2010) expand upon the work of Gillespie et al. (1999) and contended that financial returns, emotional returns and social returns on investment influenced the investment profile of the diaspora.

Moreover, according to Djajić and Vinogradova (2015) (also consistent with the diaspora "target earning" theory), migrants' primary motivation is to accumulate enough savings to start a business or purchase some other assets upon return to home country (perhaps on temporary visit or permanent basis). The "target earning" theory adequately explains the savings behaviour of migrants and feeds into the income theory narrative on the propensity to consume, where aggregate demand is composed of demand 'C' for consumption and demand 'I' for investment goods (Bliss, 2014).

In one of the early appraisals of the Keynesian model (see Ramsey, 1928), it is pressumed that consumption is a linear function of income 'y' of the form; $C = k + by$ (a > 0; 0 < b < 1) where, C and y represent consumption and income respectively, k is autonomous consumption and, b is the behavioral consumption or the Marginal Propensity Consumption (MPC) that cannot be deferred for the sake of investment (Fujita, 2016). Nonetheless, the more income 'y' a person obtains, the less proportion he or she spends in direct consumption 'C' of goods (Bliss, 2014) while the remainder translates into savings and subsequently investment. Alternatively, an investment 'I' is described as expenditures other than the consumption C expenditures which is nothing but income 'y' minus consumption 'C'.

Hence, savings 'S' is equal to investment 'I'. Savings are often transferred to borrowers in two forms. First, owners of funds buy bonds (issued by states and firms) and stocks (issued by firms), and recipients of the funds then use the money to buy investment goods (Becker, 2016). Second, owners of funds deposit savings into banks. The banks subsequently lend the money to states and firms, which use it to buy investment goods (Bronfenbrenner, 2017). Within this framework of savings analysis, we address the question on the value of the diaspora bond to be issued.

2.2.2 An Overview of Diaspora Finance

Mobilizing finance through the diaspora has gained traction within the World Bank, as a strategy to bridge the financing gap in the developing world (Ketkar & Ratha, 2011). The flow of remittances from the diaspora remains a key and stable source of financing for their home countries, surpassing ODA and FDI (excluding China). It was recently found that, the outlook in remittance is somewhat larger or equivalent to, the official foreign exchange reserves, in the case of many Africa countries (Ratha, 2016). According to Cattaneo (2005) diaspora finance wields a positive effect on the receiving country's balance of payment position and as well as influencing economic growth via investment and savings as pathways. The effective application of diaspora finance to priority areas such as climate mitigation or adoption projects could help the developing world achieve its infrastructure-related sustainable development goals (Rwigema, 2023).

Amid the greatest recession in 2008, diaspora workers transferred US$336 billion to their countries of origin (Ratha et al., 2010). According to the World Bank this is almost three times the amount of official aid flows from OECD member states. The World Bank (2019) estimates most recent remittance incomes have reached US$689 billion, representing annual growth rates that are well above 10%, and equivalent to about 2.5% of the gross national income of the developing world with most remittances into developing countries coming from Europe and the US (Arthur, 2016). Notwithstanding the stylized facts about the buoyant nature of diaspora finance, Plaza and Ratha (2011) argue that their efficacy depends on sending countries financial innovativeness and capacity to build trust to mobilize the resources of the diaspora through special investment vehicles such as diaspora bonds.

According to Ketkar and Ratha (2010), diaspora bonds have several appealing prospects. First, diaspora bonds offer diaspora investors the opportunity to help their country of origin while they also provide an investment opportunity. Second, the uniqueness of diaspora bonds is viewed from the fact that they constitute a risk management strategy for the home country as they tend to transfer the risk of currency devaluation and default of payment onto their diaspora members. This is on the premise that they may be willing to take on certain financial burdens for the sake of patriotism (see Licuanan et al., 2015). Third, states issuing diaspora bonds are also likely to benefit from the leverage of offering below the market interest rates.

This is because diaspora investors do not request a high-country risk premium as the capital markets would require.

2.2.3 *Testable Hypotheses*

Given that, there is limited evidence that explores diaspora financing for preventive climate projects, we expect the following:

H1: The diaspora will invest in bonds issues to finance climate change.
H2: The migrants' connection with their home country positively correlates with participation in diaspora bond for climate change projects.
H3: The migrant is more likely to participate in long-term diaspora bond for climate change projects.

2.3 Methodology

We employed two different methods in this study.

2.3.1 *Cross-Sectional Survey*

We surveyed 1265 migrants from five countries in Europe during 2021 and 2022. Based on literature, proxy variables were identified for which survey questions are constructed. The main outcome variable is derived from the following question: Would you buy a diaspora bond for a climate change project? The question seeks the diaspora's willingness to invest in the bond specific to address climate change. We construct a binary variable equal to 1 if the respondent answered "Yes" and 0 if the answer is "No". Following this the questionnaire solicited responses to evaluate the respondents' connection to country of origin and how the bond should be designed (i.e., bond characteristics). The frequency of travel to country of origin is the proxy for Connection to Country of Origin. The Bond Characteristics are ascertained by seeking preferences of climate change projects, bond maturity period, frequency of coupon payment, bond issuer, outlet for the purchase of the bond and legal jurisdiction under which the bond is issued. The descriptive statistics are in Table 2.1.

Table 2.1 presents descriptive statistics of the variables and are self-explanatory.

Given the binary nature of our dependent variable of interest (the probability of participation in diaspora bond), and the interest in determining the probability of participation conditional on the various bond, countries, and migrant

Table 2.1 Summary statistics

	No	Yes	Grand total
Bond participation	12.49	87.51	100
Gender			
Female	4.27	35.89	40.16
Male	8.22	51.62	59.84
Migrant age group [years]			
20–30	0.32	7.51	7.83
31–40	6.72	45.53	52.25
41–50	3.64	29.64	33.28
51–60	1.82	4.82	6.64
Educational level			
Master's degree or PhD	0.55	9.01	9.56
Other qualifications	11.94	78.5	90.44
Income			
Low income [below $65,000]	10.67	79.6	90.27
Upper income [above $65,000]	1.82	7.91	9.73
Connection to country of origin			
1–2 years	10.04	63.95	73.99
3–5 years	1.98	14.31	16.29
6–10 years	0.47	9.25	9.72
Maturity			
1–5 years	11.54	81.42	92.96
6–10 years	0.48	5.06	5.54
Above 10 years	0.47	1.03	1.5
Frequency			
Coupon payment (12 months)	6.49	40.55	47.04
Coupon payment (3 months)	4.74	20.87	25.61
Coupon payment (6 months)	1.26	26.09	27.35
Outlet			
Financial markets	0.47	1.74	2.21
Mobile money	0	4.11	4.11
Origin bank	2.53	26.4	28.93
Settlement bank	9.49	55.26	64.75
Law			
Origin law	2.53	31.07	33.6
Settlement law	9.96	56.44	66.4
Project			
Mitigation	7.98	54.31	62.29
Adaptation	4.51	33.2	37.71
Issuer			
State	2.53	15.81	18.34
Government	8.38	66.96	75.34
Local authority	1.58	4.74	6.32

(continued)

Table 2.1 (continued)

	No	Yes	Grand total
Remittance			
Yes	1.26	4.03	5.29
No	11.23	83.48	94.71

Note: The study includes migrants from the following countries: Brazil, Ghana, India, Nigeria, and Romania

characteristics, we estimate the model in Eq. (2.1) below using the probit model. This allowed us to estimate the relationship between diaspora bond participation and migrant, country, and bond characteristics in a way that forces the fitted values to lie between zero and 1. The results in Table 2.1 report discrete probability changes. All estimations control for migrant's origin fixed effects.

$$\Pr\left(Y_i = 1 | X_i\right) = \Phi\left(X_i^T \beta\right) \tag{2.1}$$

where Y_i represents bond participation by migrant of i, Φ is the standard normal cumulative distribution function (CDF) of the unit normal distribution, X_i is a place holder for migrant, country, and diaspora bond characteristics outlined in Table 2.1, and βs are parameters to be estimated.

2.3.2 *Semi-Structured Interviews*

We collected qualitative data through semi-structured interviews (Husband, 2020). The interviews were conducted with diaspora investors and academic researchers with expertise in diaspora bonds and investment decisions. Conducting the semi-structured interviews allowed us to explore the perceptions of the interviewed diaspora investors or experts about the diaspora's willingness to invest in a bond specific to address climate change in a more flexible way. In total, we conducted 17 interviews from May 2021 until May 2022. The participants interviewed were found via personal contacts and a subsequent snowball sampling. The diaspora investors were asked "would you buy a diaspora bond for a climate change project?" The question seeks the diaspora investor's willingness to invest in the bond specific to address climate change. To understand the experts view about the possibility of the diaspora buying a diaspora bond for a climate change project, the experts interviewed were asked "in your expert opinion do you think the diaspora will invest in a bond designed for climate change projects in their home country? The diaspora investors interviewed were also asked "how often do you travel to your country of origin? The aim of this question is to evaluate the diaspora investor's' connection to the country of origin. To understand whether the diaspora's connection to their country of origin could influence their decision to invest in climate change projects, the experts interviewed where asked "in your expert opinion do you think the diaspora's connection to their home country could influence their decision to invest in climate change projects in their country of origin?"

2.4 Results and Discussions

2.4.1 *Survey Results and Discussions*

Table 2.2, Column (1) presents the baseline estimations of the bond characteristics and how they influence diaspora preference for the bond. Because the independent variables are discrete, the coefficients show how $\Pr(Y_i = 1)$, is predicted to change as the respective variable changes from 0 to 1. The reference categories are in the footnotes of Table 2.2. The diaspora bonds with a short coupon payment (3 months) and a long maturity (10 years) are preferred; the participation decreases with the length of maturity, as the coefficients are significant at 1%. The diaspora is 1.5% less likely to invest in a bond with a coupon maturity of 6 or 12 months relative to a coupon payment of 3 months, all else equal. This could be attributed to the risk aversion of the diaspora (Krasniqi & Williams, 2019). More specifically, the diaspora is 2.5% less likely to buy a bond that matures between 1 and 10 years than longer; the result is significant at 1%. The findings corroborate (Huynh & Xia, 2021.) who suggested investors favor long-long term climate bonds.

Columns (2) and (3) progressively add characteristics of the issuing country and diaspora characteristics to determine their impact on the bond participation. We include variables through which the bond is purchased: financial markets, mobile money, or through a bank in the issuing country relative to the settlement country of the migrant. Results in column (4) show the outlet for purchasing the bond has no significant impact on participation vis-à-vis the bond being issued in the migrant's settled country. Column 3 shows that diaspora bond participation is gender neutral. The results suggest migrants without a postgraduate degree are 2.2% more likely to participate in the bonds in comparison with migrants with postgraduates. This may be explained by the higher risk aversion amongst higher education attainers (Black et al., 2018). In addition, higher-income earners, above USD 65,000, are more likely to participate in diaspora bonds than low earners; these findings are corroborated by Painter (2020). Both the survey results and the interview responses from the diaspora investors and experts suggest that migrants' connection with the home country positively correlates with participation in climate change diaspora bond. Overall, the study shows that diaspora bonds that pay frequent coupons, have longer maturity, and target high-income earners who with strong ties to the country of origin are more successful at raising finance. Given the above outcomes, the framework below (Fig. 2.1) innovates the theory of change by augmenting impactful investment to support climate projects. The diagram suggests diaspora finance (remittance for investment) is not merely for consumption alone but also for impact investing. Thus, this innovative approach extends the literature by illustrating the importance of diaspora in impact investing.

Table 2.2 Probit regression results: determinants of diaspora bond participation

	(1)	(2)	(3)	(4)
Coupon payment (12 months)	−1.549***	−1.400***	−1.195***	
	(0.380)	(0.384)	(0.428)	
Coupon payment (6 months)	−1.472***	−1.524***	−1.383***	
	(0.355)	(0.356)	(0.372)	
Bond maturity (1–5 years)	−2.499***	−2.166***	−2.493***	
	(0.621)	(0.760)	(0.829)	
Bond maturity (6–10 years)	−2.006***	−1.775**	−2.079**	
	(0.704)	(0.843)	(0.924)	
Issuance based on settlement country law		0.278	0.012	
		(0.371)	(0.391)	
Issuance through financial markets		0.634	0.061	
		(0.719)	(0.783)	
Issuance through origin bank		0.571	−0.143	
		(0.381)	(0.455)	
Migrant gender (male)			0.161	0.263
			(0.216)	(0.202)
Migrant age (31–40)			0.715	0.600
			(0.565)	(0.551)
Migrant age (41–50)			0.495	0.396
			(0.584)	(0.568)
Migrant age (51–60)			1.042*	1.155*
			(0.632)	(0.612)
Migrant education [postgraduate]			2.244***	1.938***
			(0.515)	(0.465)
Migrant income [high income]			0.984**	0.933***
			(0.383)	(0.332)
Migrant remittance [1 = yes]			−1.042***	−1.027***
			(0.382)	(0.359)
Most recent travel home [3–5 years]			−0.494*	−0.528**
			(0.252)	(0.244)
Most recent travel home [6–10 years]			−1.272**	−1.304***
			(0.528)	(0.477)
Project type [mitigation]		0.116	0.172	
		(0.213)	(0.232)	
Constant	2.159**	1.308	−0.187	−3.393***
	(0.847)	(1.047)	(1.390)	(0.804)
Origin effects	Yes	Yes	Yes	Yes
Observations	1265	1265	1265	1265
Log likelihood	−434.645	−427.02	−400.883	−421.74

Note: Dependent variable is Diaspora Bond Participation [1 = Yes, 0 = No]. The reference group for coupon payment is 3 months. That for Bond Maturity is >10 years. The reference group for Issuance law is origin law, and that for the outlet is settlement bank. While gender reference group is female, the age reference group is between 20 to 30, education reference group is migrants'education below the postgraduate level, that for remittance is, No and home travel is less than 2 years. Finally, the reference group for project type is adaptation. ***Significant at the 1% level, **Significant at the 5% level, *Significant at the 10% level. Because the independent variables are discrete, the coefficients show how $\Pr(Y_i - 1)$,is predicted to change as the respective variable changes from 0 to 1. Robust standard errors are in parentheses. *** $p < 0.01$, ** $p < 0.05$

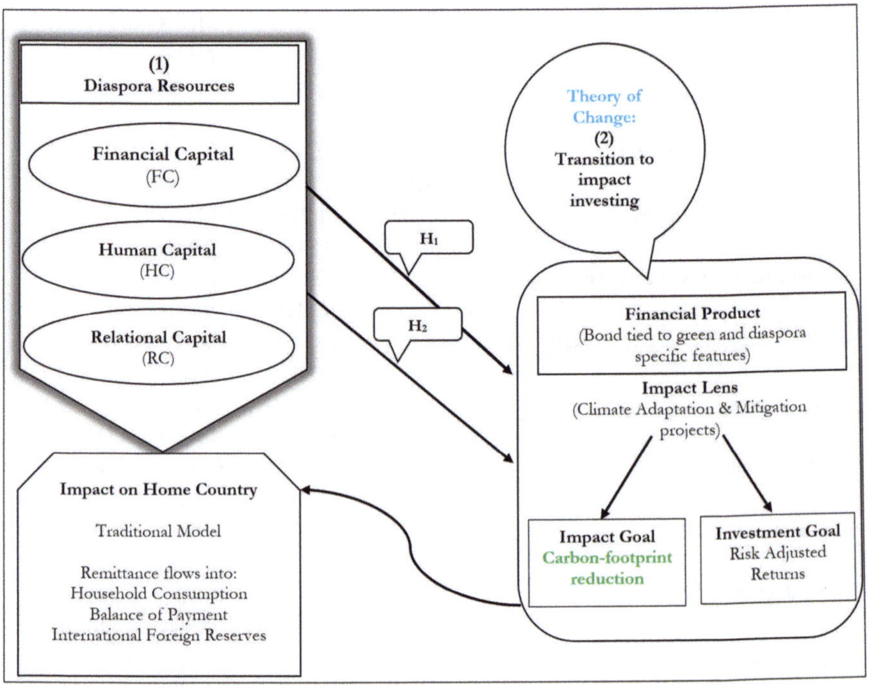

Fig. 2.1 Diaspora impact investing. Source: own elaboration

2.4.2 *Semi-Structured Interviews Results and Discussions*

All the diaspora investors interviewed confirmed that they will buy a diaspora bond for climate change project in their country of origin. One respondent for example stated that "I will definitely invest in any bond that aims to reduce the effects of climate change in any part of Africa". Similarly, all the experts interviewed stated that in their opinion the diaspora will invest in bonds designed for climate change projects in their country of origin. Most of the experts opined that the negative effect of climate change on communities recorded in the developing world could be a stimulus for the diaspora investment in such projects. With regards to the question on how often the respondents travel to their country of origin, all the diaspora investors interviewed confirmed that they frequently travel to their country of origin. All the experts interviewed stated that in their opinion the diaspora's connection to their home country does influence their decision to invest in climate change projects in their country of origin.

2.5 Conclusions

Given the pivotal role of the diaspora in economic and social development within their country of origin, this paper investigated the role of diaspora finance for climate projects. Thereby, the paper fills a major void in knowledge. In summary, the connection of migrants with their home country is positively correlated with participation in the bond. Diaspora bonds with frequent coupons, longer maturity that targets high-income earners are more likely to be successful. Impact investing diaspora bonds has the potential to partially bridge the climate finance gap in developing and emerging economies. The limitation of the study is that it considers data from migrants of only five countries and covers a limited period, from 2020 to 2021. Future studies should examine diaspora bond structure for debt burden countries and data for longer periods.

References

Aharoni, Y. (1966). The foreign investment decision process. In *International business* (pp. 87–97). https://doi.org/10.4324/9781315199689-5

Akanle, O., Kayode, D., & Abolade, I. (2022). Sustainable development goals (SDGs) and remittances in Africa. *Cogent Social Sciences, 8*(1), 2037811.

Alexander, C. (2017). Beyond the "the 'diaspora' diaspora": A response to Rogers Brubaker. *Ethnic and Racial Studies, 40*(9), 1544–1555. https://doi.org/10.1080/01419870.2017.1300302

Arthur, J. A. (2016). *The African Diaspora in the United States and Europe*. https://doi.org/10.4324/9781315612287

Banga, J. (2019). The green bond market: A potential source of climate finance for developing countries. *Journal of Sustainable Finance & Investment, 9*(1), 17–32.

Becker, G. S. (2016). *An equilibrium theory of the distribution of income and intergenerational mobility* (pp. 17–49). https://doi.org/10.4324/9781315619750-11

Bhutta, U. S., Tariq, A., Farrukh, M., Raza, A., & Iqbal, M. K. (2022). Green bonds for sustainable development: Review of literature on development and impact of green bonds. *Technological Forecasting and Social Change, 175*, 121378.

Black, S. E., Devereux, P. J., Lundborg, P., & Majlesi, K. (2018). Learning to take risks? The effect of education on risk-taking in financial markets. *Review of Finance, 22*(3), 951–975.

Bliss, C. J. (2014). *Capital theory and the distribution of income* (Vol. 4). Elsevier.

Bronfenbrenner, M. (2017). *Income distribution theory*. https://doi.org/10.4324/9780203788721

Brubaker, R. (2005). The 'diaspora' diaspora. *Ethnic and Racial Studies, 28*(1), 1–19. https://doi.org/10.1080/0141987042000289997

Capelle-Blancard, G., Crifo, P., Diaye, M.-A., Oueghlissi, R., & Scholtens, B. (2019). Sovereign bond yield spreads and sustainability: An empirical analysis of OECD countries. *Journal of Banking & Finance, 98*, 156–169. https://doi.org/10.1016/J.JBANKFIN.2018.11.011

Cattaneo, C. (2005). *International migration and poverty: A cross country analysis*. Retrieved from https://www.researchgate.net/publication/267261100

Chirambo, D. (2017). Increasing the value of climate finance in an uncertain environment: Diaspora financial resources as a source of climate finance for sub-Saharan Africa. *AIMS Environmental Science, 4*(6), 730–742.

Chowdhury, A., & Jomo, K. S. (2022). The climate finance conundrum. *Development, 65*(1), 29–41.

Cohen, R., Fischer, C., & Fischer, C. (2018). Diaspora studies. In *Routledge handbook of diaspora studies* (pp. 1–10). https://doi.org/10.4324/9781315209050-1

Djajić, S., & Vinogradova, A. (2015). Overshooting the savings target: Temporary migration, investment in housing and development. *World Development, 65*, 110–121. https://doi.org/10.1016/j.worlddev.2014.01.015

Du, Y., & Takeuchi, K. (2019). Can climate mitigation help the poor? Measuring impacts of the CDM in rural China. *Journal of Environmental Economics and Management, 95*, 178–197.

Das, A., Brown, L., McFarlane, A., & Campbell, K. (2021). Remittances and reverse flows in Jamaica. *The Journal of Developing Areas, 55*(4), 211–233.

Fujita, Y. (2016). Piketty's capital-income theory reconsidered for a small open economy with increasing savings rate. *Open Journal of Statistics, 6*(01), 25–30. https://doi.org/10.4236/ojs.2016.61004

Gillespie, K., Riddle, L., Sayre, E., & Sturges, D. (1999). Diaspora interest in homeland investment. *Journal of International Business Studies, 30*(3), 623–634. https://doi.org/10.1057/palgrave.jibs.8490087

Goertz, G. (2006). *Social science concepts: A user's guide*. Retrieved from https://books.google.co.uk/books?hl=en&lr=&id=vwNxIyT-M94C&oi=fnd&pg=PP2&dq=Goertz+2006&ots=cRq-4LiS85&sig=MldO9HBzca3AlZO395LsZMBjnwQ&redir_esc=y#v=onepage&q=Goertz2006&f=false

Graham, C. (2020). Managing climate change: The role of multi-stakeholder partnerships in building climate resilience in sub-Saharan Africa. *Interdisciplinary Journal of Partnership Studies, 7*(2), 4–4.

Grossman, J. (2019). Toward a definition of diaspora. *Ethnic and Racial Studies, 42*(8), 1263–1282. https://doi.org/10.1080/01419870.2018.1550261

Hong, H., Sraer, D., & Yu, J. (2017). Inflation bets on the long bond. *The Review of Financial Studies, 30*(3), 900–947. https://doi.org/10.1093/rfs/hhw090

Husband, G. (2020). Ethical data collection and recognizing the impact of semi-structured interviews on research respondents. *Education Sciences, 10*(8), 206.

Huynh, T. D., & Xia, Y. (2021). Climate change news risk and corporate bond returns. *Journal of Financial and Quantitative Analysis, 56*(6), 1985–2009.

Ketkar, S. L., & Ratha, D. (2010). Diaspora bonds: Tapping the diaspora during difficult times. *Journal of International Commerce, Economics and Policy, 01*(02), 251–263. https://doi.org/10.1142/S1793993310000147

Ketkar, S. L., & Ratha, D. (2011). Viewpoint: Diaspora bonds for funding education. *Migration Letters, 8*(2), 153–172. Retrieved from www.migrationletters.com

Krasniqi, B. A., & Williams, N. (2019). Migration and intention to return entrepreneurial intentions of the diaspora in post-conflict economies. *Post-Communist Economies, 31*(4), 464–483.

Lainer-Vos, D. (2013). The practical organization of moral transactions: Gift giving, market exchange, credit, and the making of diaspora bonds. *Sociological Theory, 31*(2), 145–167.

Lapshyna, I. (2019). Do diasporas matter? The growing role of the Ukrainian diaspora in the UK and Poland in the development of the homeland in times of war. *Central and Eastern European Migration Review, 8*(1), 51–73.

Licuanan, V., Omar Mahmoud, T., & Steinmayr, A. (2015). The drivers of diaspora donations for development: Evidence from The Philippines. *World Development, 65*, 94–109. https://doi.org/10.1016/j.worlddev.2014.05.010

Maara, J. N., Manda, D. K., & Kiiru, J. M. (2019). Remittances and household expenditure allocation behavior in Kenya. *African Journal of Economic Review, 7*(1), 85–108.

Markowitz, H. (1952). Portfolio selection. *The Journal of Finance, 7*(1), 77–91. https://doi.org/10.1111/j.1540-6261.1952.tb01525.x

Mecagni, M. M., Kriljenko, M. J. I. C., Gueye, C.A., Mu, M. Y., Yabara, M. M., & Weber, M. S. (2014). *Issuing international sovereign bonds: Opportunities and challenges for sub-Saharan Africa*. IMF Departmental Papers/Policy Papers, (2014/007).

Mikutowski, M., Karathanasopoulos, A., & Zaremba, A. (2019). Return seasonalities in government bonds and macroeconomic risk. *Economics Letters, 176*, 114–116. https://doi.org/10.1016/J.ECONLET.2019.01.012

Miller, M. H., Grundy, B. D., & Bruce D. (1961). *Selected works of Merton H. Miller: A celebration of markets* (4th ed.). Retrieved from https://books.google.co.uk/books?hl=en&lr=&id=CIni3oHnprEC&oi=fnd&pg=PA42&dq=Modigliani+(1961)+&ots=yudBqnxzEm&sig=2RO36wxHqekyYJq2RWGuplvTsak#v=onepage&q=Modigliani(1961)&f=false

Monasterolo, I. (2020). Climate change and the financial system. *Annual Review of Resource Economics, 12*, 299–320.

Moyo, G. (2021). Reimagining the future of development finance. In A. Agency (Ed.), *Finance and developmental states* (pp. 183–206). Springer International Publishing.

Mpofu, F. Y. (2022). Green taxes in Africa: Opportunities and challenges for environmental protection, sustainability, and the attainment of sustainable development goals. *Sustainability, 14*(16), 10239.

Nielsen, T. M., & Riddle, L. (2010). Investing in peace: The motivational dynamics of diaspora investment in post-conflict economies. *Journal of Business Ethics, 89*(S4), 435–448. https://doi.org/10.1007/s10551-010-0399-z

Nyame-Asiamah, F., Amoako, I. O., Amankwah-Amoah, J., & Debrah, Y. A. (2020). Diaspora entrepreneurs' push and pull institutional factors for investing in Africa: Insights from African returnees from the United Kingdom. *Technological Forecasting and Social Change, 152*, 119876.

Nnyanzi, J. B., Kilimani, N., & Oryema, J. B. (2022). How important are remittances to savings? Evidence from the Latin America and the Caribbean countries. *IZA Journal of Development and Migration, 13*(1).

Olabisi, M., & Stein, H. (2015). Sovereign bond issues: Do African countries pay more to borrow? *Journal of African Trade, 2*(1–2), 87–109. https://doi.org/10.1016/J.JOAT.2015.08.003

Painter, M. (2020). An inconvenient cost: The effects of climate change on municipal bonds. *Journal of Financial Economics, 135*(2), 468–482.

Peavy, J. W. (1990). Returns on initial public offerings of closed-end funds. *Review of Financial Studies, 3*(4), 695–708. https://doi.org/10.1093/rfs/3.4.695

Podsakoff, P. M., MacKenzie, S. B., & Podsakoff, N. P. (2016). Recommendations for creating better concept definitions in the organizational. *Behavioral, and Social Sciences Organizational Research Methods, 19*(2), 159–203. https://doi.org/10.1177/1094428115624965

Plaza, S., & Ratha, D. (Eds.). (2011). *Diaspora for development in Africa*. World Bank Publications.

Presbitero, A. F., Ghura, D., Adedeji, O. S., & Njie, L. (2016). Sovereign bonds in developing countries: Drivers of issuance and spreads. *Review of Development Finance, 6*(1), 1–15. https://doi.org/10.1016/J.RDF.2016.05.002

Ramsey, F. P. (1928). A mathematical theory of saving. *The Economic Journal, 38*(152), 543. https://doi.org/10.2307/2224098

Ranjan, A., Kharat, R., & Deka, P. (Eds.). (2023). *Environment, climate change and migration in South Asia*. Taylor & Francis.

Ratha, D. (2016). *Migration and remittances factbook 2016*. World Bank Publications.

Ratha, D., Mohapatra, S., & Silwal, A. (2010). *Remittance flows to developing countries remained resilient in 2009, expected to recover during 2010-11*. Retrieved from https://openknowledge.worldbank.org/bitstream/handle/10986/10931/586260BRI0Migr10BOX353808B01PUBLIC1.pdf?sequence=1

Rizvi, S. Z. A., Jamil, S., & Shaikh, A. I. (2019). Diaspora, remittances and dependence on Arab countries: A case of Pakistan. *Liberal Arts and Social Sciences International Journal (LASSIJ), 3*(2), 74–84.

Rwigema, P. C. (2023). G20 and African Union development: Building alliances for sustainable development. *The Strategic Journal of Business & Change Management, 10*(1), 38–79.

Salia, S., & Bempong Nyantakyi, E. (2022). *Diaspora bonds can help fill climate finance gaps in developing economies*. Africa at LSE.

Senga, C., Cassimon, D., & Essers, D. (2018). Sub-Saharan African Eurobond yields: What really matters beyond global factors? *Review of Development Finance, 8*(1), 49–62. https://doi.org/10.1016/J.RDF.2018.05.005

Sheffer, G. (2006). Transnationalism and ethnonational Diasporism. *Diaspora: A Journal of Transnational Studies, 15*(1), 121–145. https://doi.org/10.1353/dsp.0.0029

Sangiorgi, I., & Schopohl, L. (2021). Explaining green bond issuance using survey evidence: Beyond the greenium. *The British Accounting Review, 55*, 101071.

Stern, N. (2022). A time for action on climate change and a time for change in economics. *The Economic Journal, 132*(644), 1259–1289.

Taghizadeh-Hesary, F., & Yoshino, N. (2019). The way to induce private participation in green finance and investment. *Finance Research Letters, 31*, 98–103.

Welde, T. B., Emovwodo, S. O., Saud, M., & Wardhani, B. L. S. W. (2022). Nigeria and Ethiopian diaspora remittances; engagement, policy reforms and poverty reduction. *Migration and Development, 11*(2), 174–190.

World Bank. (2019). *Price tag for sustainable infrastructure spending in developing countries is 4.5% of GDP* [online]. Accessed July 30, 2023, from https://www.worldbank.org/en/news/press-release/2019/02/19/price-tag-for-sustainable-infrastructure-spending-in-developing-countries-is-45-of-gdp

Dr Samuel Salia is an Associate Professor of Finance at Birmingham City University (UK) where he currently leads research and teaches finance. He holds a PhD in Finance from Birmingham City University. He is a member of the UK Institute of Consulting and has consulted for international organisations including the African Union and GIZ. Before joining BCU, Samuel was a Senior Lecturer in Finance and Faculty Head of Doctoral Training (Business and Law) at De Montfort University. Before this, he was a Lecturer in International Finance and Programme Director for MSc International Banking and Finance at the University of Wolverhampton. He has worked as a Management Consultant with the Ghana Ministry of Employment (MDPI) and as Managing Director of SAS Capital Money Lending Limited and has also held academic appointments abroad. He has had over eleven years of banking and consultancy experience in the SME sector, specialising in entrepreneurial finance. The findings of Samuel's research have influenced the practice of ethnic minority businesses in the UK, financial institutions, and the policy of regional bodies in Africa. For example, he recently worked on a BAL HEIF-funded project that provided training and support to Afro-Caribbean-owned businesses in the Midlands (UK) in response to COVID-19 challenges. He has also worked on projects such as evaluating the impact of services of Opportunity International Savings and Loans-Ghana, and Village Savings and Loans Associations. As a Technical Advisor, he developed a policy booklet for the African Heads of State and Governments on the AU 2021 theme of the year. He has served as a keynote speaker at national and international conferences. His focus has recently been on exploring issues of diaspora (migrant) remittance, FinTech, and investment in developing countries. Samuel has published extensively on issues relating to access to finance, green finance, SME innovation, and entrepreneurial training. His work has been published in the International Journal of Finance and Economics (ABS ranking 3*), International Journal of Entrepreneurial Behaviour and Research (ABS ranking 3*), IEEE Transactions on Engineering Management (ABS ranking 3*) Journal of Small Business and Enterprise Development (ABS ranking 2*) among others. Samuel has examined and supervised Ph.D. students, and on the strength of his research, he has received research funding totalling £26,000. He has served as a reviewer for highly ranked academic journals including the International Journal of Entrepreneurial Behaviour and Research, and the Journal of Small Business and Enterprise Development among others.

Javed Hussain is Professor of Entrepreneurial Finance at Birmingham City University where he currently leads the Accounting and Finance Group. Professor Hussain completed his PhD (1996) and M. Soc. Sci (1987) in Money, Banking, and Finance from the University of Birmingham and a first degree in Economics, BA (Hons) From Birmingham Polytechnic (1985). Currently, Professor Hussain supervises several Ph.D. in the areas of corporate, micro, and small business finance. He also takes postgraduate courses on Research Methods and International Financial Strategy. Before joining Birmingham City University Professor Hussain held posts in finance within public and private sector organisations. He was a financial analyst with the Forward Trust Group (now a subsidiary of HSBC bank) and before that, he worked for Birmingham City Council. He has collaborated on several research projects funded by public sector clients. He has published extensively on issues of bank finance for SMEs with a particular focus on ethnic firms and has co-authored papers and chapters in several journals and books. He is currently co-editing Reading in Entrepreneurial Finance book with

Dr Jonathan Scott. Furthermore, he is conducting collaborative research on differences in entrepreneurship and SME financing between developed and developing countries. In particular, considering the issues of SMEs within the Malaysian context. Professor Hussain regularly presents papers at national and international conferences and engages in research with colleagues from several other UK institutions, Professor Paul Mosley on microfinance, Dr. Paul Stuart, University of West of Scotland, on the presence of venture capital amongst ethnic minorities and Dr. Jonathan Scott, Teesside University on entrepreneurship. He is a peer referee for several international journal publications. You may contact Professor Javed Hussain informally to explore your research interests or possible collaborative projects within his specialist area of interest.

Eugene Bempong Nyantakyi, PhD, is Chief Research Economist at the African Development Bank. He is also currently on leave as an Assistant Professor of Global Trade at Oklahoma State University. He worked as an economist and private sector development specialist at the World Bank Group and has taught economics at West Virginia University and Whitworth University. He holds a PhD in Economics from West Virginia University. His primary research and academic interests are in the areas of global trade and finance, with a secondary focus on entrepreneurship and private sector development in emerging and developing economies. His work has been published in major international economics and entrepreneurship journals as well as in numerous reports of the World Bank Group and African Development Bank.

Eric Ofosu-Hene, PhD, is a Senior Lecturer in Accounting and Finance. Prior to joining Leicester Castle Business School, he was a Senior Lecturer in Actuarial Science and Finance in Asia Pacific University of Innovation and Technology (Malaysia), before that he was a Lecturer in Insurance, Finance and Risk Management at the University of Ghana Business School. Eric has over 13 years of combined experience in Academia and in Industry. He has consulted for several organisations including PwC(Ghana) and the National Pensions Regulatory Authority (Ghana) drawing on his Enterprise Risk Management and Pensions Management Expertise. Eric has a PhD in Actuarial Science from University of Kent, a Double Masters with Distinction in Actuarial Management and Actuarial Science from Heriot-Watt University and is a Qualified Accountant with the Association of Chartered Certified Accountants (UK).

Dr. Yahaya Alhassan is the Head of Academic Operations at the University of Sunderland in London. Dr. Alhassan is responsible for leading the integration and execution of the University of Sunderland's strategic and operational priorities across all academic programmes at the London campus (UoSiL). He also oversees the development and implementation of the Academic Programme Offer, as well as the integration of the University's Research and Innovation Strategy. Alongside his leadership role, Dr. Alhassan maintains an active research profile. His current research explores investment in financial technology (FinTech) and firm growth, with several of his papers published in high-ranking ABS 3* journals. He has co-edited books, authored multiple book chapters in finance and enterprise, and frequently presents at academic conferences, contributing meaningfully to the field of finance since 2019. Dr. Alhassan has over 20 experience in teaching, academic leadership, and management, gained through his roles at the University of Sunderland in London as well as previous positions in the higher education and consultancy sectors. He holds a PhD in Business Management (Finance) from Anglia Ruskin University, an MBA in Finance and a Master of Education from the University of Sunderland, and a BA (Hons) in Business Management from Arden University. He is also a Senior Fellow of the Higher Education Academy (HEA).

Chapter 3
Eco-marketing and Green Finance synergy for Eco-hotels in Central Uganda

Florence Prescah Muheebwa and Michael Omeke

3.1 Introduction

The development of eco-hotels in Central Uganda presents a promising opportunity for advancing sustainable tourism, promoting environmental conservation, and generating inclusive economic benefits. However, despite this potential, eco-hotels in the region remain underdeveloped, underfinanced, and largely invisible in both domestic and international markets. Many of these enterprises struggle to effectively position themselves as environmentally responsible brands due to limited eco-marketing capacity, lack of certification, and minimal use of digital green branding strategies (MTWA, 2020a; UNEP, 2022).

Moreover, access to green finance remains a major constraint. Most eco-hotel operators are small and medium-sized enterprises (SMEs) that face challenges in meeting the eligibility criteria for climate-smart funding and sustainability-linked financial products. Financial institutions are often reluctant to offer green credit to tourism enterprises due to limited awareness, risk perceptions, and weak regulatory incentives (NPA, 2023). As a result, the scaling of eco-friendly infrastructure and innovation in hospitality services remains inadequate.

This mismatch between sustainable tourism aspirations and implementation hinders Uganda's ability to fully leverage its tourism sector for green growth, as outlined in Uganda Vision 2040 and the Fourth National Development Plan (NDP IV). It also undermines the country's progress toward key Sustainable Development Goals (SDGs), including SDG 8 (decent work), SDG 12 (responsible consumption), and SDG 13 (climate action).

Addressing this problem requires an integrated approach that combines eco-marketing synergies with access to innovative green finance to support the viability,

F. P. Muheebwa (✉) · M. Omeke
Kyambogo University, Kampala, Uganda
e-mail: fmuheebwa@kyu.ac.ug; momeke@kyu.ac.ug

Y. Alhassan et al. (eds.), *Financial Innovation and Sustainable Enterprise in Developing and Emerging Economies*, Research Series on Responsible Enterprise Ecosystems, https://doi.org/10.1007/978-3-032-04500-3_3

visibility, and long-term sustainability of eco-hotels. This study, therefore, seeks to explore how marketing and financing strategies can be aligned to strengthen eco-hotel enterprises in Central Uganda and contribute to national and global sustainability agendas.

3.2 Literature Review

3.2.1 Theoretical Foundations Supporting Sustainable Eco-hotel Development

This study is underpinned by two key theories including the Sustainable Livelihoods Framework (SLF) (Chambers & Conway, 1992) offers insight into how rural enterprises leverage diverse assets human, social, financial, natural to build resilience. Green finance and eco-marketing can enhance these assets, promoting livelihood sustainability. Additionally, the Diffusion of Innovations Theory (Rogers, 2003) explains how new sustainable business practices and financial products spread among eco-hotel entrepreneurs. Adoption depends on perceived benefits, communication channels, and social networks, highlighting the role of education and partnership. Together, these theories provide a comprehensive lens to analyze how eco-marketing and green finance interact to foster sustainable competitive advantage, stakeholder engagement, livelihood resilience, and innovation diffusion in Central Uganda's eco-hotel sector.

3.2.2 Eco-marketing Practices in Sustainable Tourism

Eco-marketing, often termed green marketing, refers to strategies that promote environmentally responsible products and services by integrating sustainability values into branding, communication, and delivery (Peattie & Crane, 2005). In the context of tourism, eco-marketing emphasizes low-impact experiences, nature conservation, and community benefit. The adoption of eco-marketing in sustainable tourism serves both ecological and economic purposes by appealing to environmentally conscious travelers and differentiating services in a competitive market (Dolnicar & Leisch, 2008). Key strategies in eco-tourism marketing include eco-branding which means creating a distinctive green identity using labels, certifications, and narratives of sustainability (Font & Buckley, 2001), digital storytelling which means using websites, blogs, and social media to convey authentic environmental values and immersive experiences (Carvache-Franco et al., 2020), experiential marketing which means engaging visitors in sustainable activities that create emotional connections and promote positive word-of-mouth (Williams & Soutar, 2009) as well as eco-certification which means programs like Green Key or

EarthCheck enhance trust and market visibility, especially in global eco-conscious markets (Honey, 2008).

Despite the potential, small eco-hotels in developing regions like Uganda face notable challenges including limited marketing expertise whereby many rural operators lack training in digital marketing, branding, or sustainability communication (UNWTO, 2022). Another challenge is low visibility and market access. Without strong platforms or promotional alliances, eco-hotels often fail to reach target segments such as international ecotourists or responsible domestic travelers (Tumusiime, 2018). Greenwashing risks is another challenge. Inadequate monitoring or exaggerated claims can lead to consumer mistrust and undermine eco-brand credibility (Parguel et al., 2011).

Recent literature highlights the interconnectedness between eco-marketing and financial mechanisms for enterprise sustainability. Green finance such as climate-smart microloans, sustainability-linked credit lines, and eco-grants can enhance eco-tourism offerings when paired with effective marketing (IFC, 2019a, b; Kato & Kratzer, 2018). Studies show that eco-tourism ventures with access to finance are better able to invest in renewable energy, eco-friendly infrastructure, and professional branding (Stavrou & Renko, 2020). Financial literacy is critical, as many eco-entrepreneurs fail to leverage available funds due to limited knowledge of eligibility, application procedures, or credit management (Muriithi, 2017).

Strategic alliances especially with NGOs, local government, and community-based organizations facilitate marketing efforts through co-branding, joint visibility campaigns, and shared infrastructure (Akampumuza & Hayombe, 2017). Such collaborations also foster authenticity and inclusiveness in eco-tourism narratives, which appeal to the values of ethically minded travelers (George et al., 2019).

In Uganda, eco-tourism is a growing niche, especially around national parks and rural communities. However, market development is constrained by weak institutional support for eco-certification and eco-brand development, inadequate integration of eco-tourism into national and district-level tourism promotion strategies (Ministry of Tourism, Wildlife and Antiquities, 2020b) as well as fragmented digital presence and lack of storytelling platforms tailored for eco-enterprises. Recent efforts by organizations such as the Uganda Tourism Board (UTB) and NGOs have begun addressing these gaps through training programs and digital toolkits (NPA, 2023). Yet, scaling impact requires a national framework that integrates eco-marketing with sustainable financing.

The literature affirms the study's finding that eco-marketing and green finance must be synergized to scale eco-hotel growth. Successful case studies emphasize digital storytelling, eco-branding, and financial innovation as mutually reinforcing tools. To replicate and scale these models in Uganda, there is a need for capacity-building for eco-hotel operators in both branding and financial management, public–private partnerships to develop digital platforms and access to green finance as well as policy support for eco-certification and climate finance alignment with SDGs.

3.2.3 Green Finance Instruments and Access in Eco-tourism

Green finance refers to financial investments that deliver environmental benefits within the broader context of sustainable development (OECD, 2017). In tourism, green finance supports eco-friendly infrastructure, renewable energy adoption, waste management, and low-impact hospitality services (UNEP, 2021). It enables enterprises to reduce their carbon footprint while meeting the growing demand for sustainable tourism offerings (Beck et al., 2017). Eco-tourism enterprises, particularly in developing economies such as Uganda, often face financial constraints in transitioning to sustainable models (IFC, 2019a, b). Access to targeted financial instruments can mitigate these constraints and enhance eco-value propositions. Green finance enhances not only environmental sustainability but also economic resilience and competitiveness of rural tourism enterprises (Kato & Kratzer, 2018).

There are instruments that have shown relevance and potential for application in eco-tourism settings. For instance, climate-smart microloans or small-scale loans targeted at eco-preneurs to invest in renewable energy, water conservation, or sustainable infrastructure. These have proven effective in East African agri-tourism and eco-hospitality projects (Stavrou & Renko, 2020). Another instrument is sustainability-linked credit lines or financing instruments tied to environmental performance indicators such as waste reduction, use of solar power, or eco-certification. Enterprises achieving sustainability milestones benefit from reduced interest rates or extended repayment periods (UNDP, 2019). Green bonds and grants is another instument. Although more prominent in public or large-scale investments, donor-supported green grants and municipal green bonds can provide funding for eco-hotel clusters, community conservation tourism, or green innovation hubs (World Bank, 2020). Impact investing and blended finance is another instrument. These tools attract private investors by combining commercial returns with social and environmental impact. NGOs and international agencies often de-risk such investments in rural eco-tourism (Nyaga & Were, 2017). Another instrument is the mobile-based microfinance platforms or leveraging fintech to deliver accessible, low-cost credit to rural eco-tourism entrepreneurs. These tools lower transaction costs and expand reach to women and youth (Munyua et al., 2021).

Despite availability, access to green finance remains limited in many low-income tourism contexts due to information asymmetry. Many eco-enterprises are unaware of available financial products or lack the literacy to apply (Muriithi, 2017). Another challenge is inadequate credit history. Informal or small-scale eco-hotels often lack formal documentation or collateral required by traditional financial institutions. Furthermore, policy and regulatory gaps is another challenge. Weak national green finance frameworks hinder integration of tourism in broader climate finance strategies (Kiss & Barr, 2018). Additionally, gendered access disparities present another challenge. Women-run eco-tourism ventures face greater challenges in accessing formal finance due to social and institutional constraints (Kimbu & Ngoasong, 2016).

Scholars and policy experts propose several interventions to expand financial access in the eco-tourism space. For example, financial literacy and capacity-building can be a good strategy. Training eco-entrepreneurs on investment readiness, business planning, and sustainability reporting increases bankability (Jack & Suri, 2017) can help improve accessibility. Partnerships with NGOs and Fintech firms can be another strategy. These collaborations can co-create loan products, lower lending risks, and facilitate group-based lending models (IFC, 2019a, b). Another strategy can be Government and donor incentives. Tax rebates, loan guarantees, and co-financing schemes encourage financial institutions to serve the ecotourism sector (UNEP, 2021) can be of great use in improving access. Finally, community-based financial models can be a good strategy to address access challenge. Village savings and loans associations (VSLAs) or eco-cooperative funds allow rural groups to mobilize internal resources and qualify for external support (Kumbhar, 2012).

Uganda's tourism sector offers strong potential for green finance integration, particularly in regions like Central Uganda that boast natural and cultural assets. However, the uptake of climate finance remains fragmented due to lack of tailored financial products for eco-tourism SMEs, low alignment between tourism policy and Uganda's green growth strategy as well as minimal participation of eco-tourism in national climate finance dialogues. Nonetheless, recent initiatives by the Ministry of Tourism and the Uganda Green Growth Development Strategy highlight emerging windows for green finance targeting community tourism and eco-hotels (NPA, 2023).

The reviewed literature strongly supports the study's assertion that synergizing green finance and eco-marketing is critical for scaling eco-hotel development. Climate-smart microfinance, donor-supported green grants, and mobile-based platforms offer viable paths for eco-hotel growth especially when complemented by financial literacy and institutional support. The study's call for capacity-building and policy incentives is consistent with global best practices. A coordinated green finance framework featuring accessible instruments, financial training, and stakeholder partnerships is vital to unlocking the sustainability potential of eco-tourism in Uganda and beyond.

3.2.4 Challenges and Opportunities in Integrating Eco-marketing with Green Finance

The integration of eco-marketing and green finance represents a synergistic approach to scaling sustainable tourism enterprises. Eco-marketing enhances the visibility and credibility of eco-hotels, increasing their appeal to both tourists and investors who are increasingly prioritizing sustainability criteria (Chen & Chang, 2013). Concurrently, green finance provides the necessary capital to implement environmentally sustainable practices promoted through marketing.

Despite its potential, this integration faces obstacles such as information asymmetry, weak institutional support, and fragmented stakeholder coordination

(Mourad, 2016). For instance, financial institutions may lack understanding of eco-tourism value propositions, while entrepreneurs may underutilize marketing to demonstrate sustainability credentials to financiers. Opportunities lie in developing innovative financing models that incorporate marketing milestones or certifications as loan conditions, and in fostering multi-stakeholder partnerships for knowledge exchange (Odoom et al., 2020).

Despite a growing body of research on eco-marketing and green finance individually, significant gaps remain in understanding their combined impact on sustainable tourism enterprises, especially within emerging economies like Uganda. Nost studies on eco-marketing focus on consumer behavior and green branding effectiveness in developed markets (Han et al., 2010; Font & McCabe, 2017), with limited empirical evidence from the context of eco-hotels in Sub-Saharan Africa. There is a scarcity of research examining how eco-marketing strategies are practically implemented by small and medium-sized eco-tourism enterprises, particularly in rural areas of developing countries where resources and capabilities are limited (Khan et al., 2019). Although green finance has received increasing attention globally (UNEP, 2022; Gangi et al., 2020), there is insufficient exploration of the accessibility and suitability of green financial products for eco-hotels in low-income settings. The literature often overlooks the challenges SMEs face in accessing climate-smart loans, sustainability-linked financing, or grants, and how these financial tools can be tailored to local realities (Zhang et al., 2021). The integration of eco-marketing and green finance remains an underexplored area. Existing studies tend to treat marketing and finance as separate silos, without considering the potential synergies that arise from linking marketing strategies with innovative financing mechanisms to drive sustainable growth (Odoom et al., 2020; Mourad, 2016). There is a lack of holistic frameworks that combine key theoretical perspectives—such as Resource-Based View, Stakeholder Theory, Sustainable Livelihoods, and Diffusion of Innovations to guide sustainable enterprise development in eco-tourism. This theoretical gap limits comprehensive understanding of how internal resources, stakeholder engagement, livelihood impacts, and innovation adoption intersect to influence eco-hotel success in developing regions. Addressing these gaps is critical to designing effective interventions that support eco-hotels in Central Uganda to scale sustainably, align with national development priorities, and contribute meaningfully to the Sustainable Development Goals.

3.3 Research Methodology

This study adopts a mixed methods research design, integrating both quantitative and qualitative approaches to provide a comprehensive understanding of the relationship between eco-marketing practices and green finance accessibility among eco-hotels in Central Uganda. The convergent parallel design was used, where both qualitative and quantitative data were collected simultaneously, analyzed independently, and then merged for interpretation (Creswell & Plano Clark, 2018). This design allowed triangulation of findings to enhance the validity, depth, and policy relevance of the study.

The study was conducted in Central Uganda, a region characterized by ecotourism potential due to its biodiversity, proximity to urban centers, and presence of emerging eco-hospitality businesses. Key districts included Wakiso, Mpigi, Mukono, and Buikwe, which host several eco-hotels and nature-based lodges. The study population (N) of 1000 individuals included Eco-hotel owners/managers involved in sustainable tourism and hospitality practices, financial institutions offering green finance products (e.g., banks, microfinance institutions, development partners), tourism regulatory authorities and NGOs promoting eco-tourism and sustainability in Uganda as well as the domestic and international tourists visiting eco-hotels, whose perspectives were essential in evaluating eco-marketing effectiveness. A stratified random sampling technique was employed to select eco-hotels based on type (e.g., lodge, resort, community-based hotel) and location. The study surveyed 100 eco-hotel owners/managers and 100 tourists, yielding a total of 200 quantitative respondents. The sample size was derived from the study population using the Krejcie and Morgan's Table. Purposive sampling was used to select 20 key informants, including eco-hotel managers, finance providers, officials from the Uganda Tourism Board (UTB), Ministry of Tourism, and NGO representatives. These participants were selected based on their knowledge of green financing or eco-marketing strategies.

Structured Questionnaires were administered to eco-hotel operators and tourists. Eco-hotel survey focused on eco-marketing strategies, financing sources, awareness and access to green finance, and operational sustainability. Tourist survey focused on awareness of eco-hotels, perception of green marketing practices, and factors influencing patronage. Semi-structured Interviews were conducted with key informants to explore experiences, challenges, and policy insights regarding eco-marketing and green finance. Document Review involved analyzing relevant policy papers, green financing frameworks, eco-certification reports, and marketing materials.

Data were coded and analyzed using STATA software. Descriptive statistics (means, frequencies, percentages) were used to profile respondents and identify patterns. Inferential statistics (correlation and regression analysis) were applied to examine the relationship between eco-marketing strategies and access to green finance. Interview transcripts were analyzed using thematic content analysis (Braun & Clarke, 2006). NVivo software supported the coding and organization of themes related to eco-innovation, marketing-finance synergies, institutional barriers, and enabling factors. Findings from both strands were compared and interpreted concurrently to identify convergence, divergence, and complementarity. Joint displays were created to illustrate how quantitative trends aligned or contrasted with qualitative insights.

Ethical clearance was obtained from a recognized Institutional Review Board. Participants were informed about the study objectives, assured of confidentiality, and required to provide written informed consent. Anonymity and voluntary participation were guaranteed throughout data collection and reporting.

While the mixed methods approach strengthened the study's depth and credibility, some limitations were noted: including access to green finance information was restricted by institutional confidentiality, some hotel managers had limited documentation on eco-marketing or financing history and time and logistical constraints slightly limited the number of site visits.

Despite these limitations, the study produced robust and actionable findings relevant to eco-hospitality, green finance, and sustainable tourism policymaking in Uganda.

3.4 Results and Discussion

3.4.1 Profile of Respondents

A total of 200 participants were surveyed quantitatively: 100 eco-hotel operators/managers and 100 domestic/international tourists. In addition, 20 key informants were interviewed, including financial institution representatives, tourism officials, and NGO staff. For Eco-hotel respondents, 60% were located in peri-urban areas (e.g., Mukono, Mpigi), 40% in rural zones (e.g., Buikwe, Kayunga). For ownership structure, 48% were privately owned, 37% community-based, and 15% NGO-supported enterprises. For tourist profile, 55% were domestic travelers, 45% international, with 72% indicating environmental sustainability as a factor in accommodation choice (Table 3.1).

3.4.2 Eco-marketing Practices Employed by Eco-hotels

82% of eco-hotels reported using at least one form of green marketing (e.g., eco-certification labels, nature-based storytelling). Only 36% used digital platforms to promote their sustainability efforts. 45% of tourists recalled encountering eco-messages when choosing their accommodation.

Key informants noted that eco-marketing was largely informal, with many SMEs lacking strategic communication plans. Most relied on word-of-mouth or basic web

Table 3.1 Profile of respondents

Category	Distribution
Eco-hotel location	60% peri-urban, 40% rural
Ownership structure	48% private, 37% community-based, 15% NGO-supported
Tourist origin	55% domestic, 45% international
Tourist sustainability preference	72% consider sustainability when choosing accommodation

listings. Several respondents cited low digital literacy and limited marketing budgets as key barriers (Table 3.2).

These findings affirm previous research (Font & McCabe, 2017; Khan et al., 2019) suggesting that eco-marketing is underutilized in emerging economies. Although awareness of green branding exists, strategic application is weak, especially among smaller operators. This aligns with the sustainable marketing theory, which emphasizes the need to develop marketing capabilities as strategic assets.

3.4.3 Accessibility and Use of Green Finance

Only 28% of eco-hotels had accessed any form of green or sustainability-linked financing. 72% relied on personal savings or traditional commercial loans, often at high interest rates. Awareness of green finance products was low, with only 31% familiar with terms such as "climate finance" or "green credit lines (Table 3.3)."

Interviewees from financial institutions confirmed that eco-tourism businesses rarely meet eligibility criteria for green loans duc to lack of collateral, formal registration, or audited financial records. NGOs and development partners highlighted the absence of tailored financial products for sustainable tourism.

Consistent with UNEP (2022) and Gangi et al. (2020), these results indicate a critical mismatch between the supply and demand of green finance in the eco-tourism sector. The findings underscore a need for financial innovation tailored to the realities of eco-hotel SMEs. The Diffusion of Innovations Theory reinforces that financial institutions, government, and tourism actors must coordinate to create enabling financial environments.

3.4.4 Challenges and Opportunities in Integrating Eco-marketing and Green Finance

Four themes emerged from interviews including ack of integration between finance and marketing functions within eco-enterprises, missed opportunities to use eco-certification or green achievements as a marketing-finance leverage point, weak institutional support in providing technical assistance or bridging the information

Table 3.2 Eco-marketing practices employed by eco-hotels

Marketing practice/observation	Percentage/Insight
Use of any green marketing	82%
Use of digital platforms	36%
Tourists recalling eco-messages	45%
Common barriers	Low digital literacy, limited budget

Table 3.3 Accessibility and use of green finance

Financial indicator	Observation
Accessed green finance	28%
Used personal/traditional loans	72%
Awareness of green finance	31%
Main barriers	Collateral, lack of documentation

gap, potential for blended finance models that reward verified marketing achievements (e.g., loan incentives for certified eco-brands).

These insights support earlier findings (Mourad, 2016; Odoom et al., 2020) that integration is not automatic and requires enabling policies, training, and innovation. Applying the Diffusion of Innovations Theory, adoption of eco-finance and green branding remains slow due to perceived complexity and lack of communication networks.

3.4.5 A Conceptual Framework for Sustainable Enterprise Growth

Based on the findings, a conceptual model is proposed where eco-marketing capability and green finance access jointly influence the sustainability and competitiveness of eco-hotels. This relationship is mediated by factors such as institutional support, access to training, stakeholder collaboration and innovation diffusion.

The model draws on both theories SLF, and Diffusion of Innovations to explain how internal and external enablers shape sustainable enterprise outcomes.

3.4.6 Policy and Managerial Recommendations

Based on the findings, the study recommends the following:

For Policy Makers, establish a green finance framework tailored to eco-tourism SMEs, integrate eco-marketing capacity-building into Uganda Tourism Board (UTB) programming, and encourage public-private partnerships to co-develop marketing and finance platforms.

For Financial Institutions, develop low-collateral loan products linked to sustainability performance (e.g., green certifications) and partner with tourism bodies to raise awareness and improve financial literacy among eco-entrepreneurs.

For Eco-Hotel Operators, invest in digital marketing and eco-certification to build brand credibility, collaborate with local tourism associations for marketing and lobbying efforts, collect and report sustainability metrics to attract impact investors and tourists.

The study demonstrates that eco-marketing and green finance are interdependent levers for sustainable tourism development. In Central Uganda, however, both remain underutilized due to structural, institutional, and capacity barriers. Unlocking their synergy requires coordinated efforts across stakeholders and innovations in both financial product design and marketing practices. The results contribute to theory and practice by offering a grounded framework and context-specific insights for scaling sustainable eco-hospitality in developing economies.

3.5 Conclusion and Recommendations

3.5.1 *Summary of Findings*

This study examined the integration of eco-marketing strategies and green finance in promoting the sustainability and competitiveness of eco-hotels in Central Uganda, using a mixed methods approach. The findings reveal that while a majority of eco-hotels engage in some form of eco-marketing, their strategies are often informal, underdeveloped, and rarely digital. Only a small fraction of the enterprises accessed green financial instruments, with most relying on traditional funding mechanisms. Barriers to green finance access include limited awareness, lack of collateral, and misalignment between financial products and tourism sector needs.

The integration of eco-marketing with green finance was found to be weak, primarily due to limited institutional support and a lack of targeted training. However, stakeholders recognized the potential for synergy particularly where green certifications and sustainability reporting could serve both marketing and financing functions. A conceptual framework was proposed to demonstrate how internal capabilities and external enablers influence the sustainable growth of eco-hotels.

3.5.2 *Contributions to Knowledge*

This study contributes to the literature on sustainable tourism and entrepreneurship in several ways. It offers one of the few empirical investigations into the synergy between eco-marketing and green finance in the eco-tourism context of a developing country. It applies an integrated theoretical lens (Sustainable Livelihoods Framework, and Diffusion of Innovations Theory) to explore sustainable enterprise development. It proposes a context-specific conceptual model for sustainable eco-hospitality growth in Sub-Saharan Africa. It generates policy-relevant evidence that aligns with Uganda Vision 2040, NDP IV, and the SDGs, especially SDGs 8, 12, 13, and 17.

3.5.3 Practical Recommendations

For Policy Makers and Regulators, they should develop a national green finance policy tailored to tourism SMEs, including eco-hotel loan products linked to sustainability metrics. They should provide tax incentives or subsidies to eco-hotels investing in renewable energy, waste management, or green certifications. They should integrate eco-marketing and finance modules into government tourism training programs.

For Financial Institutions, they should create low-interest green credit schemes accessible to informal or community-based eco-enterprises. They should collaborate with the Uganda Tourism Board (UTB) and Ministry of Tourism to raise awareness about green finance instruments and eligibility requirements.

For Eco-Hotel Operators, they should invest in digital eco-marketing tools, such as interactive websites, social media, and green storytelling to enhance visibility and customer trust. They should seek eco-certification and sustainability reporting to improve both marketing appeal and eligibility for green finance. They should build local networks and associations to collectively negotiate financing, training, and policy support.

3.5.4 Limitations and Future Research Directions

While the study provides valuable insights, it is not without limitations. The sample size, though adequate for mixed methods, was limited to Central Uganda and may not reflect experiences in other eco-tourism regions. Additionally, access to financial data from private institutions was constrained by confidentiality restrictions.

Future research should conduct longitudinal studies to assess the long-term impact of green finance and eco-marketing investments on eco-hotel performance. Future research should expand the geographic scope to include eco-tourism hotspots in other Ugandan regions such as Western and Northern Uganda). Future research should quantitatively test the proposed conceptual model using structural equation modeling or other advanced analytical tools. Future research should investigate consumer willingness to pay for eco-branded tourism in Uganda to better inform marketing strategies.

References

Akampumuza, P., & Hayombe, P. (2017). Tourism, poverty alleviation, and nature conservation: Evidence from communities adjacent to Queen Elizabeth National Park, Uganda. *Journal of Tourism and Cultural Change, 15*(1), 61–78. https://doi.org/10.1080/14766825.2016.1150284

Beck, T., Demirgüç-Kunt, A., & Levine, R. (2017). Finance, inequality, and the poor. *Journal of Economic Growth, 12*(1), 27–49. https://doi.org/10.1007/s10887-007-9010-6

Braun, V., & Clarke, V. (2006). Using thematic analysis in psychology. *Qualitative Research in Psychology, 3*(2), 77–101. https://doi.org/10.1191/1478088706qp063oa

Chambers, R., & Conway, G. (1992). *Sustainable rural livelihoods: Practical concepts for the 21st century* (IDS Discussion Paper 296).

Carvache-Franco, M., Carvache-Franco, O., Carvache-Franco, W., & Hernández-Lara, A. B. (2020). Motivation and segmentation of ecotourism in protected natural areas: *A study in Ecuador. GeoJournal of Tourism and Geosites, 28*(1), 260–269. https://doi.org/10.30892/gtg.28121-471

Chen, Y.-S., & Chang, C.-H. (2013). Greenwash and green trust: The mediation effects of green consumer confusion and green perceived risk. *Journal of Business Ethics, 114*(3), 489–500.

Creswell, J. W., & Plano Clark, V. L. (2018). *Designing and conducting mixed methods research*(3rd ed.). Sage Publications.

Dolnicar, S., & Leisch, F. (2008). An investigation of tourists' patterns of obligation to protect the environment. *Tourism Management, 29*(4), 672–681. https://doi.org/10.1016/j.tourman.2007.07.002

Font, X., & Buckley, R. (2001). *Tourism ecolabelling: Certification and promotion of sustainable management*. CABI.

Font, X., & McCabe, S. (2017). Sustainability and marketing in tourism: Its contexts, paradoxes, approaches, challenges and potential. *Journal of Sustainable Tourism, 25*(7), 869–883.

Gangi, F., Mustilli, M., Marzano, V., & Barbera, F. (2020). Financing sustainability in tourism: The role of green bonds. *Sustainability, 12*(11), 4607.

George, R., Mair, H., & Reid, D. (2019). *Rural tourism development: Localism and cultural change*. Channel View Publications.

Han, H., Hsu, L.-T. J., & Sheu, C. (2010). Application of the theory of planned behavior to green hotel choice: Testing the effect of environmentally friendly activities. *Tourism Management, 31*(3), 325–334.

Honey, M. (2008). *Ecotourism and sustainable development: Who owns paradise?* Island Press.

IFC. (2019a). *Digital financial services in Africa*. World Bank Group.

IFC. (2019b). *Digital financial services in Africa: Beyond the Kenyan success story*.

Jack, W., & Suri, T. (2017). *American Economic Review, 104*(1), 183–223.

Kato, M. P., & Kratzer, J. (2018). *ACRN Journal of Entrepreneurship Perspectives, 2*(1), 31–59.

Khan, S., Tuškej, U., & Škerlavaj, M. (2019). How social media marketing activities enhance customer equity in tourism? The mediating role of consumer engagement. *Tourism Management, 75*, 194–205.

Kimbu, A. N., & Ngoasong, M. Z. (2016). Women's empowerment and tourism entrepreneurship: Evidence from Cameroon. *Tourism Planning & Development, 13*(2), 105–109. https://doi.org/10.1080/21568316.2015.1135278

Kiss, A., & Barr, A. (2018). Credit, collateral and entrepreneurship: Evidence from a field experiment in Uganda. *Development in Practice, 28*(7), 897–910. https://doi.org/10.1080/09614524.2018.1493099

Kumbhar, V. M. (2012). *Journal of Rural Development, 31*(2), 223–238.

Ministry of Tourism, Wildlife and Antiquities. (2020a). *Tourism development plan 2020–2025*. Government of Uganda.

Ministry of Tourism, Wildlife and Antiquities. (2020b). *Tourism sector development plan*.

Mourad, M. (2016). Sustainable consumption practices in tourism: An empirical investigation of Egyptian tourists. *Journal of Cleaner Production, 111*, 355–363.

Munyua, A., Maina, K., & Waithaka, E. (2021). Green microfinance and sustainable rural livelihoods: Evidence from Kenya. *International Journal of Development and Economic Sustainability, 9*(1), 1–15.

Muriithi, S. M. (2017). African small and medium enterprises (SMEs) contributions, challenges and sustainability strategies. *European Journal of Research and Reflection in Management Sciences, 5*(1), 36–48.

NPA. (2023). Fourth National Development Plan (NDP IV), 2025/26–2029/30.

Nyaga, R., & Were, M. (2017). Access to credit and the performance of small and medium enterprises in Kenya. *African Development Review, 29*(S1), 69–84. https://doi.org/10.1111/1467-8268.12234

Odoom, R., Anning-Dorson, T., & Acheampong, G. (2020). Green financing and sustainable business performance: The role of eco-innovation. *Business Strategy and the Environment, 29*(2), 897–908.

OECD. (2017). *Green finance and investment: Mobilising bond markets for a low-carbon transition*. OECD Publishing. https://doi.org/10.1787/9789264272323-en

Parguel, B., Benoît-Moreau, F., & Larceneux, F. (2011). How sustainability ratings might deter 'greenwashing': A closer look at ethical corporate communication. *Journal of Business Ethics, 102*(1), 15–28. https://doi.org/10.1007/s10551-011-0901-2

Peattie, K., & Crane, A. (2005). Green marketing: Legend, myth, farce or prophesy? *Qualitative Market Research, 8*(4), 357–370.

Rogers, E. M. (2003). *Diffusion of innovations* (5th ed.). Free Press.

Stavrou, E., & Renko, M. (2020). Rural entrepreneurship and microenterprise growth: The role of access to finance and innovation. *Small Business Economics, 55*(2), 339–356. https://doi.org/10.1007/s11187-019-00210-1

Tumusiime, D. M. (2018). In M. C. Hall & S. Gössling (Eds.), *Tourism and development in sub-Saharan Africa* (pp. 123–139).

UNDP. (2019). *Sustainable development goals report 2019*.

UNEP. (2021). *Green finance for sustainable tourism*.

UNEP. (2022). *State of finance for nature*. United Nations Environment Programme. https://www.unep.org/resources/state-finance-nature-2022

UNWTO. (2022). *Tourism and rural development: A policy perspective*.

Williams, P., & Soutar, G. N. (2009). Value, satisfaction and behavioral intentions in an adventure tourism context. *Annals of Tourism Research, 36*(3), 413–438. https://doi.org/10.1016/j.annals.2009.02.002

World Bank. (2020). *Digital economy for africa initiative: Country diagnostics*.

Zhang, J., Geng, Y., Shao, S., Song, X., & Dong, L. (2021). A bibliometric analysis on green finance: Current status, development, and future directions. *Environmental Science and Pollution Research, 28*(43), 60648–60666. https://doi.org/10.1007/s11356-021-14738-2

Florence Prescah Muheebwa, PhD, is a Lecturer, Tourism and Hospitality Marketing in the Department of Management and Administrative Sciences, School of Management and Entrepreneurship at Kyambogo University, Kampala, Uganda. Her academic and research interests span Sustainable Entrepreneurship, Social Entrepreneurship, and Innovation Entrepreneurship, with a particular focus on promoting inclusive, resilient, and impact-oriented business models. Dr. Muheebwa is dedicated to empowering communities through sustainable entrepreneurial education, applied research, and policy-relevant scholarship. She actively engages in projects that foster sustainability, youth empowerment, and enterprise development, and contributes to academic discourse through publications, mentorship, and collaboration with local and international institutions.

Dr. Omeke Michael is a Senior Lecturer in the department of Accounting, Finance and MicroFinance, School of Management and Entrepreneurship at Kyambogo University, Uganda. He has over 15 years of experience in teaching, research and consultancy in the areas of Accounting, Finance, Microfinance and Sustainable Business development. His academic work focuses on financial inclusion, rural and agritourism finance, microfinance innovations, and the intersection between finance and entrepreneurship in developing economies. His research and professional engagement are grounded in fostering inclusive financial systems that promote rural transformation.

Part II
Financial Technologies and Sustainable Enterprise Development

Chapter 4
Financial Technologies and Sustainable Enterprise Development in Developing Economies

Joseph Asare

Synopsis
Financial technology (Fintech) has revolutionized enterprises in developing economies by transforming operations, financial management, and product development. It has enabled the adoption of emerging technologies to drive revenue, growth, and accessibility. Fintech provides benefits such as reduced costs, increased accessibility, and financial inclusion, but also poses risks like cybercrime and regulatory oversight. The sector is capital-intensive and relies on funding from various sources. Fintech in developing economies faces challenges like fraud and regulatory risks. Sustainable enterprise development involves conducting business activities that contribute positively to the environment, economy, and society. Fintech adoption facilitates cost reduction, economic growth, and financial inclusion. Human capital is crucial for the success of Fintech, and enterprises must invest in enhancing talent. Fintech contributes to sustainable growth by facilitating economic efficiency, access to finance, and innovation. It rationalizes the traditional financial sector, enhances resource allocation, and improves capital for enterprises. Understanding Financial Technologies and enterprise development in developing economies is crucial for sustainable development (2024).

J. Asare (✉)
Ghana Communication Technology University, Accra, Ghana
e-mail: jasare@gctu.edu.gh

Y. Alhassan et al. (eds.), *Financial Innovation and Sustainable Enterprise in Developing and Emerging Economies*, Research Series on Responsible Enterprise Ecosystems, https://doi.org/10.1007/978-3-032-04500-3_4

4.1 Financial Technologies Overview in Developing Economies

4.1.1 Introduction

Enterprises in developing economies are experiencing the impacts of the rapid development of financial technologies (Fintech) due to the many changes and advances brought about in enterprises' operations and financial management. Financial technology is believed to have revolutionized various enterprises' activities, especially in dealing with financial and nonfinancial institutions, customers, trading, insurance, and risk management. The advent of technology-based financial innovations is utilized by enterprises in the production and trading sectors, as well as enterprises in the banking and insurance sectors, which also use financial technologies in their operations and product development. Technology-based financial products and services support both small and big businesses, including information and communication technology enterprises and start-ups. Leveraging emerging technologies such as artificial intelligence, data, edge computing, blockchain, and digital financial services to drive revenue, promote growth, and make enterprise products and services more accessible and efficient should be the focus of enterprises in developing economies. The changes in operations, activities, products, and services, from physical services to more advanced services based on digital technology, have changed people's behavior regarding how enterprises in developing economies currently operate. The term financial technology contrasts with traditional finance, whereby technology is applied to develop and provide financial products and services. Especially the operations and marketing of financial products with the view of making the product easily and readily accessible to the customer, while at the same time reducing transaction costs without compromising the potential for competitive advantage against the existing financial system.

Financial technology is widely considered to provide significant benefits ranging from reduced costs to an increase in easy and readily accessible products and services at convenience. However, one cause for worry is the potential risks associated with the use of financial technology by enterprises for digital financial, operating, and other transactions, which increase their vulnerability to cybercrime, and the lack of regulatory oversight in most developing economies. This requires that policymakers in developing economies carefully study these risks and the associated benefits to guarantee that all activities of enterprises that are conducted through the use of and promotion of financial technologies and the associated compliance are regulated to protect consumers for guaranteed financial stability. Some empirical studies have shown that the risk associated with certain kinds of financial technologies may originate from the disruptive nature of those technologies. Because there are technological developments that lead to disruptive innovations in financial technology, they have had a tremendous impact on the development of financial sector products and services (Palmié et al., 2020). The disruptive innovations also created a condition that has changed how various start-up businesses traditionally ought to operate in developing countries. For example, the growth in the use of mobile phones in developing economies has supported opportunities for the use of mobile financial services such as Mobile Financial Receipt and Payment Services, which strive to provide convenient financial services (Lee, 2018). The use of mobile financial receipt and payment services not only makes it easy for consumers to access account, product, and service information, but it also enables enterprises to access customer data and reach out to customers for financial transactions through the use of mobile phones. Further, financial technologies promote financial inclusion, which supports enterprise growth through the improved buying capabilities of customers. In addition, the emergency of financial technologies is gradually helping to reduce income inequality and poverty and increase access to capital and opportunities for deprived communities. Furthermore, a significant feature of the use of financial technologies in developing economies is that the development of digital financial innovation has boosted job creation, economic growth, and entrepreneurship. And further increased financial transaction efficiency and transparency, reducing the potential for trust issues.

4.1.1.1 Understanding Financial Technologies

Presently, the financial sector continues to experience rapid technological and digital advancements through the implementation of innovative financial technologies that have influenced processes, products, and services provided by financial institutions. Financial technological advances have altered the traditional financial ecosystem, posing challenges to enterprises that in the past dominated the mainstream service offerings. This disruption has surfaced opportunities for innovations that seemed unacceptable in the past but currently appear to influence the way enterprises pay, receive money, and perform varied financial services with convenience, ease, efficiency, and enhanced product and service delivery (Tashtamirov, 2023). The key drivers of financial technology are financial innovation and digital technology, which have also generated much interest in recent years.

Financial Innovation

The process of creating new financial products, services, and technologies that aim to meet the evolving needs of the market (Tashtamirov, 2023). A significant potential of financial innovation is the ability to increase efficiency and lower costs. However, it also poses significant challenges for the financial system. The emergent technologies are continuously reforming the financial and enterprise ecosystems, driving innovation, transforming customer experiences, and enhancing the overall efficiency of enterprise operations.

a. Forms of Financial innovation

Table 4.1 explains various forms of financial innovations.

Table 4.1 The forms of financial innovations

Financial Innovations	Definition
Technological advancements	A continuous process of innovation, improvement, and integration of new tools, techniques, and systems to enhance efficiency, productivity, and convenience in various fields. It has revolutionized the way we live, work, and communicate and has opened new frontiers for exploration and discovery (Ebimene et al., 2024)
Risk Management techniques	The development of sophisticated risk management tools, including credit default swaps, securitization, and catastrophe bonds, that aid enterprises in performing avoidance, retention, spreading, loss prevention, and reduction of risks (CSU, 2024)
New products and services	The introduction of novel financial instruments, such as derivatives, exchange-traded funds (ETFs), or peer-to-peer lending platforms, offer innovative ways to manage risk, allocate capital, or access financing. Also, enterprises exploit advanced technology to improve the functionality of their existing and new products and enhance their services in an attempt to satisfy customers' needs and improve enterprise performance (Kocak et al., 2017; Chen et al., 2014)
Business models	The adoption of innovative business models, including financial and nonfinancial institutions, crowdfunding platforms, or digital finance and financial services, disrupts traditional financial and banking services by offering more affordable, accessible, and tailored solutions to customers. Also, technological advancements aid financial institutions to streamline their operations and reduce costs associated with maintaining physical branches (GCB, 2023)
Regulatory changes	The significance of technological advancement is also observed in the implementation of new regulations or frameworks, such as the Dodd-Frank Act and Basel III, that aim to enhance stability, transparency, and consumer protection within the financial system, as well as encourage innovation and competition. Technological innovations are believed to increase trust in the financial sector, which drives financial growth. In using Ghana as a case, digital finance is utilized to build trust in financial institutions and promote financial inclusion (Ofori-Acquah et al., 2023)

Source: The author, 2024

Most importantly, financial innovation performs a crucial role in facilitating investment, driving economic growth, expanding financial inclusion, capital formation (Jain, 2024).

Digital Technology

The application of a wide range of technologies, services, tools, and applications, including the usage of various forms of software and hardware to execute activities through electronic means to create, store, process, transmit, and display information, including the use of mobile phones, robots, personal computers, radio, digital television, etc. (Rice, 2003).

Digital The use of electronic technology to represent and manipulate data. That is converting information into binary code, which consists of 0s and 1s, and processing it using computers or other digital devices. In the context of technology, computing, communications, and programming, digital in general refers to the digitalization of various processes and the use of digital platforms and tools.

How Does Digital Technology Work? Digital technology functions on the theory of encoding information into binary code, using a combination of 0s and 1s to represent data and instructions. By performing calculations and executing commands based on the code provided, the binary codes can be understood by computers and digital devices. The results are then decoded back into a human-readable format for interpretation and use (Lenovo, 2024).

Forms of Digital Technology

There are several forms of digital technologies, however the most relevant today that support enterprise growth and development are shown in Fig. 4.1 as digital technology parachute:

The Table 4.2 explains thc various forms of digital technologies.

The recognition of the association between innovation and digital technology and the challenges associated with the development of enterprise business models and entrepreneurial start-ups is crucial. Therefore, enterprises need to consider it critical to leverage technology and innovation to manage the mass of customers and infrastructure to unlock the full market potential and value proposition. The significance is that entrepreneurial ecosystems and start-up environments often determine

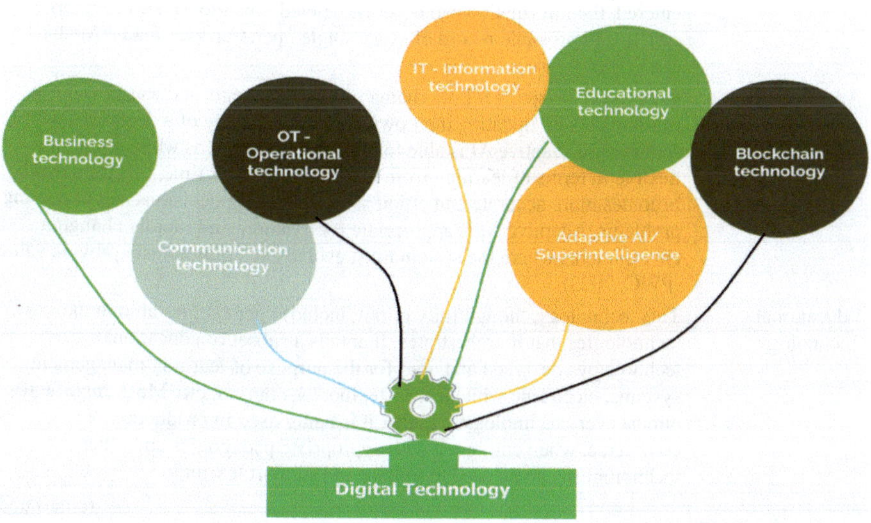

Fig. 4.1 Digital technology parachute. Source: Author, 2024. (Further developed based on Digital Adaption, 2023)

Table 4.2 Forms of digital technology

Financial Innovations	Definition
Business Technology	Enterprises are now operating in an in an environment where information technology is changing the landscape around them, transitioning from the back room of an organization into the hands of customers, employees, and society. The strategy used by enterprises for organizing and coordinating technology management across the entire enterprise is what constitutes business technology. It may also be described as the set of tools, management practices, organizational structures, and technology governance intended to ensure that the use of technology is enhanced across the enterprise with the overarching aim of satisfying customer needs and expectations (BTS, 2024)
Communication Technology	Information and communication technology (ICT) is influencing every aspect of human life. They are playing salient roles at workplaces, businesses, etc. ICT is recognized as a catalyst for change in the areas of handling and exchanging information, changing working conditions, and accessing information and communication technologies. Technologies that provide access to information through telecommunication and focus primarily on communication technologies, including wireless networks, the internet, cell phones, and other communication mediums, constitute ICT (Ratheeswari, 2018)
Blockchain Technology (BT)	Blockchain technology is software; a protocol for the secure transfer of unique instances of value (e.g., money, property, contracts, and identity credentials) via the internet without requiring a third-party intermediary such as a bank or government; email over IP; voice over IP; or money over IP. Most importantly, BT is a dispersed database of records or public ledger of all operations or digital events that have been performed and shared among active parties. Each transaction in the ledger is verified by the agreement of a majority of the contributors in the system. Also, once entered, the information can never be deleted. The blockchain contains a certain and provable record of every single operation ever made (Michael et al., 2005)
Adaptive AI/ superintelligence	Adaptive AI systems follow changes in environments and learn from new runtime data by updating their own codes. Consisting of a decision-making framework, adaptive AI is able to make faster decisions while remaining flexible in terms of learning from newer issues. Over time, this framework becomes more accurate and efficient while making decisions and/or solving problems. Adaptive AI is appropriate for dynamic and rapidly changing environments where the system must evolve and continuously provide value (PWC, 2023)
Educational Technology	This technology, thoughtfully or not, includes pedagogies among the technologies that it orchestrates. It entails a subset of educational technologies designed and used for the purpose of learning management systems, electronic whiteboards, textbooks, courses, etc. Most importantly, almost every technology, whether it is being used in production or commerce, when combined with appropriate pedagogies and other technologies, can be used to initiate and support learning

(continued)

Table 4.2 (continued)

Financial Innovations	Definition
IT—Information Technology	This implies resources used by a firm in the processing and management of its data. Including hardware, software, communications (voice, data, and video), and associated personnel. That is any activity that involves information processing and integrated communication through electronic equipment (Victoria, 2020). IT is crucial in all aspects of enterprise development
Operational Technology	All information systems used for managing, operating, and monitoring automation systems and other "shop floor" systems. Information technology is expanding into this area even more than before. Many manual operations presently start with an IT-enabled check. E.g., the servicing of cars and other operations that used to be purely manual are now assisted by operational technology. Such as a laser-assisted wheel alignment machine (Sofigate, 2019)

Source: The Author, 2024

the geographical phenomena that foster the growth and scaling-up of enterprise development.

4.2 Financial Technology and New Technologies (Types, Products, and Services)

4.2.1 Introduction

Financial technology is unlike other inventions because it directly impacts the efficiency of the financial sector. It is for this reason that investments and savings are intermediated in an economy to effect growth. Fintech is considered an integral part of the current digital economy that has produced advances that have transformed the way enterprise operates and have also shaped productivity and growth across advanced economies over the years. Typically, it is the more open financial markets that witness the rapid development of fintech. The examples are mobile money and t-cash payment systems, which operate in Ghana, Nigeria, and other developing economies and demonstrate most of the success of fintech since its emergence a few years ago. Using mobile phones, fintech has effectively transformed phones into payment accounts, thereby increasing financial access, and financial inclusion for those who previously could not access traditional banking services. One effective way Fintech has disrupted the financial sector is by increasing efficiency across developing economies. Although traditional financial services are equally delivered with technology, fintech has been radically disruptive in the way financial services are conducted by allowing for greater consumer choice and freedom. Using fintech products such as embedded financial services, digital payment solutions, lending, digital wallets, mobile money, remittances, artificial intelligence, and blockchain, among others, there has been freedom in the offering of financial products, and use of financial services (Ibrahim, 2022).

4.2.1.1 Historical Revolution of Fintech

The application of technology to financial service delivery and products can be traced as far back as the nineteenth century, through investment and adaptation in communications infrastructure such as the telegraph and transatlantic cable, which enabled the transmission of financial information across borders (Barbiroli, 1997). The early to mid-twentieth century of technology was characterized by the creation of a centralized funds transfer service as well as the adoption of credit cards to reduce cash payments. However, the latter twentieth century saw banks leading the development of Fintech by converting from analogue to digital platforms of service delivery, including ATMs, digital stock exchanges, and SWIFT (Society for Worldwide Interbank Financial Telecommunications), a communication protocol designed to facilitate the movement of large-volume cross-border payment transactions between financial institutions (Volcker, 2009; Hills, 2002). Also, the introduction of e-commerce and online banking amalgamated due to the global adoption of bank mainframe computers, leading to the transition of the financial sector into a digital era during the early years of the twenty-first century (Welch, 1999). The disruption of the traditional banking system is reported to have heightened after the global financial disaster that happened in 2008 revealed a lot of weaknesses in the financial sector, generating disbelief from consumers in the banks' products and service delivery (SSG, 2009). A significant effect on the financial world took place in 2009 with the introduction of Bitcoin and other cryptocurrencies. Current fintech innovation is marked by the adoption of blockchain and related technologies. In the near future, fintech is expected to leverage the increasingly sophisticated technologies that are in the hands of progressively sophisticated customers with innovations in enterprise models (Gomber, 2018).

4.2.2 Defining Financial Technology (Fintech)

4.2.2.1 Fintech System Model

What is your understanding of FinTech? According to Leong and Sung (2018), most people are unclear or even do not know what fintech is all about. Some people are of the view that FinTech mainly focuses on some technical aspects, such as e-payment and blockchain, without considering the general view. This weak public understanding and the lack of a clear definition of fintech have led to many practical problems associated with fintech. This leads to the discouragement of enterprises from considering relevant fintech in enterprise development. Consequentially, the pipeline of fintech impacts on enterprises has been minimal or negatively affected. Also, the shortage of FinTech professionals has stimulated the need to stimulate knowledge on FinTech (Jackson et al., 2023). The application of technology for the provision of financial services connotes financial technology. That is the infusion of technology into finance through the integration of digital and technological tools in the delivery of financial services and products. The scope of fintech includes the deployment, design, and adoption of software and applications to automate the delivery of financial services to enhance the development and delivery of financial products and services by traditional banks within and beyond the banking halls (Dewi & Viverita, 2022; Anyfantaki, 2016). Also, the rapid development of technology has prompted the advent of various innovation efforts in the financial sector, one of which is financial technology. The adaptation of fintech services by financial institutions and enterprises, which promoted enterprise growth and reduced firms risk-taking behavior, thereby increasing stability, supported the relationship between the development of fintech and traditional financial services.

Financial technology (Fintech) entails advanced technology that improves and automates the delivery and use of financial services and products. The fundamental of fintech is that it is applications that support enterprises, entrepreneurs, and consumers to effectively manage their financial processes and operations by utilizing specially designed computers, devices, software, and algorithms that smartly perform financial activities and operations. Currently, fintech is creating a possibility for enterprises to use competitive alternatives to traditional financial intermediaries, markets, and infrastructure. Further, the prevalent adoption of modern technologies offers advantages but also poses risks, such as data insecurity. However, fintech offers many efficiencies in financial operations by offering better and more directed products and services and strengthening financial inclusion in developing countries. However, it could also establish risks that could undermine trust, competition, financial stability, and monetary policy transmission in developing economies (Ibrahim, 2022; Girma & Huseynov, 2024; Jackson et al., 2023).

The Fig. 4.2 the fintech system model that shows the core components of fintech.

Finance and Investment Like any other sector, finance plays a very crucial role in the fintech sector and may be described as highly capital-intensive. The sources of funding for the most significant fintech projects in developing countries such as Ghana, Nigeria, and South Africa are from the US. There is substantial investment from Asia too, including China. In 2021, Nigeria raised US$400 million, and most of that came from Asian investors (BCG, 2023). Fintech investment funding and deal sizes in Africa are smaller than in the rest of the world. The three markets in Africa average fintech investment between $3 million and $10 million. This is because the African market is a 'frontier market' with weak regulations and structures. However, the market is the fastest-growing in the world and proves that investment is storming up (4C Group, 2024). In 2021, the global fintech market will reach $210 billion; however, global investment in fintech will drop in 2023 compared to the last five years by $113.7 billion from the 4547 deal. This represents a 42% decline from the $196.3 billion reported in 2022 and may be considered the

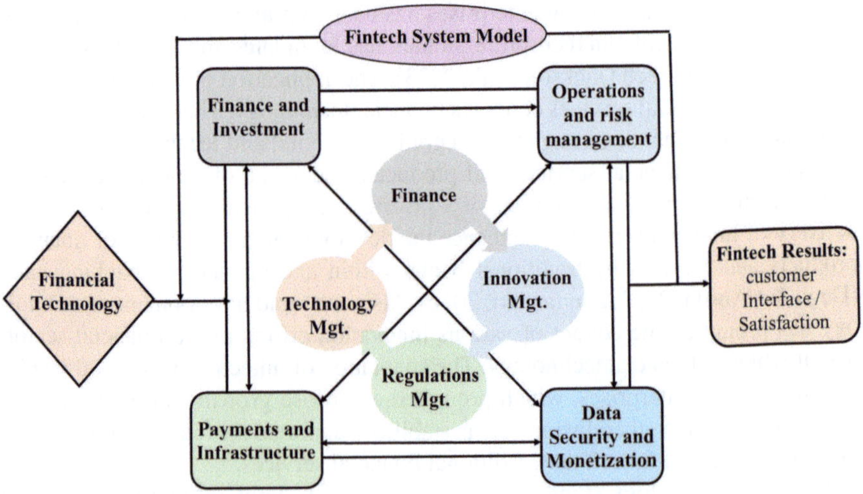

Fig. 4.2 Fintech system model. Source: Author's Developed Model, 2024

weakest result since 2017 (Duffy, 2024). This downturn in investment in fintech could be attributed to interest rates and persistent inflation in various regions, the conflicts in Ukraine and the Middle East, and declining valuations, which led to a growing concern and an act of caution for fintech investors.

Payments and Infrastructure In most developing economies, such as Ghana, the fintech market is rapidly developing, with digital payments, digital capital raising, digital investment, digital assets, and challenger banks (fintech firms that use software, apps, and other technologies to streamline mobile and online banking) emerging as some of the most significant trends. Digital payments in most developing economies, including Nigeria, Ghana, and Kenya, have seen an unprecedented surge in popularity, with consumers increasingly relying on mobile payment solutions for their day-to-day transactions (Statista, 2024; Adjasi et al., 2023). Also, investment digital assets and platforms are also gaining traction, with most customers in developing economies seeking easy-to-use and low-cost investment options. Further, raising digital capital has become the other of the day for SMEs and start-ups because it provides an effective way to access funding. Also, there is a rise of digital assets, NFTs, and cryptocurrencies in developing economies, creating new opportunities for investors and traders. Furthermore, fintech firms that use software, apps, and other technologies to streamline mobile and online banking have disrupted the traditional banking and financial industry through the provision of innovative and customer-oriented solutions that cater to the needs of today's digitally knowledgeable consumers (Lensink et al., 2022; Prakash, 2024).

Operation and Risk Management **Fintech** in most developing economies over the past few years has witnessed fraudsters using advanced technologies to pose more dangerous schemes and greater risks for enterprises (Ifechukwu, 2022). This calls for the development of management systems to confront this new reality. The risks faced in the fintech industry are regulatory risk, anti-money laundering (AML), countering terrorist financing (CTF), fraud risk, consumer risk, merchant risk, and outsourcing risk. In 2022, 70% of financial institutions lost over $500 k to fraud, while the market capitalization of the industry also fell to $156 billion (Kereibayev, 2023).

Data Security and Monetization Data is equivalent to a dollar in the digital world. Data is considered a currency that can be reinvested into enterprises products and services to improve user experience, marketing, etc. Data around general interests, users' engagement, spending habits, etc. has proven to be valuable for enterprises to understand and deliver low-cost, quality, and innovative products and services to customers (Nesbitt-Ahmed, 2023). Enterprises around the world are deeply dependent on information and communication technology; therefore, there is a need to ensure that data and information are secured, managed, and used in the most effective way. Information management standards provide best practice frameworks to support enterprises in efficiently and securely managing their data and complying with regulations. However, some fintech entities have a greater risk of business failure or insolvency than established financial service providers due to untested business models, inexperience, and market factors that affect their long-term viability. This can also lead consumers whose funds are held or administered by a fintech entity to face greater risk of data theft and losses if the provider becomes insolvent or their business ceases to operate (Boeddu et al., 2021). All industries benefit from data monetization in some capacity because it optimizes the supply chain, lowers operating costs, supports scheduled deliveries, and contributes to the rise in enterprise sales (Arkadiusz, 2022).

Financial Management and Innovation Management Managing and regulating innovation is very important. Technology is not just transforming the provision of financial services on continents such as Africa by altering traditional financial sectors; it is also facilitating the creation of alternative financial products and services using FinTech innovation by enterprises emerging from outside of the traditional financial sector (CCAF, 2021). FinTech has been transformative in all economies, particularly in the developing economies of Africa, providing innovative solutions to promote economic growth, financial inclusion, and reduced poverty (Celik, 2019). In addition, fintech has promoted market solutions by developing important solutions to overcome obstacles to reducing barriers to financial inclusion, economic development, increasing competition in payments, and other financial services. On the contrary, fintech evolution has led to challenges for regulators, who are responding by altering existing regulatory frameworks and creating new regulatory and innovation initiatives that are designed to support existing and new approaches while protecting consumers from harm (Richard, 2023; Agelyne & Musau, 2021; Budiarti & Jannah, 2022).

Technology Management Fintech is considered by many to be a relatively recent innovation development, and it has changed so quickly over the last decade due to the advancements in technology being applied to the finance sector (Milanesi, 2022). Fintech is not a new phenomenon because financial institutions sought to streamline their service delivery and cut costs by using technology many years ago. The technologies that highlight fintech business models vary considerably. This includes machine learning, blockchain technology, artificial intelligence (AI), machine learning, and other big data functions (Idian et al., 2023).

Regulations Management Fintech in Sub-Saharan Africa (SSA) has experienced significant growth over the years in countries such as Kenya, Ghana, and Nigeria. Such growth may be attributed to the widespread adoption of digital payments and mobile technology, which has paved the way for the usage of most digital financial services and policymakers' support for fintech innovation (Sussu, 2024). Most developing countries have put in place robust policy frameworks for digital financial services. However, some policy frameworks for fintech in developing countries are uneven in comparison. While certain developing countries have initiated digital financial activity-specific regulations, others have yet to release rules or guidance pertaining to such activity or may be in their early stages of developing them (Mas, 2011). Most importantly, existing legislation to control fintech operations is considered sufficient, depending on the jurisdiction and the business models involved. Whereas some developing countries may put in place certain regulators as a soft touch for market stimulation, other regulatory bodies in certain developing economies may be a response or in reaction to specific risks aimed at addressing, imposing limits, or protecting a specific sector. Therefore, policymakers in developing economies have a role in fostering the safe development of the fintech industry, aiming to enhance individual and enterprise access to financing and operational efficiencies (OECD, 2024).

4.2.3 Benefits of Fintech in Enterprise Development

Regardless of the related challenges and risks associated with fintech in developing countries, fintech also presents huge benefits for the adoption and use of fintech, including:

Efficiency Fintech adoption in enterprises and other sectors facilitates cost reduction in both operations and financial-related transactions because it supports the absence of the application of transactions without physical assets, thereby reducing overhead costs (Berger, 2023). Further, fintech impacts increase enterprises' economic added value and are more productive than those that do not adopt financial technology (Sedunov, 2016).

Financial Inclusion The existing fintech facilitates financial inclusion by allowing people without a traditional bank account to undertake financial transactions (receipts, payments, savings, or other financial activities). In general, in developing countries such as Ghana, Kenya, and Nigeria, fintech has enabled over 90% of people who do not have bank accounts to access finance and financial services using mobile phones (GSMA, 2023). Additionally, fintech is significantly helping enterprises to develop, grow, and support efforts to increase financial inclusion (Kurniasari et al., 2021).

Inclusive Growth in most developing economies, there are reported economic disparities and inequality (Tabash et al., 2024). However, the adoption of fintech plays a crucial role in overcoming economic inequalities and promoting access to quality financial products and services. Thereby improving the people's overall economic condition in developing countries. Also, fintech helps to improve enterprise performance and guarantees continuity (Desiyanti et al., 2023; Heath-Brown, 2015).

Enhances Product and Service Experience The adoption of fintech products and services supports access more quickly by using financial technology. Fintech products and services such as online banking, mobile payments, and digital wallets make financial transactions easier and enhance the customer experience, especially when faced with financial decision-making (Meena, 2023).

Innovation Fintech offers avenues and advanced methods that make it easier to gather and use financial data, develop business models, improve innovative services, new products, and markets, and create new financial instruments. Fintech also supports the update of established enterprise models to be more innovative and creative. In addition, fintech facilitates the performance of financial transactions using various applications that are faster, cheaper, and more secure. Also, fintch promotes the quality of innovation, strengthens cooperation, and structures industrial structures through the efficient use of financial technology resources (Ye et al., 2023; Gomber, 2018).

4.3 Sustainable Enterprise Development and Fintech in Developing Economies

4.3.1 Introduction

The introduction of fintech technologies is expected to disrupt enterprise development systems in developing economies at all levels, necessitating the cultivation of fresh talent, which, in turn, requires an immediate and proactive response from higher enterprises and the business community. The incorporation of fintech in enterprise development and fostering growth requires professionals who possess a comprehensive understanding of various fields and can address real-world enterprise challenges. Fintech is not limited to only advanced economies and high-tech business programs; it can also benefit a wide range of enterprises, irrespective of their location on the globe. Fintech in enterprise development can range in support for small and medium enterprises, smallholder farms, manufacturing, agro-processing, leading information and communication technology institutional support, etc. in developing countries. It should be noted that fintech is not a solution to all enterprise development and growth problems; however, when applied appropriately, it can serve as an enabler of enterprise development in developing countries. A demonstration of the practical application and monetization efforts of newly developed fintech technology is crucial for its long-term adoption and circulation among enterprises (Debora et al., 2023). By leveraging fintech innovation, enterprises can offer accessible and affordable products and services to underserved communities, reducing barriers that prevent individuals from accessing certain products and services. Also, through digital platforms, mobile banking, and innovative payment solutions, enterprises can offer products and services to customers regardless of their location to attain sustainable enterprise development (Siano et al., 2020).

4.3.2 Understanding Sustainable Enterprise Development

A sustainable enterprise is an institution that can meet and anticipate the needs of present and future customers and stakeholders through initiating activities that accelerate positive social change, innovating new business strategies, and protecting and enhancing business performance while preserving environmental honesty. The incorporation of the principles of sustainability into each of the enterprise decisions, the use of greener than traditional competition, the supply of environmentally friendly products or services that replace demand for nongreen products and/or services, and making an enduring commitment to environmental principles in all business operations are features of sustainable enterprise (Zu, 2013). The notion of sustainable development is dear in the world of business. That term comprises three characteristics: social, economic, and environmental, which must be balanced with each other. This concept must be known by all enterprises and entrepreneurs in their operational activities and the starting of businesses. In addition, enterprises are expected to become sustainable to be able to survive the challenges that confront them. That is, there is a correlation between sustainable development and entrepreneurs who set up and run enterprises. Therefore, entrepreneurial orientation toward sustainability can accelerate the creation of sustainable enterprises (Rahmana & Bawono, 2021). **Sustainable enterprise development is a strategy that satisfies the needs of enterprises while maintaining employee well-being, ecological balance, and community welfare. The concept involves conducting enterprise activities in a manner that contributes more to the environment, economy, and society than it takes from them (AfriBlocks Network,** 2024).

In most developing economies, such as countries on the African continent, sustainability business practices extend beyond environmental deliberations to include social development. Enterprises in Africa recognize the importance of inclusive community engagement and fair operational practices and the promotion of gender equality, fair wages, providing decent work, contributing to poverty alleviation, enhancing social well-being, supporting local communities, and fostering sustainable economic growth (Chatterjee et al., 2021). Sustainable enterprise development is an approach that considers the concurrent fulfillment of social, economic, and environmental goals. It encompasses a long-term strategy that determines that enterprises should operate responsibly and with future generations in mind. Sustainable enterprise development aims to make enterprises's efforts measurable. Figure 4.3 is a sustainable enterprise model.

Economic and sustainable enterprise development goals involve attaining financial growth and profits, which are essential for the success and functioning of an enterprise. Every sustainable development goal entails economic objectives to be achieved ethically and with respect for the community in which the enterprise operates and the natural environment.

Social enterprises operate with employees; therefore, sustainable enterprise development should focus on creating high-quality jobs, taking care of employee well-being, promoting fairness in the workplace, promoting diversity and equality, and engaging with local communities. To attain sustainable enterprise development, enterprises should also consider the impact of their activities on society and customers by aspiring to deliver quality products and services that meet consumer needs and respect for their rights.

Environmentally, enterprises sustainable development entails aiming to minimize their negative impact on the natural environment because of their operation. Further, for sustainability, enterprises should endeavor to efficiently use resources, reduce greenhouse gas emissions, protect biodiversity, promote sustainable energy, minimize waste and pollution, and manage water. Enterprises should implement ecological practices that involve reducing raw material consumption, using

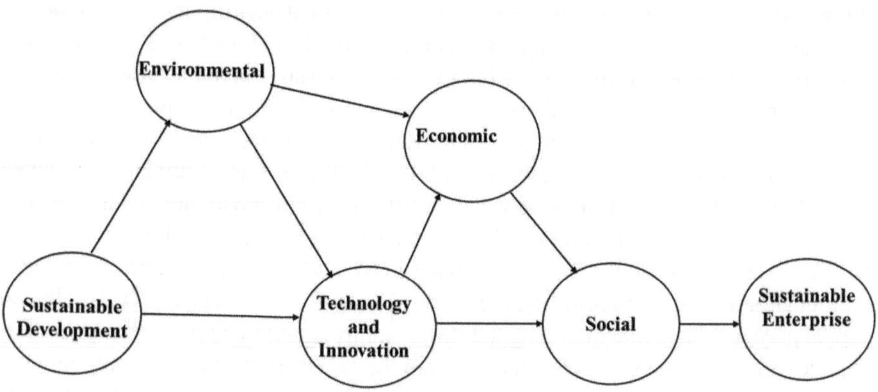

Fig. 4.3 Sustainable enterprise model. Source: Author, 2024

renewable energy, recycling, various other actions, and investing in clean transportation technology (Koźmińskiego, 2023).

4.3.2.1 Enterprise Development and the Drivers of Sustainable Enterprise Development

Enterprise development is the process of developing small or medium-sized companies. Enterprise development is different from other forms of business development as the purpose is for the enterprise rather than an individual. However, an important distinction is that the sustainability of the enterprise depends on whether it is worth more than the sum of its parts or whether it is becoming more than how it was started. The purpose of enterprise development differs, either for positive societal change or commercial reasons. Recently, investors want to see that their enterprises grow fast in order to maximize the return on their investment. Mostly, in developing economies, enterprise development is done to benefit society and stimulate economic activity, with a specific focus on economic empowerment. Also, enterprise development could be more specific, with a focus on developing a specific sector, region, ethnic group, or promoting gender equality. Enterprise development approaches differ significantly and can vary from mentoring, financial investment, grants, training for staff with a focus on improving production, service delivery, or supply chain management (Gancarczyk & Zabala-Iturriagagoitia, 2023; Oppong et al., 2014).

Most of the time, small and medium enterprises in developing economies pay little or no attention to sustainable development aspects when choosing and investing in business opportunities. This is attributed to the disparity between components of sustainability implemented in enterprises. When enterprises disregard community rights and environmental sustainability, it will have a consequential impact on enterprise continuity. In other words, environmental, economic, and social factors must support and satisfy each other to make a positive contribution to enterprise development. In this regard, the concept of sustainable development is needed (Cassar & Friedman, 2009). Sustainability enterprise development is driven by various factors, and enterprises are motivated to adopt sustainable practices because of internal environment factors such as financial, employee, benefits, and management attitude (Zhivkova, 2022). Further, enterprises are motivated to adopt technology and innovative activities towards attaining sustainability in order to attain sustainable development. In this regard, factors such as investments in innovation activities, innovation performance, and skills needed to support sustainability-focused innovation play a significant role in driving sustainable innovation in enterprises (Grigorescu et al., 2019). Also, enterprises are driven to recognize that sustainable marketing can benefit their businesses as it validates resilience during economic downturns, generates higher market returns, and ensures compliance with environmental and social requirements (Chavadi & Manickam, 2023). Human capital plays a critical role in driving the sustainability agenda within an enterprise; this includes embedding sustainable strategies into the organizational culture, aligning talent with emerging technology and innovation realities, and promoting and supporting employees' skills development in information and communication technologies.

4.3.3 *Factors that Affects Enterprise Development in Developing Economies*

Like most developing countries, enterprise growth in developing countries in Africa has been very challenging due to many economic, social, environmental, political, and technological factors. **Access to credit**—the effect of accessibility to credit on enterprise growth and operations—is important for its survival and growth. Also, policymakers appear not to have pursued financial sector policies that boost financial intermediaries to design appropriate products and services for enterprises. Enterprises in Ghana, a West African country, are noted to lack adequate access to credit, posing a major limitation to small and medium enterprise development (Nkua et al., 2013).

Technology, innovation, and globalization—most enterprises in Ghana are believed to have been affected by technology and innovation, which have promoted competition and globalization in Ghana. Globalization has ushered in technological changes and greater levels of competition. Technological advancement has brought about various challenges that influence enterprise competitiveness and the global market. Therefore, enterprises must properly strategize to embrace the changes in the global marketplace and cultures (Ocioo et al., 2014).

Impact of government policy: Most enterprises in developing economies are faced with the challenge of unfavorable government policies that negatively impact their growth and operations. In addition, some enterprises get inadequate financial support from financial institutions due to certain government policies. Further, an unstable macroeconomic environment limits the development of enterprises, and this can be overcome by advocating for loan guarantee schemes and formalizing enterprise policies.

Intellectual capital issue: the competitiveness of enterprises in the current knowledge-based economy demands employees with high intellectual abilities who can explore the challenges that confront enterprise operations. Intellectual capital has become a lubricant for modern economies to become competitive in knowledge-based economies. However, most enterprises in developing economies struggle to acquire employees with high intellectual abilities (Khalique et al., 2011).

The application of modern technologies—most enterprises in developing economies acknowledge that the operation and development of a service that uses modern technologies are not yet fully accepted by many enterprises in developing countries. This is mainly due to market structure and technical reasons that have become obstacles to enterprise. This makes it imperative to also understand the influence of technology and innovation on enterprise operations, growth, and development in developing economies (Decker et al., 2006).

Exposure to modern technology: The extent of technological advancement in most developing economies determines the success of enterprises. Most developing economies are said to be at an initial stage of adopting technology, and once technological apparatus is in place to encourage big and small enterprises, it will be possible for enterprises in developing economies enterprise to move at a faster pace than enterprises in developed economies.

Education, knowledge, and skills are major sources of enterprise strength. Unfortunately, most prospective enterprises in developing economies are unable to scale through due to a lack of the requisite knowledge and skills needed to develop. A thorough understanding of the business environment and its dynamics remains an absolute tool for success. Current and prospective enterprises must continuously seek knowledge and requisite skills in order to excel in many positive ways in the currently technologically driven world (Ojonugwa & Omale, 2016).

4.4 Fintech and Enterprise Development in Developing Economies

Enterprises (micro, small, medium, and large) play a significant role in developing economies, constituting the basic source of entrepreneurial ideas, materials, processes, and services that other sectors of the economy cannot do or do not want to do. In an attempt to benefit from the cost advantage of economies of scale, most enterprises in developing economies implement policies that will enable them to improve their operation capacity for a long period in the form of investments in technology, machines, tools, devices, and the labor force. Also, enterprises in developing economies are faced with problems maintaining large-scale investment. Because their economies are small, they possess a more elastic structure when compared to developed economies (Ackah & Vuvor, 2011). In addition, the introduction of fintech has brought many changes and advances to enterprise operations in developing economies. Fintech has revolutionized various activities, especially financial, trading, operations, product development and service delivery, and risk management.

The emergence of technology-based financial service innovations is not only utilized by financial companies in the financial sector but also encourages the development of enterprises and other technology-based non-financial services. Fintech products such as data, artificial intelligence, blockchain, and edge computing enterprises, start-up businesses, technology companies, and financial institutions are leveraging emerging technologies to make financial services more accessible and efficient for all. The change in financial products and services from physical services to more advanced products and services on digital platforms has succeeded in changing enterprise and customer behavior regarding how to use financial services (Feyen et al., 2021). The adoption of fintech based on the perspective of enterprises in developing countries is influenced by the ease of use, access, and performance of financial services and activities. The development of fintech has changed the way and attitude of enterprises in conducting financial transactions. However, the potential benefits of fintech have not been fully adopted simultaneously by enterprises, especially in developing countries, due to several conditions related to socio-culture, cost, knowledge of use, and demographics, which result in different perspectives on fintech (Asma, 2023).

4.4.1 *Leveraging Fintech for Sustainable Enterprise Development*

Innovation and fintech are rapidly changing how traditional financial services are served, especially having a significant impact on the banking industry. Compared with developed countries, fintech has kept on moving forward at a high speed compared to developing countries (Berger, 2003). Fintech innovation has proved to have an impact on the real economy and high total factor productivity. In most developing economies, such as countries in Sub-Saharan Africa, fintech has advanced enterprise innovation and entrepreneurship by providing platforms for startups and small businesses to access funding and investment. Also, crowdfunding campaigns, accelerator programs, and venture capital investments have stimulated the growth of innovative enterprises and ventures, driving economic development and attracting investments from both local and international sources (CCAF, 2021). Figure 4.4 shows fintech's role in sustainable enterprise development in developing economies.

Fintech and Human Capital Factors in Enterprise Development Human capital may be defined as the knowledge, experience, and skills of a group of people or a person seen as something valuable that an enterprise or economy can use (Oxford Learner's Dictionaries website). It could also mean a person's character, knowledge, and intelligence, which enable them to develop to their full potential in all areas of their personal, social, and economic well-being. Or a collection of attributes, skills, and knowledge that each of us possesses and that can be used to boost

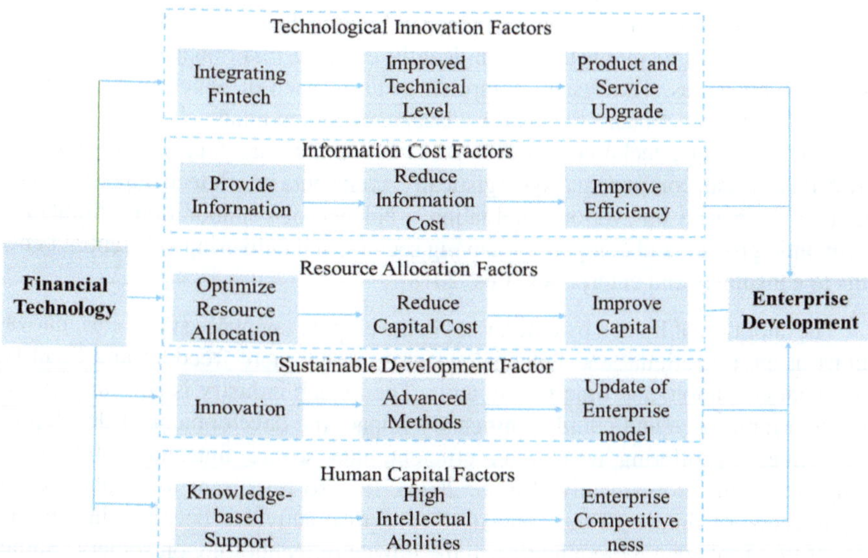

Fig. 4.4 Fintech for sustainable enterprise development. Source: Author, 2024. Further developed abased on the impact mechanism of fintech on the transformation of enterprise, Sumei et al. (2022)

productivity (Lockhart, 2019). Is it people or technology that drives FinTech growth? (Deloitte, 2022). It should be noted, however, that human capital is the key factor in the success of fintech today. Enterprises in developing economies must know that they would benefit more in the long run if they invested in enhancing human capital rather than following the old-fashioned method of downsizing and firing employees (Hanini et al., 2023).

The development of fintech is increasingly concealing the distinction between financial products and services and technology sectors. FinTech brings out the best of both of these sectors to disrupt financial services and enterprises by enhancing the customer experience, increasing the speed of service, and reducing operating costs through digitization. In terms of human capital development, fintech helps to attract, engage, and retain talent, which is key because talented individuals drive the growth of enterprises. However, the focus on growth often reduces the priority of investing time and resources in building a long-term people strategy, as fintech offers most of these benefits. Fintech plays a key role in enterprise development; however, attracting highly talented employees such as data analysts is crucial to driving the growth of enterprises (Deloitte, 2022). Fintech provides knowledge-based support and requires employees with high intellectual abilities, which together would make the enterprise highly competitive.

Fintech and Sustainable Enterprise Development The truth about FinTech is that it contributes to the sustainable growth of businesses, nations, and societies by facilitating economic efficiency, access to finance, financial inclusion, and environmentally friendly digital financial solutions that are often perceived as disruptors of traditional financial institutions (Sheth, 2024). Also, the FinTech system is an is an interdependent network and complex that combines technology with financial products and services to innovate to significantly enhance traditional institutions and financial processes. The system comprises entities, each of which plays a crucial role in shaping the modern financial landscape, including financial customers, start-ups, governments, technology developers, and traditional financial institutions. Together, these components synergistically contribute to fintech's predominant goals of fostering innovation, facilitating a balance of collaboration, stimulating economic growth. and competition among sectors, and delivering substantial benefits to consumers and enterprises (Lee, 2018).

The adoption of fintech by enterprises in developing countries stimulates innovations in the operational and financial systems, grants more freedom and security, financial education, and time-saving tools. The fintech industry is currently evolving at a rapid pace and could significantly impact the development of developing economies by offering accessible, efficient, and secure financial solutions to empower them economically (Russu, 2024). It is so important to emphasize the significance of fintech in the context of enterprise activities because, in the vast majority, people pay more attention to the impact of technology on society (Sumei et al., 2022). Also, fintech is vital that some developing countries have decided to implement reforms to support small and medium enterprise non-bank financing, which have nurtured non-bank funding sources, alternative equity markets for small and medium enterprises, venture capital, microfinance, and leasing (Safitri, 2020; Mavilia & Pisani, 2020). Also, many developing countries have placed great emphasis on the need to digitalize business activities in their domestic economies. Those developing economies have put digitalization at the center of applied reforms (Setianto et al., 2022). Unfortunately, the low level of technological advancement in some developing countries has limited the impact of those reforms, and this is common in developing countries where small and medium enterprises lack public support and access to public finance. Fintech supports enterprise innovation, the use of advanced technology and methods for operations, and the updating of existing systems.

Fintech and Resource Allocation Factors for Enterprise Development Fintech has rationalized the traditional financial sector, enhanced the effect of resource allocation for real enterprises, and enabled financing to overcome the limits of time, presence, and distance to meet the capital needs of different types of enterprises (Sumei et al., 2022). The use of big data sets (online peer-to-peer loan platforms) to support lending makes it easier for people and enterprises to access loans through online lending (Tao & Lin, 2017). Also, crowd funding has emerged as a new type of start-up financing that can support entrepreneurial ventures and small and medium enterprises. Fintech technologies, such as cloud computing, block chain, and other digital technologies, are used to automatically input enterprise user transaction records, customer information, demand queries, and other information into the cloud system. This data can then be integrated into a data system by an enterprise in a secured form that cannot be tampered with (Chetan, 2017). Based on the historical data recorded in the cloud, such as loan records, payment orders, consumption records, etc., enterprises can use artificial intelligence technology and big data modeling to make intelligent judgments on customer behaviors, risk probability, forecast demand, and investment decisions. Fintech facilitates improved resource allocation, reduces the cost of capital, and improves the capital of enterprises.

Fintech and Technology Innovation for Enterprise Development An examination of the relationship between financial development and corporate innovation and the impact of equity markets and credit markets on corporate innovation using a big data set from the global market revealed that a better developed equity market can improve corporate innovation. This shows that fintech might promote technical advancement through the financial market mechanism (Hsu & Tian, 2014). Also, fintech technologies such as data, artificial intelligence, and cloud computing enable physical enterprises to precisely locate and judiciously predict customer needs, realize the change of products from standard mode to personalized customization, and design products more suitable for the long-tail group (2023). Further, fintech enables the upgrading of enterprises products and services, such as their production equipment, production technologies, and production methods, to directly optimize the production mode and resource utilization efficiency of the enterprises, leading to the overall development of enterprises to a more advanced production form. Further, the use of big data technology, mobile internet, technology, and other groundbreaking elements by enterprises delivers knowledge and improves enterprise performance. Further, fintech significantly supports low-cost diffusion, increasing returns to scale, and diminishing marginal returns to improve product quality and optimize the product structure of enterprises. This leads to the upgrading and promotion of the transformation of the entity enterprises (Jianwei et al., 2021; Sumei et al., 2022). Fintech supports integrated services and operations of enterprises, improves technical levels, and upgrades products and services.

Fintech and Information Cost for Enterprise Development Information cost considers the degree of difficulty in obtaining the required information for ecosystem services in enterprise development. Also, by extending the principle of information costs, this would mean the related implication of the value of a product, or the future gains to be expected from rational decisions, and the amount of information gathered on production costs, which is subtractable from the gross income on the same monetary scale (Pelletier et al., 2021). There is a need to lessen the extraordinarily wide discrepancy in the extent to which rich and poor countries are enjoying the benefits of technology, often referred to as the digital divide (James, 2003). The application of fintech and innovation reduces the unequal cost of information in transactions. The use of big data analysis and cloud computing facilitates precision and customized financial services for enterprises, reducing unproductive intermediary costs (Damilola, 2024). In addition, a lack of information about the financial market affects an enterprise's ability to access funding. However, fintech improves the credit investigation level of financial institutions for enterprises, reducing the asymmetric cost of information (Adhami et al., 2018). In addition, fintech supports the streamlining of the approval of processes and the examination of business processing by enterprises. This helps to save both the examination and approval time, improve the efficiency of business processing, meet customer satisfaction, and fully provide enhanced services (Gomber, 2018).

4.5 Highlights

- Enterprises in developing economies are experiencing the impacts of the rapid development of financial technologies (Fintech) due to the many changes and advances brought about in enterprises' operations and financial management.
- Financial technology is unlike other inventions because it directly impacts the efficiency of the financial sector.
- Fintech is considered an integral part of the current digital economy that has produced advances that have transformed the way enterprise operates and have shaped productivity and growth across advanced economies over the years.
- Regulations Management: Fintech in Sub-Saharan Africa (SSA) has experienced significant growth over the years in countries such as Kenya, Ghana, and Nigeria. Such growth may be attributed to the widespread adoption of digital payments

and mobile technology, which has paved the way for the usage of most digital financial services and policymakers' support for fintech innovation (Sussu, 2024).

- The adoption of fintech based on the perspective of enterprises in developing countries is influenced by the ease of use, access, and performance of financial services and activities.
- This study believes that financial technologies are the catalyst for sustainable enterprise development in developing countries.

4.6 Conclusions

Financial technology (Fintech) has revolutionized various aspects of enterprises in developing economies, transforming their operations, financial management, and product development. Fintech has enabled enterprises to leverage emerging technologies such as artificial intelligence, data, edge computing, blockchain, and digital financial services to drive revenue, promote growth, and make products and services more accessible and efficient. Fintech provides significant benefits, including reduced costs, increased accessibility, and convenience of financial products and services. It has also promoted financial inclusion, supported enterprise growth, and reduced income inequality and poverty. Additionally, Fintech has boosted job creation, economic growth, and entrepreneurship, while increasing financial transaction efficiency and transparency.

However, Fintech also poses risks, including vulnerability to cybercrime and lack of regulatory oversight in developing economies. The use of Fintech may also lead to disruptions in traditional financial systems, and policymakers must carefully study these risks to ensure that Fintech activities are regulated to protect consumers and guarantee financial stability.

Financial innovation and digital technology are key drivers of Fintech, generating interest in recent years. Financial innovation has the potential to increase efficiency, lower costs, and drive economic growth, but it also poses significant challenges for the financial system. Digital technology, on the other hand, has transformed the financial and enterprise ecosystems, driving innovation, and enhancing the overall efficiency of enterprise operations.

Financial technology refers to the infusion of technology into finance, integrating digital and technological tools in the delivery of financial services and products. The scope of Fintech includes the deployment, design, and adoption of software and applications to automate the delivery of financial services, enhancing the development and delivery of financial products and services by traditional banks and beyond.

The fintech sector is highly capital-intensive and relies on funding from various sources, including the US and Asia. In 2021, Nigeria raised $400 million, mostly from Asian investors. Fintech investment funding and deal sizes in Africa are smaller than in the rest of the world, averaging between 3 million and 10 million. The global fintech market reached $210 billion in 2021, but global investment in fintech is expected to decline in 2023 due to interest rates, inflation, and declining valuations.

In developing economies, the fintech market is rapidly developing, with digital payments, digital capital raising, digital investment, digital assets, and challenger banks emerging as significant trends. Digital payments have seen an unprecedented surge in popularity, with consumers relying on mobile payment solutions for daily transactions. Investment in digital assets and platforms is also gaining traction, providing easy-to-use and low-cost investment options.

Fintech in developing economies faces risks such as fraud, regulatory risk, anti-money laundering, and consumer risk. In 2022, 70% of financial institutions lost over 500 k to fraud and the market capitalization of the industry fell to fell in 156 billion. To mitigate these risks, management systems need to be developed to confront the new reality.

Data is a valuable asset in the digital world, and enterprises rely on information and communication technology to manage and secure their data. Data monetization optimizes supply chains, lowers operating costs, and contributes to enterprise sales. However, fintech entities face a greater risk of business failure or insolvency, which can lead to data theft and losses.

Managing and regulating innovation is crucial in fintech. Technology has transformed the provision of financial services, facilitating the creation of alternative financial products and services. Fintech has promoted market solutions, overcoming obstacles to financial inclusion, economic development, and increasing competition in payments and other financial services. Fintech is a relatively recent innovation development, and it has changed rapidly over the last decade due to advancements in technology. Fintech business models vary, including machine learning, blockchain technology, artificial intelligence, and big data functions.

Fintech in Sub-Saharan Africa has experienced significant growth, attributed to the widespread adoption of digital payments and mobile technology. Policymakers have a role in fostering the safe development of the fintech industry, aiming to enhance individual and enterprise access to financing and operational efficiencies. Fintech presents huge benefits for enterprise development, including efficiency, financial inclusion, inclusive growth, enhanced product and service experience, and innovation. Fintech adoption facilitates cost reduction, increases economic added value, and promotes financial inclusion. It also helps enterprises to develop, grow, and support efforts to increase financial inclusion.

Sustainable enterprise development involves conducting business activities in a way that contributes more to the environment, economy, and society than it takes from them. In developing economies, sustainable business practices extend beyond environmental considerations to include social development, inclusive community engagement, fair operational practices, and the promotion of gender equality.

The goals of sustainable enterprise development include attaining financial growth and profits, creating high-quality jobs, taking care of employee well-being, promoting fairness in the workplace, and engaging with local communities. Enterprises should also focus on minimizing their negative impact on the natural environment, using resources efficiently, reducing greenhouse gas emissions, and promoting sustainable energy.

Human capital plays a critical role in driving the sustainability agenda within an enterprise. This includes embedding sustainable strategies into the organizational culture, aligning talent with emerging technology and innovation realities, and promoting and supporting employees' skills development in information and communication technologies.

Enterprises in developing economies face various challenges, including limited access to credit, unfavorable government policies, intellectual capital issues, and the need to adopt modern technologies. These challenges can be overcome by advocating for loan guarantee schemes, formalizing enterprise policies, and acquiring employees with high intellectual abilities.

Fintech has revolutionized various activities, especially financial, trading, operations, product development, and service delivery, and risk management. It has also changed the way enterprises conduct financial transactions and has the potential to drive sustainable enterprise development in developing economies. However, the adoption of fintech is influenced by factors such as ease of use, access, and performance of financial services and activities.

Human capital is the key factor in the success of fintech. Enterprises in developing economies must invest in enhancing human capital rather than following the old-fashioned method of downsizing and firing employees. Fintech helps to attract, engage, and retain talent, which is key to driving the growth of enterprises.

Fintech contributes to the sustainable growth of businesses, nations, and societies by facilitating economic efficiency, access to finance, financial inclusion, and environmentally friendly digital financial solutions. It is an interdependent network that combines technology with financial products and services to innovate and enhance traditional institutions and financial processes. The fintech system comprises entities such as financial customers, startups, governments, technology developers, and traditional financial institutions. These components work together to foster innovation, facilitate collaboration, stimulate economic growth, and deliver benefits to consumers and enterprises.

The adoption of fintech by enterprises in developing countries stimulates innovations in operational and financial systems, grants more freedom and security, financial education, and time-saving tools. Fintech can significantly impact the development of developing economies by offering accessible, efficient, and secure financial solutions. Fintech supports enterprise innovation, the use of advanced technology and methods for operations, and the updating of existing systems. It rationalizes the traditional financial sector, enhances resource allocation, and enables financing to overcome the limits of time, presence, and distance.

Fintech facilitates improved resource allocation, reduces the cost of capital, and improves the capital of enterprises. It uses big data sets to support lending, crowdfunding, and other digital technologies to automatically input enterprise user transaction records and customer information. Fintech enables physical enterprises to precisely locate and predict customer needs, realize product customization, and design products suitable for the long-tail group. It also enables the upgrading of enterprises' products and services, leading to the overall development of enterprises to a more advanced production form.

Fintech reduces the unequal cost of information in transactions by using big data analysis and cloud computing to facilitate precision and customized financial services for enterprises. It also improves the credit investigation level of financial institutions for enterprises, reducing the asymmetric cost of information. This study believes that financial technologies are the catalyst for sustainable enterprise development in developing countries. Fintech supports integrated services and operations of enterprises, improves technical levels, and upgrades products and services.

References

4C Group. (2024). What the future holds for fintech in Africa? *Itweb*. https://www.itweb.co.za/article/what-the-future-holds-for-fintech-in-africa/wbrpOMg2WXg7DLZn

Ackah, J., & Vuvor, S. (2011). *The challenges faced by small & medium enterprises (SMEs) in obtaining credit in Ghana*. School of Management. https://www.diva-portal.org/smash/get/diva2:829684/FULLTEXT01.pdf;The

Adhami, S., Giudici, G., & Martinazzi, S. (2018). Why do businesses go crypto? An empirical analysis of initial coin offerings. *Journal of Economy Business, 100*, 64–75.

Adjasi, C., Hamilton, C., & Lensink, R. (2023). Fintech and financial inclusion in developing countries. In T. Walker, E. Nikbakht, & M. Kooli (Eds.), *The fintech disruption: How financial innovation is transforming the banking industry* (pp. 297–327). (Palgrave Studies in Financial Services Technology). Palgrave Macmillan. https://doi.org/10.1007/978-3-031-23069-1_12

AfriBlocks Network. (2024). *The role of sustainability in African Business practices: Paving the way for a brighter future*. AfriBlocks Network: https://blog.afriblocks.com/en/the-role-of-sustainability-in-african-business-practices-paving-the-way-for-a-brighter-future

Agelyne, M., & Musau, S. M. (2021). Financial technology and financial inclusion of small and medium enterprises in Kabati Market Kitui County, Kenya. *International Journal of Academic Research in Business and Social Sciences, 11*(4). https://doi.org/10.6007/IJARBSS/v11-i4/9679

Anyfantaki, S. (2016). The evolution of financial technology. *Economic Bulletin, 1*(44), 47–62.

Arkadiusz, S. (2022). *Industries that data monetization can transform*. Linkedin. https://www.linkedin.com/pulse/industries-data-monetization-can-transform-arek-skuza/

Artur Victoria, A. (2020). *Information Technology*. https://doi.org/10.13140/RG.2.2.15684.78728

Asma, R., Atma H., & Asrid, J. (2023). Financial technology issues from developing countries perspective: Role and challenges a systematic literature review. *International Journal of Innovative Research in Multidisciplinary Education, 2*(11), 572–578. https://doi.org/10.58806/ijirme.2023.v2i11n05

Barbiroli, G. (1997). *The dynamics of technology: A methodological framework for technoeccfionomic analyses*. Springer Science+Business Media B.V. 1997, ISBN 978-0-7923-4756-9. https://doi.org/10.1007/978-94-017-3280-2

Berger, A. N. (2003). The economic effects of technological progress: Evidence from the banking industry. *Journal of Money, Credit and Banking, 35*(2003), 141–176.

Berger, A. N. (2023). The economic effects of technological Progress: Evidence from the banking industry. *Journal of Money, Credit, and Banking. The Ohio State University Press, 35*(2), 141–176. https://doi.org/10.1353/mcb.2003.0009

Boeddu, G., Chien, J., & Istuk, I. (2021). *Consumer risks in Fintech new manifestations of consumer risks and emerging regulatory approaches*. The World Bank. Policy Research Paper. https://documents1.worldbank.org/curated/en/515771621921739154/pdf/Consumer-Risks-in-Fintech-New-Manifestations-of-Consumer-Risks-and-Emerging-Regulatory-Approaches-Policy-Research-Paper.pdf

Boston Consult Group (BCG). (2023). Africa's Fintech market poised for significant growth. *African Business.* https://www.bcg.com/news/26june2023-africas-fintech-market-poised-significant-growth

Budiarti, I., & Jannah, A. M. (2022). Financial inclusion of Islamic banking and financial technology as a growth factor for MSMEs. *Jurnal Ilmu Keuangan Dan Perbankan, 12*(1), 25–33.

Business Technology Standard (BTS). (2024). *Introduction to Business Technology*. BTS. https://www.managebt.org/book/introduction/introduction-to-business-technology/

California State University (CSU). (2024). *What are the essential techniques of risk management.* CSU. https://hr.fullerton.edu/risk-management/information-and-document-requests/information-management/essential-techniques-of-risk-management.php

Cassar, G., & Friedman, H. (2009). Does self-efficacy affect entrepreneurial investment? *Strategic Entrepreneurship Journal, 3*(3), 241–260.

CCAF. (2021). *FinTech regulation in sub-Saharan Africa, Cambridge Centre for Alternative Finance at the University of Cambridge Judge Business School, Cambridge*. CCAF. https://www.jbs.cam.ac.uk/wp-content/uploads/2021/11/2021-11-fintech-in-sub-saharan-africa.pdf

Celik, K. (2019). *FinTech and ML/TF risks*. World Bank. https://thedocs.worldbank.org/en/doc/187851572546448957-0130022019/original/Day3KuntayCelikWBFinTECHRisks002.pdf

Chatterjee, I. Cornelissen, J., & Wincent, J. (2021). Social entrepreneurship and values work: The role of practices in shaping values and negotiating change. *Journal of Business Venturing, 36*(1), 106064. ISSN 0883-9026. https://doi.org/10.1016/j.jbusvent.2020.106064

Chavadi, C., & Manickam, T. (2023). Importance of sustainable marketing initiatives for supporting the sustainable development goals. *Advances in marketing, customer relationship management, and e-services book series*, 149–169. https://doi.org/10.4018/978-1-6684-8681-8.ch008

Chen, Y., Tang, G., Jin, J., Xie, Q., & Li, J. (2014). CEOs transformational leadership and product innovation performance: The roles of corporate entrepreneurship and technology orientation. *Journal of Product Innovation Management, 31*(S1), 2–17. https://doi.org/10.1111/jpim.12188

Chetan, G. S. (2017). The fintech book: The financial technology handbook for investors, entrepreneurs and visionaries. *Finance Annual Journal, 73*(2), 136–137.

Damilola Ol.Og. (2024). Conceptualizing cloud computing in financial services: opportunities and challenges in Africa-US contexts. *Computer Science & IT Research Journal, 5*(4), 757–767. P-ISSN: 2709-0043, E-ISSN: 2709-0051. https://doi.org/10.51594/csitrj.v5i4.1020

Debora, J., Kwamie, D., Sarkis, J., & Robert Sarnie, R. (2023). Advancing Fintech through a transdisciplinary approach. *iScience, 26*(9), 107694. ISSN 2589-0042. https://doi.org/10.1016/j.isci.2023.107694

Decker, M., Schiefer, G., & Bulander, R. (2006). Specific challenges for small and medium-sized enterprises (SME) in m-business. In *Proceedings of the International Conference on E-Business (ICE-B 2006)* (pp. 169–174); Setúbal, Portugal. INSTICC Press.

Deloitte. (2022). Human capital challenges of a fast-growing sector: FinTech. *Deloitte*. https://www2.deloitte.com/content/dam/Deloitte/uk/Documents/blogs/deloitte-uk-human-capital-challenges-of-a-fastgrowing-sector-FinTech.pdf

Desiyanti, R., Azilah Husin, N., Elvira, R., Sefnedi, S., Dwi Putri, T., & Chrismondari, C. (2023). The influence of financial literacy, financial management, and financial technology on business performance and sustainability of micro, small, and medium enterprises in Sumatera, Indonesia. *Jurnal Manajemen Universitas Bung Hatta, 18*(2), 231–244. https://doi.org/10.37301/jmubh.v18i2.23238

Dewi, R., & Viverita, V. (2022). Digital business and economic's research cluster. *Financial Technology*. Conference: The 4th Kuala Lumpur international multidisciplinary academic conference 2022 (KLIMAC 2022).

Duffy, S. (2024). Global fintech investment collapses in 2023. Interest rates and inflation combined with geopolitical tension to sabotage investor confidence. *The Banker*. https://www.thebanker.com/Global-fintech-investment-collapses-in-2023-1707725810#:~:text=Global%20investment%20in%20fintech%20nosedived,recent%20Pulse%20of%20Fintech%20report

Ebimene, T. K., Oluwabunmi, D. B., & Quadri, O. G. (2024). Reskilling the workforce for technological advancement: Prospects and implications for health information management professionals. *Igi Global*. https://doi.org/10.4018/979-8-3693-3669-4.ch01. ISBN13: 9798369336694|ISBN13 Softcover: 9798369347652|EISBN13: 9798369336700.

Feyen, E., Frost, J., Gambacorta, L., Natarajan, H., & Saal, M. (2021). *Fintech and the digital transformation of financial services: Implications for market structure and public policy*. BIS Papers No 117, ISSN 1682-7651 (online) ISBN 978-92-9259-486-2.

Gancarczyk, M., & Zabala-Iturriagagoitia, M. J. (2023). The process of the growth of small and medium-sized enterprises (SMEs). *Journal of Entrepreneurship, Management and Innovation*. ISSN: 2299-7326 (Online first) 2299-7075 (Print), DOI prefix: 10.7341

GCB Bank PLC. (2023). *Digital Landscape Bank*. GCB Bank. https://www.gcbbank.com.gh/research-reports/sector-industry-reports/357-digital-landscape-of-banks-2023-final-v1/file

Girma, A. G., & Huseynov, F. (2024). The causal relationship between FinTech, financial inclusion, and income inequality in African Economies. *Journal of Risk and Financial Management, 17*(1), 2. https://doi.org/10.3390/jrfm17010002

Gomber, P. (2018). On the Fintech revolution: Interpreting the forces of innovation, disruption, and transformation in financial services. *Journal of Management Information Systems, 35*(1), 220–265. https://doi.org/10.1080/07421222.2018.1440766

Grigorescu. A., Maer-Matei, M.M, Mocanu, C., & Ana-Maria, Z. (2019). Key drivers and skills needed for innovative companies focused on sustainability. *Sustainability, 12*(1), 102. https://doi.org/10.3390/SU12010102

GSMA Mobile Money. (2023). Tthe state of the industry report on Mobile money 2023. *GSMA*. https://www.gsma.com/sotir/wp-content/uploads/2023/04/GSMA-SOTIR-2023_Web.pdf

Hanini, I. C. H., Mohd, E. Y., & Juliana Reesha, J. M. J. (2023). The role of human capital on driving Fintech Force. *International Journal of Academic Research in Business and Social Sciences, 13*(12). E-ISSN: 2222-6990. https://doi.org/10.6007/IJARBSS/v13-i12/19876

Heath-Brown, N. (2015). *Asian Development Bank Institute. 1385*, 76–76. https://doi.org/10.1007/978-1-349-57823-8_117

Hills, J. (2002). *The struggle for control of global communication: The formative century*. Urbana, USA University of inois Press. ISBN 0252027574.

Hsu, P. X., & Tian, Y. X. (2014). Financial development and innovation. *Journal of Financial Economics, 112*(1), 116–135.

Ibrahim, A. Z. (2022). *The role of financial Technology (FINTECH) in changing financial industry and increasing efficiency in the economy*. Common Market for Eastern and Southern Africa. https://www.comesa.int/wp-content/uploads/2022/05/The-Role-of-Financial-Technology.pdf

Idian M. J, Mohammad K. H., & Terzungwe, S., (2023). Artificial intelligence, blockchain, machine learning, and customer relationship management. *Bincang Sains dan Teknologi, 2*(01),16–20. https://doi.org/10.56741/bst.v2i01.276. LicenseCC BY-SA 4.0.

Ifechukwu, A. (2022). *Regulating Fintech in developing economies: Examining the risks, policies and Nigeria's path to financial prosperity*. SSRN: https://ssrn.com/abstract=4312289 or https://doi.org/10.2139/ssrn.4312289

Jackson, D., Dunbar, K., Sarkis, J., & Sarnie, R. (2023). Advancing Fintech through a transdisciplinary approach. *iScience, 26*(9), 107694. ISSN 2589-0042. https://doi.org/10.1016/j.isci.2023.107694

Jain, N. (2024). *What is financial innovation? Definition, examples, strategies, and emerging technologies*. Ideascale: https://ideascale.com/blog/what-is-financial-innovation-definition/

James, J. (2003). Bridging the Global Digital Divide. Cheltenham, UK: *Edward Elgar Publishing*. Retrieved Sep 26, 2025. From https://doi.org/10.4337/9781843767169

Jianwei, L., Li, N., & Xiang, C. (2021). The impact of Fintech on corporate technology innovation based on driving effects. *Mechanism Identification, and Heterogeneity Analysis., 2021*. https://doi.org/10.1155/2021/7825120

Kereibayev, O. (2023). *Risk management in Fintech and how Artificial Intelligence can help*. Sumber: https://sumsub.com/blog/risk-management-in-fintech-and-how-artificial-intelligence-can-help/

Khalique, M., Isa, A. H., Shaari, J. A. N., & Ageel, A. (2011). Challenges faced by the small and medium enterprises (SMEs) in Malaysia: An intellectual capital perspective. *International Journal of Current Research., 33*(6), 398–401.

Kocak, A., Carsrud, A., & Oflazoglu, S. (2017). Market, entrepreneurial, and technology orientations: Impact on innovation and firm performance. *Management Decision, 55*(2), 248–270. https://doi.org/10.1108/MD-04-2015-0146

Koźmińskiego, L. A. (2023). *Sustainable business development - What does it really mean?* kozminski.edu: https://www.kozminski.edu.pl/en/review/sustainable-business-development-what-does-it-really-mean

Kurniasari, F., Gunardi, A., Putri, F. P., & Firmansyah, A. (2021). The role of financial technology to increase financial inclusion in Indonesia. *International Journal of Data and Network Science, 5*(3), 391–400. https://doi.org/10.5267/j.ijdns.2021.5.004

Lee, I. (2018). Fintech: Ecosystem, business models, investment decisions, and challenges. *Business Horizons, 61*(1), 35–46. https://doi.org/10.1016/j.bushor.2017.09.003

Lenovo. (2024). *What is digital?* Lenovo. https://www.lenovo.com/us/en/glossary/digital/?orgRef=https%253A%252F%252Fwww.google.com%252F

Lensink, R., Hamilton, C., & Adjasi, C. (2022). *Advanced introduction to financial inclusion* (1st ed.). Edward Elgar. 326 C. ADJASI Et al.

Leong, K., & Sung, A. (2018). FinTech (Financial Technology): What is it and how to use technologies to create Business value in Fintech way? *International Journal of Innovation, Management and Technology, 9*(2). https://www.ijimt.org/vol9/791-M775.pdf

Lockhart, A. B. (2019). What is human capital? Everything you need to know. *World Economics*. https://www.weforum.org/agenda/2019/06/what-is-human-capitalknow/#:~:text=In%20the%201960s%2C%20the%20term,be%20put%20to%20productive%20use

Mas, I. (2011). Why are banks so scarce in developing countries? A regulatory and infrastructure perspective. *Critical Review, 23*(1–2), 135–145. https://doi.org/10.1080/08913811.2011.574476

Mavilia, R., & Pisani, R. (2020). Blockchain and catching-up in developing countries: The case of financial inclusion in Africa. *African Journal of Science, Technology, Innovation and Development, 12*(2), 151–163. https://doi.org/10.1080/20421338.2019.1624009

Meena, R. (2023). The Impact of Financial technology on Financial Services: A Comprehensive Analysis. *RESEARCH REVIEW International Journal of Multidisciplinary, 8*(3), 185–192. https://doi.org/10.31305/rrijm.2023.v08.n03.022

Michael, C., Nachiappan, P. Sanjeev, V., Vignesh, K., & Fairchild, S. (2005). *BlockChain Technology beyond bitcoin*. Berkeley University of California. Sutardja Center for Entrepreneurship & Technology Technical Report. https://scet.berkeley.edu/wp-content/uploads/BlockchainPaper.pdf

Milanesi, D. (2022). *The rise of financial Technology (Fintech) innovation and the future of the banking and financial system*. A comparative analysis of the Fintech legislative and regulatory frameworks in the United States, Europe, and the United Kingdom

Nesbitt-Ahmed, O. (2023). *Why FinTechs can't afford to NOT monetize their data in 2023*. Intive: https://intive.com/insights/why-fintechs-cant-afford-to-not-monetize-their-data-in-2023

Nkua, J. K., Tanyeh, J. P., & Gaeten, K. (2013). Financing small and medium enterprises (SMEs) in Ghana: Challenges and determinants in accessing bank credit. *International Journal of Research in Social Sciences, 2*(3), 12–25.

Ocioo, C. E., Akaba, S., & Worwal-Brown, D. (2014). Globalization and competitiveness: Challenges of small and medium enterprises (SMEs) in Accra, Ghana. *International Journal of Business and Social Science, 5*(4), 287–296.

OECD. (2024). *FinTech lending in sub Saharan Africa*. OECD. https://www.oecd.org/finance/FinTech-lending-in-Sub-Saharan-Africa.pdf

Ofori-Acquah, C., Avortri, C., & Preko, A. (2023). Taking stock of policies, regulations, and initiatives that leverage Technology to build trust: Lessons from Ghana's Financial Sector. *Global Social Welfare, 10*, 9–17. https://doi.org/10.1007/s40609-022-00260-9

Ojonugwa, A., & Omale, S. A. (2016). A study on factors affecting entrepreneurial development in Nigeria. *European Journal of Business and Management, 8*(12). www.iiste.org ISSN 2222-1905 (Paper) ISSN 2222-2839 (Online)

Oppong, M., Owiredu, A., & Quarmyne, R. C. (2014). Micro and small scale enterprises development in Ghana. *European Journal of Accounting Auditing and Finance Research, 2*(6), 84–97.

Palmié, M., Wincent, J., Parida, V., & Caglar, U. (2020). The evolution of the financial technology ecosystem: An introduction and agenda for future research on disruptive innovations in ecosystems. *Technological Forecasting and Social Change, 151*(June), 119779. https://doi.org/10.1016/j.techfore.2019.119779

Pelletier, M. Heagney, E., & Kovač, M. (2021). Valuing recreational services: A review of methods with application to New South Wales National Parks. *Ecosystem Services, 50*, 101315. ISSN 2212-0416. https://doi.org/10.1016/j.ecoser.2021.101315

Prakash, P. (2024). *How fintech innovation is driving digital transformation for communities across the globe*. IBM. https://www.ibm.com/blog/how-fintech-innovation-is-driving-digital-transformation-for-communities/

PricewaterhouseCoopers (PWC). (2023). Adaptive AI: Why businesses should adopt it? *PWC*. https://www.pwc.in/assets/pdfs/emerging-tech/adaptive-ai-why-businesses-should-adopt-it.pdf

Rahmana, F., & Bawono, A. (2021). Sustainable development toward sustainable enterprise. *Management Science Letters, 11*(2), 657–668. https://doi.org/10.5267/j.msl.2020.9.001

Ratheeswari, K. (2018). Information communication technology in education. *Journal of Applied and Advanced Research, 3*(Suppl. 1). https://doi.org/10.21839/jaar.2018.v3S1.169. ISSN 2519-9412.

Rice, M. (2003). Information and communication technologies and the global digital divide: Technology transfer, development, and least developing countries. *Comparative Technology Transfer and Society, 1*(1), 72–88.

Richard, M. (2023). *Anti-money laundering challenges faced by the fintech industry*. Shuftipro. https://shuftipro.com/blog/anti-money-laundering-challenges-faced-by-the-fintech-industry/

Russu, C. (2024). *How can FinTech help developing countries? Experts' opinions*. Development aid. https://www.developmentaid.org/news-stream/post/178806/how-can-fintech-help-developing-countries

Safitri, T. A. (2020). The development of fintech in Indonesia. *1st Borobudur international symposium on humanities, economics and social sciences, advances in social science, Education and Humanities Research*. https://doi.org/10.2991/assehr.k.200529.139

Sedunov, J. (October 14, 2016). Does Bank Technology Impact Small Business Lending Decisions?. *Journal of Financial Research*, Forthcoming. https://doi.org/10.2139/ssrn.2517332

Senior Supervisors Group (SSG). (2009). *Risk management lessons from the global banking crisis of 2008*.

Setianto, R. H., Sipayung, R. S., & Azman-Saini, W. (2022). Working capital financing and corporate profitability in the ASEAN region: The role of financial development. *Entrepreneurial Business and Economics Review, 10*(1), 51–64. https://doi.org/10.15678/EBER.2022.100104

Sheth, N. (2024). The BNPL battleground: Traditional banks vs. Fintech disruptors. *Forbes*. https://www.forbes.com/sites/nandansheth/2023/12/22/the-bnpl-battleground-traditional-banks-vs-fintech-disruptors/?sh=21fb12bc46f1

Siano, A., Raimi, L., Palazzo, M., & Panait, M. C. (2020). Mobile banking: An innovative solution for increasing financial inclusion in sub-Saharan African countries: Evidence from Nigeria. *Sustainability, 12*(23), 10130. https://doi.org/10.3390/su122310130

Sofigate. (2019). *What is Business Technology?* Sofigate White Paper, Sofigate. https://www.sofigate.com/wp-content/uploads/2019/01/sofigate_bt_whitebook_print.pdf

Statista. (2024). *FinTech—Ghana. Market Insights – Digital*. https://www.statista.com/outlook/dmo/fintech/ghana

Sumei, L., Yongkun, S., Yang, F., & Guangyou, Z. (2022). *Does fintech innovation promote enterprise transformation?* Evidence from China, Technology in Society,Volume 68, 101821, ISSN 0160-791X. https://doi.org/10.1016/j.techsoc.2021.101821

Sussu, C. (2024). *How can FinTech help developing countries?* | experts' opinions. News Stream: https://www.developmentaid.org/news-stream/post/178806/how-can-fintech-help-developing-countries

Tabash, M. I., Elsantil, Y., Hamadi, A., & Drachal, K. (2024). Globalization and income inequality in developing economies: A comprehensive analysis. *Economies, 12*, 23. https://doi.org/10.3390/economies12010023

Tao, Y., & Lin, Z. (2017). Who can get money? Evidence from the Chinese peer-to-peer lending platform. *Information Systems Frontiers, 19*, 425–441.

Tashtamirov, M. (2023). *Financial innovation and digital technology in the banking system: An institutional perspective.* SHS Web of Conferences 172, 02004 (2023) SHCMS 2023. https://doi.org/10.1051/shsconf/202317202004

Volcker, P. (2009). The only thing useful banks have invented in 20 years is the ATM. *New York Post.* https://nypost.com/2009/12/13/the-only-thing-useful-banks-have-invented-in-20-years-is-the-atm/

Welch, B. (1999). *Electronic banking and treasury security* (2nd ed.). Woodhead Publishing, ISBN-10:1855733366.

Ye, Y., Xu, Z., & Chen, W. (2023). The heterogeneous effect of financial technology on green total factor productivity in China. *Journal of Innovation and Knowledge, 8*(3), 100390. https://doi.org/10.1016/j.jik.2023.100390

Zhivkova, S. (2022). Sustainability and the reasons for its adoption in the companies. *Proceedings of CBU in Economics and Business, 3*, 75–80. https://doi.org/10.12955/peb.v3.296

Zu, L. (2013). Sustainable enterprise development. In S. O. Idowu, N. Capaldi, L. Zu, & A. D. Gupta (Eds.), *Encyclopedia of corporate social responsibility*. Springer. https://doi.org/10.1007/978-3-642-28036-8_253

Joseph Asare, PhD, is a Senior Lecturer in Finance at the Business School Faculty of Ghana Communication Technology University in Ghana. He holds Ph.D. in Business Administration (Finance and Management option), master's in economics and management, and a BSc Degree in Accounting, His research interest includes Business and Project finance, investment risk analysis and control, Fintech, digital finance, financial innovation, and digital financial inclusion. He has over 15 year of research experience, and several publications in finance.

Chapter 5
Experiential Marketing Strategies, Financial Innovation and Agritourism Sustainable Enterprise Outcomes in Western Uganda

Florence Prescah Muheebwa and Arinda Christone

5.1 Introduction

Agritourism has emerged globally as a transformative approach to rural development, blending tourism with agriculture to generate diversified income streams, promote environmental stewardship, and preserve cultural heritage (Barbieri & Mahoney, 2020). In Uganda, agritourism is gaining momentum as a sustainable alternative for rural communities seeking to reduce poverty and increase socio-economic resilience. Western Uganda, endowed with rich agricultural landscapes and cultural diversity, holds significant potential for agritourism enterprise development. However, the effectiveness of these enterprises hinges on innovative strategies that appeal to evolving tourist preferences and address persistent financial barriers limiting growth and sustainability.

The integration of experiential marketing into agritourism ventures offers promising avenues for enhancing tourist engagement and satisfaction. Experiential marketing emphasizes the creation of memorable, emotionally resonant interactions that go beyond traditional product promotion (Schmitt, 2019a, b). In the context of agritourism, this can involve farm-to-table culinary experiences, participatory harvesting, guided storytelling, and immersive cultural performances. Such approaches are aligned with modern tourist demands for authentic, meaningful, and educative experiences (Pine & Gilmore, 2013; Tussyadiah, 2020). However, despite growing

F. P. Muheebwa (✉)
Kyambogo University, Kampala, Uganda
e-mail: fmuheebwa@kyu.ac.ug

A. Christone
Finance, Accounting and Microfinance Department, School of Management and Entrepreneurship, Kyambogo University, Kampala, Uganda
e-mail: carinda@kyu.ac.ug.

Y. Alhassan et al. (eds.), *Financial Innovation and Sustainable Enterprise in Developing and Emerging Economies*, Research Series on Responsible Enterprise Ecosystems, https://doi.org/10.1007/978-3-032-04500-3_5

interest in experiential travel, many agritourism operators in Uganda continue to rely on conventional marketing methods, which limit their ability to effectively differentiate and competitively position themselves in the regional and global tourism market.

Simultaneously, financial innovation particularly in the form of green microfinance, mobile money solutions, and crowdfunding is reshaping the landscape of small and medium-sized enterprises (SMEs) in rural tourism (UNWTO, 2022). The intersection of digital finance and agritourism offers practical solutions to critical issues such as limited access to capital, irregular cash flow, and insufficient customer reach. Financial innovation promotes inclusive growth by lowering entry barriers, especially for youth and women entrepreneurs in rural Uganda. Yet, the extent to which these financial tools are adopted by agritourism enterprises and their influence on sustainability outcomes remains underexplored in empirical literature.

This study addresses these gaps by investigating how experiential marketing strategies and financial innovation can enhance the performance and sustainability of agritourism enterprises in Western Uganda. Specifically, the research aims to examine the relationship between immersive marketing techniques and visitor outcomes such as satisfaction, loyalty, and engagement. It also seeks to assess how innovative financial mechanisms influence enterprise performance, customer retention, and local economic empowerment.

The relevance of this research is underscored by its alignment with Uganda's Vision 2040, which emphasizes transforming the country into a modern, prosperous society through innovation, tourism development, and inclusive growth. Moreover, the Fourth National Development Plan (NDP IV) prioritizes sustainable tourism, agro-industrialization, and financial inclusion as strategic areas for achieving socio-economic transformation. At a global level, this study contributes to the achievement of several Sustainable Development Goals (SDGs), notably SDG 8 (Decent Work and Economic Growth), SDG 9 (Industry, Innovation, and Infrastructure), SDG 12 (Responsible Consumption and Production), and SDG 17 (Partnerships for the Goals).

Understanding the dynamic interplay between experience-based marketing and innovative finance is not only timely but essential for policymakers, development agencies, and private actors seeking to build resilient rural economies. By focusing on agritourism in Western Uganda, this study highlights localized strategies that can be scaled up to other regions facing similar developmental challenges. It provides empirical insights and practical recommendations that can inform policy, guide enterprise strategy, and ultimately contribute to the transformation of Uganda's tourism and rural development sectors in line with national and global development goals.

5.2 Literature Review

5.2.1 *Theoretical Review*

This study is anchored on two interrelated theoretical perspectives i.e. the Experience Economy Theory (EET) and the Resource-Based View (RBV). These frameworks provide an analytical lens through which the relationship between experiential marketing, financial innovation, and sustainable agritourism enterprise outcomes can be understood.

The EET, first introduced by Pine & Gilmore (1999), posits that economic value creation has evolved from goods and services to experiences. In this framework, experiences are viewed as distinct economic offerings that are staged by enterprises to engage customers on emotional, physical, intellectual, or even spiritual levels. Within tourism, this theory has been widely adopted to explain how customer satisfaction and loyalty are shaped by co-created, immersive experiences rather than the passive consumption of services (Pine & Gilmore, 2013). In agritourism, this theory becomes particularly salient, as visitors increasingly seek participatory, authentic, and educational experiences that connect them with local agricultural life and cultural heritage (Kastenholz et al., 2019). Hands-on farming, farm-to-table meals, storytelling, and interactive environmental learning serve as staged experiences that align with the core tenets of the Experience Economy. These experiences, when thoughtfully designed and emotionally engaging, enhance the value proposition of agritourism enterprises and contribute to long-term brand loyalty and word-of-mouth promotion (Kim & Chen, 2020). By applying this theory, the study frames experiential marketing not just as a promotional tool, but as a core strategy for co-creating value with tourists and generating sustainable demand for rural tourism products. This is particularly crucial in contexts like Western Uganda, where competitive differentiation and cultural engagement are critical to enterprise survival and growth.

The Resource-Based View (Barney, 1991) serves as the second theoretical pillar of this study. RBV asserts that organizations gain and sustain competitive advantage through the acquisition, development, and strategic deployment of valuable, rare, inimitable, and non-substitutable (VRIN) resources. In agritourism, such resources may include unique cultural heritage, biodiversity, local know-how, experiential designs, and technological capabilities such as mobile finance or digital marketing platforms. RBV is particularly useful in explaining how internal capabilities such as the ability to design immersive tourist experiences or adopt innovative financing solutions can be leveraged to enhance performance outcomes like customer satisfaction, repeat visitation, and enterprise profitability. Financial innovation, in this context, is conceptualized as a strategic resource that enables agritourism enterprises to overcome structural barriers such as limited capital access and irregular cash flows (Agyemang et al., 2023). Tools like mobile payments, green microfinance, and crowdfunding can thus serve as enablers of strategic resource deployment, enhancing an enterprise's agility and financial resilience. Moreover, RBV aligns with the goals of sustainable development by recognizing that intangible assets such as community knowledge, environmental stewardship, and customer relationships can be sources of long-term value creation if nurtured and protected (Mwesigwa & Nkundabanyanga, 2022). The theory therefore supports a holistic view of enterprise sustainability that encompasses economic, social, and environmental dimensions.

Together, the Experience Economy Theory and the Resource-Based View provide a robust framework for understanding the interplay between marketing and finance in agritourism. While the Experience Economy Theory addresses the demand-side dynamics of tourist engagement and satisfaction, the RBV illuminates the supply-side capabilities that enable agritourism enterprises to capitalize on market opportunities. This theoretical integration is essential given the dual focus of the study examining both customer-centered marketing strategies and enterprise-centered financial innovation. Furthermore, the theoretical approach is consistent with the priorities outlined in Uganda Vision 2040 and the Fourth National Development Plan (NDP IV), which advocate for innovation-driven rural transformation and sustainable tourism development. It also contributes to Sustainable Development Goals (SDGs) such as SDG 8 (Decent Work and Economic Growth) and SDG 9 (Industry, Innovation, and Infrastructure). By grounding the research in these complementary theories, the study not only strengthens its analytical rigor but also enhances its relevance to policy, practice, and future research on rural tourism enterprise development in sub-Saharan Africa. Agritourism, as an intersection of agriculture and tourism, has gained scholarly and policy attention due to its potential to stimulate rural development, diversify household income, and preserve cultural landscapes (Barbieri & Sotomayor, 2022). With rising consumer interest in authentic, nature-based, and participatory travel, agritourism enterprises are compelled to adopt innovative marketing strategies that create memorable and meaningful experiences. At the same time, access to financial resources through inclusive and innovative mechanisms has become central to enabling agritourism enterprise sustainability (OECD, 2021).

5.2.2 Experiential Marketing and Agritourism Enterprise Sustainability

Experiential marketing, which focuses on engaging customers through multisensory, emotional, cognitive, and social experiences, is gaining prominence in tourism literature (Schmitt, 2019a, b). It moves beyond traditional product-centric promotion to offer immersive interactions that generate personal relevance and long-term brand loyalty. In the context of agritourism, experiential marketing elements such as hands-on farming, local storytelling, eco-culinary experiences, and educational tours are shown to significantly influence visitor satisfaction and behavioral intentions (Komppula, 2018). Tourists who actively participate in harvesting, cooking, or guided nature walks tend to associate more deeply with destinations, increasing repeat visits and positive word-of-mouth referrals (Kim & Chen, 2020).

A recent study by Lin et al. (2021) found that tourists' emotional engagement with farm-based experiences was a stronger predictor of loyalty than price or convenience. Similarly, immersive storytelling and place-based narratives have been identified as powerful tools in differentiating rural tourism brands and enhancing cultural appreciation (Kastenholz et al., 2019). This aligns with the broader notion of the "experience economy," where value is co-created through interaction rather than solely derived from consumption (Pine & Gilmore, 2013).

However, despite the strategic value of experiential marketing, many smallholder agritourism operators in sub-Saharan Africa continue to rely on word-of-mouth and static advertising due to capacity constraints (Mwesigwa & Nkundabanyanga, 2022). This suggests a need for targeted training and institutional support to build the marketing capabilities of rural tourism enterprises.

5.2.3 *Financial Innovation and Agritourism Enterprise Sustainability*

Access to finance remains a critical barrier to the growth and competitiveness of rural tourism businesses in Uganda and across the Global South (World Bank, 2020). Traditional lending mechanisms often exclude small agritourism enterprises due to collateral requirements, limited credit histories, and high transaction costs. In response, financial innovation comprising mobile banking, green microfinance, peer-to-peer lending, and crowdfunding is increasingly being recognized as a tool for democratizing financial access and promoting enterprise sustainability (Agyemang et al., 2023).

In agritourism, digital financial solutions offer multiple advantages: they improve cash flow management, facilitate advance bookings, reduce reliance on intermediaries, and enable bundled service offerings (Munyambonera et al., 2022). For example, mobile-based ticketing and pay-as-you-go tourism packages have enabled rural businesses to target urban millennials and diaspora travelers with greater efficiency.

A study by Ozili (2021) affirms that fintech adoption among rural enterprises in Africa is positively correlated with revenue growth and customer retention. Moreover, green finance instruments, such as low-interest eco-loans and sustainability-linked microfinance, are increasingly being adopted by eco-tourism enterprises to support infrastructure development and renewable energy integration (UNEP, 2022).

Nevertheless, challenges remain. Many rural entrepreneurs lack the digital literacy and institutional support required to integrate financial technologies into their operations. Gender disparities in digital finance access also persist, limiting the full potential of innovation-driven financial inclusion (FAO, 2021). This necessitates multi-stakeholder collaborations to strengthen rural financial ecosystems, especially in regions like Western Uganda where agritourism is emerging.

5.2.4 *Relationship Between Experiential Marketing, Financial Innovation, and Agritourism Enterprise Sustainability*

The intersection of experiential marketing and financial innovation is increasingly recognized as a critical driver of sustainability in rural tourism enterprises, particularly in the agritourism sector. These two strategic domains when effectively integrated can enhance customer engagement, improve financial inclusion, and foster enterprise resilience in rural economies (Agyemang et al., 2023; Lin et al., 2021). Agritourism, as a hybrid model combining agriculture and tourism, offers unique opportunities to engage visitors in authentic, place-based experiences while supporting local livelihoods. Yet, sustaining these enterprises in the face of market volatility and limited access to finance requires innovation in both how services are delivered and how they are financed (UNWTO, 2021; FAO, 2021).

Experiential marketing, which centers on creating memorable and emotional consumer experiences, is a valuable strategic tool for agritourism operators seeking to stand out in a competitive tourism market. In the agritourism context, this may include farm-based storytelling, cultural immersion, culinary experiences, and participatory agricultural practices such as harvesting or animal care (Komppula, 2018). These experiences not only satisfy tourists' growing desire for authenticity but also deepen emotional bonds between visitors and destinations, increasing the likelihood of return visits and referrals (Kastenholz et al., 2019). The literature affirms that emotionally engaging, sensory-rich experiences enhance customer satisfaction and loyalty two key indicators of enterprise sustainability (Schmitt, 2019a, b; Kim & Chen, 2020). Moreover, experiential marketing creates intangible assets for rural enterprises, such as strong brand identity and positive visitor perceptions, which are difficult for competitors to replicate (Pine & Gilmore, 2013). These attributes are essential in agritourism, where differentiation through physical infrastructure is limited and enterprises often compete on the basis of authenticity and emotional value. However, small agritourism operators in sub-Saharan Africa often lack formal marketing skills or platforms for experience design and promotion, which limits the effective deployment of experiential strategies (Mwesigwa & Nkundabanyanga, 2022). Without adequate institutional support and training, the potential of experiential marketing to contribute to long-term enterprise sustainability remains underutilized.

Alongside marketing, access to reliable, affordable, and flexible financing is crucial to sustain and scale agritourism operations. Traditional financial systems frequently exclude rural entrepreneurs due to lack of collateral, credit history, or proximity to financial institutions (World Bank, 2020). In response, financial innovation such as mobile money, green microfinance, crowdfunding, and digital credit has emerged as a game changer in promoting inclusive enterprise development (Ozili, 2021). In agritourism, digital finance allows for efficient cash flow management, real-time bookings, eco-tourism package bundling, and even remote donations or sponsorships. These innovations reduce the costs and risks associated with financial exclusion, thereby enabling rural entrepreneurs to invest in service quality, infrastructure, and marketing (Munyambonera et al., 2022). Moreover, mobile money platforms can support customer relationship management and foster stronger financial discipline among small businesses (Agyemang et al., 2023). Green finance, a subset of financial innovation that supports environmentally responsible investments, has gained ground in the tourism sector. Agritourism enterprises that adopt solar energy, water recycling, or organic farming methods may qualify for preferential funding through green microcredit schemes or impact investment channels (UNEP, 2022). These funding models not only reduce environmental footprints but also enhance the long-term viability and appeal of agritourism ventures. Despite these benefits, uptake of financial innovation among agritourism operators remains uneven. Barriers include digital illiteracy, gender disparities in access to digital finance, and a lack of tailored financial products for rural tourism enterprises (FAO, 2021). Thus, enhancing financial capability and expanding access to digital tools are essential to unlock the full potential of financial innovation for enterprise sustainability.

Recent research highlights the synergistic potential of experiential marketing and financial innovation in driving agritourism sustainability. Experiential strategies can generate customer loyalty and emotional investment, while financial innovation provides the operational stability and resources needed to sustain and scale such experiences (Lin et al., 2021). For instance, an enterprise offering eco-lodge farm stays with digital pre-booking and mobile payments is likely to outperform traditional setups in customer retention, brand equity, and revenue generation. Moreover, both strategies reinforce enterprise adaptability a key sustainability attribute by responding to changing tourist behaviors and market dynamics. The integration of digital finance facilitates data-driven decision-making and personalized marketing campaigns, while immersive customer experiences generate user-generated content and social media visibility (OECD, 2021). Despite the growing recognition of this relationship in global contexts, empirical evidence from low-income countries, particularly Uganda, remains limited. Most studies address marketing or finance in isolation, overlooking their interactive influence on sustainable outcomes. This gap underscores the need for integrated research such as the current study to explore how these dual strategies jointly influence tourist satisfaction, customer retention, enterprise performance, and rural economic empowerment.

5.2.5 *Linkage with Sustainable Development and Policy Agendas*

The convergence of experiential marketing and financial innovation directly contributes to multiple Sustainable Development Goals (SDGs), including SDG 8 (Decent Work and Economic Growth), SDG 9 (Industry, Innovation and Infrastructure), and SDG 12 (Responsible Consumption and Production).

Furthermore, Uganda's Vision 2040 and the Fourth National Development Plan (NDP IV) emphasize tourism-led transformation, digital innovation, and inclusive financing as pathways for rural industrialization and community resilience (National Planning Authority, 2020). While the literature underscores the transformative potential of both experiential marketing and financial innovation, there remains a paucity of integrated empirical studies that examine their combined impact on agri-tourism enterprise outcomes particularly in the Ugandan context. This study seeks to fill that gap by exploring how these dual strategies interact to drive satisfaction, loyalty, and sustainability among agritourism enterprises in Western Uganda.

5.3 Research Methodology

This study adopted a convergent parallel mixed-methods design, combining both qualitative and quantitative approaches to provide a comprehensive understanding of how experiential marketing strategies and financial innovation affect sustainable agritourism enterprise outcomes in Western Uganda. This approach allowed for simultaneous collection and independent analysis of qualitative and quantitative data, with results integrated during interpretation to enhance validity and triangulation (Creswell & Plano Clark, 2017).

The research was conducted in Western Uganda, particularly in the agritourism-active districts of Bushenyi, Kabale, Fort Portal, and Mbarara. These districts were selected based on their agricultural richness, tourism appeal, and the presence of emerging agritourism enterprises. The target population included two groups: (1) owners and managers of agritourism enterprises, and (2) both domestic and international tourists who had visited these enterprises within the preceding 12 months.

A multistage sampling approach was employed. First, purposive sampling was used to select 12 agritourism enterprises that actively offer immersive visitor experiences such as farm-based accommodation, farm-to-table activities, and storytelling). Second, convenience sampling was applied to recruit 180 tourists at the selected sites, based on their availability and willingness to participate. This sample size is consistent with quantitative research guidelines for regression-based analysis (Hair et al., 2019).

Quantitative data were collected using a structured questionnaire administered to tourists. The instrument assessed perceived experiential marketing such as sensory appeal, emotional connection, educational interaction), satisfaction levels, loyalty intentions, and awareness or use of financial innovations (e.g., mobile payments, eco-tourism bundles). A 5-point Likert scale was employed, and the tool was pre-tested with 20 respondents for reliability, yielding a Cronbach's alpha of 0.84 indicating strong internal consistency.

Qualitative data were obtained through semi-structured interviews with agritourism enterprise owners and managers. The interviews explored the nature and implementation of experiential marketing strategies, challenges in accessing finance, adoption of digital and green financial tools, and perceived impact on enterprise sustainability. Interviews were audio-recorded with consent and later transcribed verbatim for analysis.

Quantitative data were analyzed using SPSS version 26. Descriptive statistics (means, frequencies, and standard deviations) were computed to summarize respondent profiles and key variables. Multiple regression analysis was employed to test the relationship between experiential marketing and tourist outcomes (satisfaction, repeat visits), and between financial innovation and enterprise-level outcomes (cash flow, customer retention).

Qualitative data were analyzed using reflexive thematic analysis following Braun and Clarke's (2019) six-phase approach: familiarization, initial coding, theme development, theme review, definition, and write-up. Themes were developed inductively to reflect emerging patterns around marketing practices, financial innovations, and sustainability outcomes.

The study followed standard ethical guidelines. Informed consent was obtained from all participants, participation was voluntary, and anonymity was assured. Ethical approval was granted by the Research Ethics Committee of Kyambogo University. All data were securely stored and used solely for academic purposes.

This methodological framework enabled the researcher to holistically assess the dynamic relationship between experience design, digital financial inclusion, and agritourism enterprise sustainability. The integration of both tourist and enterprise perspectives ensures the robustness and policy relevance of the findings.

5.4 Results and Findings

This section presents the key findings from both the quantitative and qualitative strands of the study. Quantitative results are based on responses from 180 tourists, while qualitative insights were drawn from interviews with 12 agritourism enterprise operators. Findings are organized around the main variables: experiential marketing, financial innovation, and agritourism enterprise sustainability (Table 5.1).

The descriptive statistics indicate high levels of experiential marketing among the sampled enterprises, with sensory appeal and tourist satisfaction recording the highest mean scores ($M = 4.21$ and $M = 4.32$ respectively). Mobile payment usage, while positive, scored slightly lower ($M = 3.95$), suggesting moderate adoption of financial innovation (Table 5.1)

Regression results reveal that all three experiential marketing dimensions significantly predict tourist satisfaction ($p < 0.01$), with sensory appeal being the strongest predictor ($\beta = 0.32$). Financial innovation variables also had a significant impact on customer retention, notably mobile payment usage ($\beta = 0.34$, $p < 0.001$). (Table 5.2)

Qualitative Insights

Thematic analysis of interviews with agritourism operators revealed three core themes: (1) Integration of farm-based storytelling to engage visitors emotionally; (2) Perceived benefits of digital finance in improving booking and cash flow; and (3) Challenges related to digital literacy and limited infrastructure. Operators who

Table 5.1 Descriptive statistics for key variables

Variable	Mean	Standard deviation
Sensory appeal	4.21	0.56
Emotional engagement	4.08	0.63
Educational interaction	4.15	0.6
Tourist satisfaction	4.32	0.52
Repeat visit intention	4.1	0.61
Mobile payment usage	3.95	0.74
Customer retention	4.05	0.65

Table 5.2 Regression analysis-predictors of tourist satisfaction and enterprise outcomes

Independent variable	Dependent variable	Beta coefficient	p-value
Sensory appeal	Tourist satisfaction	0.32	0.001
Emotional engagement	Tourist satisfaction	0.29	0.003
Educational interaction	Tourist satisfaction	0.3	0.002
Mobile payment usage	Customer retention	0.34	0.0
Eco-tourism bundling	Customer retention	0.28	0.004

adopted mobile-based ticketing and pay-as-you-go packages reported improved financial stability and stronger customer loyalty.

5.5 Conclusion and Recommendations

5.5.1 Conclusion

5.5.2 Summary of Findings

This study set out to examine how experiential marketing strategies and financial innovation contribute to the sustainability of agritourism enterprises in Western Uganda. Drawing on a mixed-methods approach involving 180 tourists and 12 agritourism operators, the findings affirm the strategic significance of both immersive customer experiences and innovative financial tools in enhancing enterprise outcomes such as tourist satisfaction, customer retention, and financial stability.

Quantitative results revealed that experiential marketing dimensions particularly sensory appeal, emotional engagement, and educational interaction are strong predictors of tourist satisfaction and repeat visit intention. These elements, when carefully designed and delivered, help to create lasting emotional bonds between tourists and rural destinations, thereby enhancing brand loyalty and promoting sustainable tourism behaviors. The regression analysis further demonstrated that financial innovation variables, especially mobile payment usage and eco-tourism bundling, significantly influence customer retention. These findings align with existing literature emphasizing the value of experience co-creation and digital finance in rural enterprise sustainability (Agyemang et al., 2023; Kim & Chen, 2020).

Qualitative insights deepened this understanding by highlighting how agritourism operators leverage farm-based storytelling, seasonal activities, and mobile booking platforms to differentiate their services and stabilize revenue. However, challenges such as limited digital literacy, infrastructural gaps, and weak institutional support were also identified as barriers to broader adoption of financial innovation and experiential marketing in rural settings.

Taken together, the study concludes that integrating experiential marketing with financial innovation offers a viable pathway for enhancing agritourism enterprise sustainability. These strategies are not only commercially beneficial but also contribute to broader development priorities under Uganda Vision 2040, the Fourth National Development Plan (NDP IV), and global commitments such as the Sustainable Development Goals particularly SDG 8 (decent work and economic growth), SDG 9 (industry, innovation and infrastructure), and SDG 12 (responsible consumption and production).

5.5.3 *Recommendations*

Government agencies and tourism training institutions should strengthen capacity for Experiential Marketing. Government agencies and tourism training institutions should collaborate to develop tailored training programs that equip agritourism operators with skills in customer experience design, storytelling, and digital promotion. This will help standardize and elevate the quality of agritourism services.

Financial service providers should expand access to green and digital Finance. Financial service providers should design inclusive financial products such as low-interest green microloans and mobile savings schemes targeted at rural tourism entrepreneurs. Partnerships with fintech companies can further enhance the accessibility and scalability of these solutions.

Government should promote digital infrastructure in rural areas. To support the adoption of mobile payments and online booking systems, investment in digital infrastructure especially internet connectivity and mobile network coverage is critical in rural tourism zones.

Policy makers should encourage policy alignment and stakeholder engagement. National tourism policy should prioritize experience-driven and digitally enabled rural tourism as a strategy for rural development. Multi-stakeholder collaboration including government, private sector, development agencies, and community actors is essential to build an enabling ecosystem for sustainable agritourism.

Government should support innovation through pilot projects and incentives. Pilot projects showcasing successful integration of experiential marketing and financial innovation in agritourism should be funded and promoted as best-practice models. Incentives, such as tax rebates or grants for digital adoption, could motivate more enterprises to follow suit.

References

Agyemang, F. S., Aboagye, A. Q. Q., & Amankwah-Amoah, J. (2023). Financial innovation and sustainable enterprise growth in emerging markets: A systematic review and research agenda. *Technological Forecasting and Social Change, 191*, 122575.

Barbieri, C., & Mahoney, E. (2020). Why is agritourism attractive to farmers? Findings from a study in the U.S. *Journal of Rural Studies, 78*, 214–223.

Barbieri, C., & Sotomayor, S. (2022). Sustainability and profitability of agritourism farms: A global perspective. *Tourism Planning & Development, 19*(1), 1–20.

Braun, V., & Clarke, V. (2019). *Reflecting on reflexive thematic analysis. Qualitative Research in Sport, Exercise and Health, 11*(4), 589–597.

Creswell, J. W., & Plano Clark, V. L. (2017). *Designing and conducting mixed methods research* (3rd ed.).

FAO. (2021). *Empowering rural women through digital financial inclusion*. Food and Agriculture Organization of the United Nations.

Hair, J. F., Babin, B. J., Anderson, R. E., & Black, W. C. (2019). *Multivariate data analysis* (8th ed.). Cengage Learning.

Kastenholz, E., Carneiro, M. J., Marques, C. P., & Lima, J. (2019). Experiencing rural tourism: A qualitative approach to understand tourist satisfaction. *Current Issues in Tourism, 22*(11), 1280–1299. https://doi.org/10.1080/13683500.2018.1439431

Kim, J.-H., & Chen, M.-H. (2020). The experiential value of agritourism: A case study of international tourists in South Korea. *Asia Pacific Journal of Tourism Research, 25*(2), 186–201.

Komppula, R. (2018). Customer engagement and experiential value in tourism services: Empirical evidence from Finland. *Journal of Hospitality and Tourism Management, 37*, 58–67.

Lin, Z., Chen, Y., & Filieri, R. (2021). Resident-tourist emotional engagement and loyalty to rural tourism destinations: The role of place attachment. Journal of Travel Research, 60(8), 1735–1753. https://doi.org/10.1177/0047287520954642

Munyambonera, E., Katabazi, A., & Twesigye, D. (2022). *Digital financial services and SME competitiveness in Uganda's rural tourism sector*. Economic Policy Research Centre Working Paper Series.

Mwesigwa, R., & Nkundabanyanga, S. (2022). Marketing capability and performance of SMEs in Uganda: The mediating role of competitive advantage. *African Journal of Economic and Management Studies, 13*(3), 373–391.

National Planning Authority. (2020). *Uganda vision 2040 and Fourth National Development Plan (NDPIII)*. Kampala.

OECD. (2021). *Financing SMEs and entrepreneurs 2021: An OECD scoreboard*. Organisation for Economic Co-operation and Development.

Ozili, P. K. (2021). Financial innovation, financial inclusion, and fintech during the COVID-19 crisis: Policy solutions for sustainability. *International Journal of Sociology and Social Policy, 41*(5/6), 421–435.

Pine, B. J., II, & Gilmore, J. H. (1999). *The experience economy: Work is theatre & every business a stage*. Boston, MA: Harvard Business School Press.

Pine, B. J., & Gilmore, J. H. (2013). The experience economy: Past, present and future. In J. Sundbo & F. Sørensen (Eds.), *Handbook on the experience economy* (pp. 21–44). Edward Elgar Publishing.

Schmitt, B. (2019a). *Experiential marketing: How to get customers to sense, feel, think, act and relate to your company and brands* (2nd ed.).

Schmitt, B. (2019b). From experiential marketing to experiential innovation. *Journal of Marketing Management, 35*(9–10), 832–856.

Tussyadiah, I. P. (2020). A review of research into automation in tourism: Launching the annals of tourism research curated collection on artificial intelligence and robotics in tourism. *Annals of Tourism Research, 81*, 102883.

UNEP. (2022). *Green finance for sustainable tourism: A guide for small enterprises.* United Nations Environment Programme. https://www.unep.org
UNWTO. (2021). *Tourism for inclusive growth: World tourism day 2021.* United Nations World Tourism Organization.
UNWTO. (2022). *Tourism and rural development: A policy perspective.* United Nations World Tourism Organization.
World Bank. (2020). *Enabling the business of agriculture 2020.* World Bank.

Florence Prescah Muheebwa, PhD is a Lecturer, Department of Management and Administrative Sciences, School of Management and Entrepreneurship at Kyambogo University, Kampala, Uganda. Her academic and research interests span Sustainable Entrepreneurship, Social Entrepreneurship, and Innovation Entrepreneurship, with a particular focus on promoting inclusive, resilient, and impact-oriented business models. Dr. Muheebwa is dedicated to empowering communities through sustainable entrepreneurial education, applied research, and policy-relevant scholarship. She actively engages in projects that foster sustainability, youth empowerment, and enterprise development, and contributes to academic discourse through publications, mentorship, and collaboration with local and international institutions.

Arinda Christone, is an Assistant Lecturer in the School of Management and Entrepreneurship at Kyambogo University, Uganda. He holds an MBA and a degree in Accounting and Finance, and is currently a CPA student. His research focuses on financial Literacy, enterprise performance, and technology in financial management, with published work in international journals including Financial Literacy and Financial Performance of Micro and Small Enterprises in Mbarara City, Uganda (International Journal of Business and Economics Research, 6(4), 536–551, 2020). Beyond academia, Arinda is a business mentor, educationist and consultant in computerized accounting systems, supporting SMEs to enhance financial performance and growth through different mentorship and training programs run by different NGOs

Chapter 6
Institutional Quality's Catalyst Role in Fintech and Economic Development: Global Evidence

John Agyekum Addae, Sheraz Ahmed, Mikael Collan, Mara Madaleno, and Gilbert Zana Naab

6.1 Introduction

Financial Technology (Fintech) has been considered a significant factor in the financial sector of a country and it is crucial to the functioning of the economy. As the economy grows, the need for fintech enhancement in the financial sector also grows. Fintech contributed substantially to the COVID-19 recovery effort while showing resiliency in the global economy and growth year-over-year (Bai et al., 2021; Charaia et al., 2021; WorldBank, 2020; Xie & Zhu, 2022). Fintech offers multiple benefits to solution providers, consumers, and economies while promoting the UN Sustainable Development Goals (WorldBank, 2020). Fintech multichannel is currently used by 64% of the global population (Najaf et al., 2020, p. 915). Global investment in FinTech reached $210 billion in 2021 (Aslam et al., 2023; KPMG, 2022; Xie & Zhu, 2022). The estimated worth of the worldwide fintech sector is expected to reach over $324 billion by 2026 (Tiwari et al., 2023).

There is a considerable number of factors that engender fintech contribution to economic development such as openness, political stability, financial liberalization, institutional quality, and regulatory factors, among others. The association between

J. A. Addae (✉) · S. Ahmed · M. Collan
LUT Business School, LUT University, Yliopistonkatu 34, Lappeenranta 53850, Finland
e-mail: john.addae@student.lut.fi; Sheraz.Ahmed@lut.fi; Mikael.Collan@lut.fi

M. Madaleno
University of Aveiro & GOVCOPP, Aveiro, Portugal
e-mail: maramadaleno@ua.pt

G. Z. Naab
Coventry University, Coventry, UK
e-mail: ad5061@coventry.ac.uk

Y. Alhassan et al. (eds.), *Financial Innovation and Sustainable Enterprise in Developing and Emerging Economies*, Research Series on Responsible Enterprise Ecosystems, https://doi.org/10.1007/978-3-032-04500-3_6

fintech and economic development has been the focus of a growing body of research (Beck et al., 2016; Bu et al., 2022; Kanga et al., 2022; Tao et al., 2022). Although the role of institutional quality has received traction in the finance-growth nexus scholarship, most studies examine the role of institutional quality in foreign direct investment and economic growth nexus (Hayat, 2019); financial development and economic growth nexus (Aluko & Ibrahim, 2020; Mohamed Sghaier, 2022; Olaniyi & Oladeji, 2021; Tinta, 2022), and natural resources management and economic development nexus (H. Khan et al., 2022; Li et al., 2023; Xu et al., 2019).

However, the degree to which fintech can act as a catalyst for economic development is intricately tied to level of instititutional quality. Despite calls for research on the association between fintech, economic growth, and institutional quality (Khan et al., 2022; Li et al., 2023), this research gap remains unexplored.

In addressing these research gaps, this study attempts to answer two research questions (1) Is there a statistical relationship between Fintech inflows and economic development across countries? (2) Can institutional quality determine the relationships between fintech inflows and economic development? We employed 2SLS regression to analyze balanced panel data of 45 countries spanning 2012–2019. We find that the combined effect of fintech and institutional quality significantly increases the economic impact on GDP.

Our study makes a significant contribution in several ways. First, we model casual relationships among fintech, economic development, and institutional quality. Second, this study contributes to SDG Goal 8, Target 10 of strengthening financial institutions and promoting a resilient financial system. Third, our study introduces the role of institutional quality in the existing cross-country evidence on the nexus between fintech and economic development. Strong evidence is found in this study to support the hypothesis that institutional quality scores act as a stimulant for fintech inflows, which in turn causes stronger economic development.

The study continues as follows. The review of the relevant literature is presented in Sect. 6.2, while Sect. 6.3 explains the research methods used. The results and subsequent discussion are reported in Sects. 6.4 respectively. The study concludes in Sect. 6.5 with policy implications and direction for future research.

6.2 Literature Review

6.2.1 Fintech and Economic Development Nexus

Fintech and economic development co-create inextricably. The economies of the world have been accelerated by the proliferation of Fintech (Beck et al., 2016). Currently, sectors of electronic commerce and cross-border payment depend significantly on the advancements and capabilities of Fintech. Recently, it has also been demonstrated in the literature that technologies promote the path of green economic development (Awais et al., 2023), once fintech becomes a valuable technological toolbox that can be utilized to improve sustainability.

The contribution of fintech towards the formalization and expansion of the economy is significant and has gained traction in recent years. Jacolin et al., (2021) demonstrates that fintech is an innovative tool that can quicken the pace of economic activity. In a similar vein, the expansion of the global production and financial ecosystem has been transformed as a result of the impact of fintech, which has also helped the expansion of local economic activity in both developed and developing countries (Lai & Samers, 2021). The study conducted by Apeti and Edoh (2023), using data extracted from 104 developing countries between 1990 and 2019, demonstrates that fintech utilization leads to a significant increase in tax revenue performance in fintech nations compared to non-fintech countries.

Another significant strand of the literature emphasizes the effect of fintech on the real economy at the cross-country level. After analyzing 137 countries from 1991 to 2015, Kanga et al. findings reveal that fintech has significant long-term impacts on GDP per capita (Kanga et al., 2022). Beck et al. (2016) examine 32 countries over the period 1996–2010 and report a positive net effect of fintech on higher economic growth and better growth opportunities.

At the country level, according to the findings of Bu et al. (2022), fintech has a significant and positive promoting effect on China's real economic growth. In the United States, Fintech has also demonstrated its ability to increase overall consumption and stimulate economic growth (Jagtiani & Lemieux, 2018). In South Korea, Shin and Choi (2019), assert that fintech exerts a more pronounced influence on production upscale and exhibits greater potential in enhancing overall national economic performance. They further found that fintech ranked the top in all 31 industries for the forward linkage effect and 22 for the background linkage effect, far outperforming the traditional banking industry.

On account of social impact, Fintech's distinct proposition of facilitating non-cash-based remote financial offerings prevents robbery attacks in SSA countries (Pelletier et al., 2020). The fight against poverty and for greater access to financial services is another front on which fintech has taken the lead (Kanga et al., 2022; Shaikh et al., 2023). Moreover, it is widely acknowledged that financial technology (fintech) plays a crucial role in advancing sustainable development goals (SDGs) and is vital in facilitating the recovery efforts of nations in the aftermath of the COVID-19 pandemic (Mansour, 2022).

The energy and natural resource sectors have benefited equally from fintech. Tao et al. (2022) 2SLS and GMM estimations confirm that fintech development can effectively mitigate greenhouse gas emissions and pave the way for a transition towards a low-carbon economy. Yang et al. (2021) find that fintech facilitates a positive impact on the ecological environment and economic structure.

Therefore, we hypothesize that: *H1: Fintech significantly and positively accelerates economic growth.*

6.2.2 Role of Institutional Quality Between Fintech and Economic Development

Prior studies anchored that "institutions matter" (Chinoda & Kapingura, 2023; Sharma et al., 2022; Singh et al., 2012). The promotion of strong institutions is a top priority of the World Bank (Singh et al., 2012) and a strong pillar towards advancing SDG Goal 8 of strengthening institutions. Institutions are legal and societal norms that both regulate and incentivize the economic ecosystem. The absence of corruption, adherence to the rule of law, and strong regulation are all indicators of high-quality institutions (Li et al., 2023).

The global risk report published by the World Bank concludes that the most significant danger to the world's economies is institutional quality deficiency (Mehmood et al., 2023). The global upsurge in public protests against corruption, bad governance, political instability, lack of rule of law, voice, and accountability highlights the significance of strong institutions (Singh et al., 2012). The pervasiveness of corruption, ineffective governance, political instability, and weak rule of law hinder the progress of fintech and economic growth. Conversely, the presence of good rule of law, high-quality regulation, and strong voice and accountability mechanisms contribute significantly to the advancement of fintech development and economic growth (Khan & Rehman, 2022).

Strong institutions increase growth-spurring tendency. Strong institutions promote a stable macroeconomic environment. Empirically, there is a strong link between institutional quality and economic growth. Vianna and Mollick (2018) used GMM to study the effect of institutional quality on economic growth in 192 Latin American countries from 1996 to 2015. They found that a 1% increase in institutional quality increases per capita production by 3.9% and global growth by 2.6%. Similarly, the World Bank predicts that increasing institution quality by 1.0% will boost per capita GDP by 1.7% in 6 years (Góes, 2015). On the contrary, Gurvich (2016) confirms that institutional constraints hinder Russia's economic development. In a comparative study of EU and non-EU countries, the findings of Radulović (2020) reveal that institutional quality and economic growth has long-term significant effect among EU and non-EU countries. Another study among North African Countries (Mohamed Sghaier, 2022) shows that institutional quality plays a significant and positive role in economic growth.

The interdependence between the institution's quality and fintech development is apparent. Institutional quality build the trust needed to attract both investors and customers to fintech offerings. According to Moe (2005), one of the leading factors in luring investors, who in turn spur innovation, is the strength of quality institutions. In the same vein, Wang et al. (2021) show that to enhance financial innovation, countries must prioritize strengthening institutions. Countries with robust institutions provide a conducive environment that fosters innovation by allowing individuals the freedom to innovate. In the context of Fintech, stringent regulation including a proper identification system is a necessary condition for FinTech uptake

(Evans & Pirchio, 2015). Moreover, institutional quality incentivizes FinTech development (Li et al., 2023).

Institutional quality plays catalyst role in shaping the impact of fintech on economic development. Strong institutional quality mechanism attracts investment and instill confidence for fintech usage which consequently fosters economic development. A positive institutional environment can create a conducive ecosystem for fintech growth. The synergetic effect of institutional quality and fintech can better amplifies economic development.

Therefore we expect that: *H2: Institutional quality contribute positively and significantly toward the relationship between fintech and economic growth.*

6.3 Method

6.3.1 Data Collection and Measurement Variables Description

This analysis makes use of data obtained from multiple sources. We extracted our panel data from 45 countries from Global Financial Development (GFD), Worldwide Governance Indicators (WGI), and World Development Indicators (WDI) spanning 2012–2019. The study measurement variable, its operational definitions, data sources, and related prior studies are all summarized in Table 6.1. Our sample size of 45 countries, including developed as well as developing countries, is presented in Table 6.3.

Table 6.1 Description of the variables, definition, source, and reference

Variable	Notation	Definition	Source	References
Dependent variable				
Economic Development	GDP	GDP growth (annual %)	WDI	Mohamed Sghaier (2022)
Independent variables				
Fintech credit flows	Fintech	New lending provided by fintech and big tech companies to GDP (%)	GFD	Cornelli et al. (2020)
Institutional Quality	IQscore	Average score for Control of Corruption; Government Effectiveness; Voice and Accountability; Political Stability; Regulatory Quality and Rule of Law.	WGI	Abeka et al. (2022), Das and Sethi (2023), Li et al. (2023)

(continued)

Table 6.1 (continued)

Variable	Notation	Definition	Source	References
Market size	Mktsize	The market size measured by GDP per capita	WDI	Bouchoucha and Benammou (2020)
Foreign direct investment	FDI	Foreign direct investment, net inflows (% of GDP)	WDI	Bouchoucha and Benammou (2020)
Financial Development	Findev	Domestic credit to the private sector	WDI	Bouchoucha and Benammou (2020)
Savings	Savings	Gross savings (% of GDP)	WDI	
Investment	Invariate	Gross capital formation (annual % growth)	WDI	Bouchoucha and Benammou (2020)
government consumption	GovCons	General government final consumption expenditure (% of GDP)	WDI	Mohamed Sghaier, (2022)
inflation	Inflation	Consumer price index (2010 = 100)	WDI	Abeka et al. (2022)

GFD = Global Financial Development; WGI=Worldwide Governance Indicators; WDI = World Development Indicators

6.3.2 *Model Estimates Specification*

In line with the study research objectives, and to test the raised hypothesis, we establish the following regression model:

$$\begin{aligned} GDP_{i,t} &= \alpha + \beta_1 Fintech_{i,t} + \beta_2 IQscore_{i,t} + \beta_3 Mktsize_{i,t} + \beta_4 FDI_{i,t} \\ &+ \gamma_1 Findev_{i,t} + \gamma_2 Savings_{i,t} + \gamma_3 Invariate_{i,t} + \gamma_4 GovCons_{i,t} \\ &+ \gamma_5 Inflation_{i,t} + \varepsilon, \end{aligned} \tag{6.1}$$

where, α = constant, $\beta_1 \ldots \beta_4$= coefficients related to primary variables, and $\gamma_1 \ldots . \gamma_5$= coefficients related to macroeconomic control variables of fixed-effect panel data regression across country (i) and year (t). The primary null hypothesis of Eq. (6.1) is that $\beta_1 = 0$. The relevant t-stat (p-value) of the coefficient determines the level of significance.

We believe that fintech inflows are endogenous (in Eq. 6.1) because the fintech credit inflows only capture the new lending provided by fintech and big-tech companies in an economy in a year. It leaves out aspects such as the quality of institutions in a country for control of corruption; government effectiveness; voice and accountability; political stability; regulatory quality and rule of Law, all of which are left unobserved and therefore are captured in the error term (ε). Therefore we propose that country-level institutional quality 'IQscore' can be considered as an instrumental variable for fintech. We run the following 2-stage least square-IV model to capture the unobserved heterogeneity of Eq. (6.1).

1st stage:

$$\begin{aligned} Fintech_{i,t} &= a_0 + a_1 IQscore_{i,t} + a_2 Mktsize_{i,t} + a_3 FDI_{i,t} + a_4 Findev_{i,t} \\ &+ a_5 Savings_{i,t} + a_6 Invariate_{i,t} + a_7 GovCons_{i,t} + a_8 Inflation_{i,t} \end{aligned} \tag{6.2}$$

2nd stage:

$$\begin{aligned} GDP_{i,t} &= \alpha + \beta_1 Fintech_{i,t} + \beta_2 Mktsize_{i,t} + \beta_3 FDI_{i,t} + \gamma_1 Findev_{i,t} \\ &+ \gamma_2 Savings_{i,t} + \gamma_3 Invariate_{i,t} + \gamma_4 GovCons_{i,t} + \gamma_5 Inflation_{i,t} + \varepsilon \end{aligned} \tag{6.3}$$

The main variable of consideration is Fintech in Eq. (6.3) and the relevant coefficient β_1 captures the relationship and its significance (p-value) between Fintech inflows and GDP growth.

6.4 Results and Discussion

Descriptive Statistics

Table 6.2 presents the descriptive statistics of the variables utilized in the models employed in this study. The mean GDP of 3.759 showcases the average economic output across the studied economies, while the standard deviation of 3.377 highlights the variability in this measure. The range from −27.995 to 13.787 underscores the diversity of economic performances across countries. Notably, the Fintech variable displays a relatively low mean (0.171) with a moderate standard deviation (0.536), indicating a potential diversity of Fintech adoption levels across economies. The fintech range from 0 to 4.389 reflects differing degrees of technological integration. The wide range in financial development (5.247–190.756) suggests substantial differences in financial sector maturity among the studied economies. Additionally, the relatively high standard deviation in FDI (7.878) and investment rate (13.473) implies variability in foreign investment patterns and investment behaviors. The mean government consumption of 14.470, coupled with a standard deviation of 5.112, showcases varying public spending levels. The range from 4.403 to 26.471 signifies distinct fiscal policies.

Table 6.3 showcases country-wise diverse economic landscapes and diverse factors that contribute to their development and growth. The analysis reveals diverse

Table 6.2 Descriptive statistics of variables

Variable	Mean	Std. Dev.	Min	Max
GDP (%)	3.759	3.377	−27.995	13.787
Fintech (%)	0.171	0.536	0	4.389
IQscore	−0.176	0.881	−2.000	1.822
Mktsize (%)	25.864	2.023	21.879	30.625
FDI (%)	4.161	7.878	−37.173	62.907
Findev	63.230	51.633	5.247	190.756
Savings	22.426	9.887	−8.315	47.616
Invariate	5.415	13.473	−30.064	160.479
GovCons	14.470	5.112	4.403	26.471
Inflation (%)	4.887	.216	4.605	6.028

Notes: See Table 6.1 for acronyms description

GDP growth rates among the countries. Cambodia and Cote d'Ivoire demonstrate high growth rates of 7.131% and 7.855% respectively, while Yemen, Rep. exhibits a negative growth rate of −6.176%. Fintech adoption percentages vary across the countries. China stands out with a high fintech adoption rate of 2.373%, while countries like Egypt and Iraq have negligible percentages. Norway followed by Luxembourg boasts of the highest institutional quality score of 1.780 and 1.703 respectively whereas Congo DR and Yemen, Rep. has the weakest institutions. Notably, the United States and China are the dominant markets with the highest market size of 30.553% and 30.098%, respectively while Liberia with 21.895% is the least market. Foreign direct investment percentages display differences in investment attractiveness. Singapore and Mozambique have a substantial FDI percentage of 24.335% and 23.022% respectively, whereas Yemen, Rep. records a negative percentage of −0.835%. Finally, the United States and Japan have high levels of financial development at 184.492 and 164.690, respectively, while Congo DR and Yemen, Rep. exhibit lower levels.

Table 6.4 exhibits the pairwise correlations between variables. There is a strong positive correlation (0.759) between institutional quality scores (iqscore) and financial development (findev). This suggests that economies with higher IQ scores tend to exhibit greater financial development. This could be because strong institutions are associated with a strong conductive environment, which in turn contributes to better financial systems and innovations. There is a relatively strong positive correlation (0.654) between market size (mktsize) and financial development (findev), meaning that large countries are expected to have a high level of financial development. Larger market sizes often indicate the presence of more opportunities for financial services and innovations. This positive correlation implies that as the market size grows, the financial sector becomes more developed to cater to the demands of the larger population. There is a moderate negative correlation (−0.436) between inflation and financial development. This suggests that as inflation increases, the level of financial development tends to decrease. High inflation rates can create uncertainty and instability in financial markets, which might hinder the growth of the financial sector.

Table 6.3 Country-wise mean statistics of primary variables

Country	GDP (%)	Fintech (%)	IQscore	Mktsize (%)	FDI (%)	Findev
Argentina	−0.183	0.022	−0.169	27.097	1.543	14.719
Brazil	0.172	0.021	−0.139	28.223	3.635	63.089
Cameroon	4.556	0.013	−1.001	24.228	2.070	13.999
China	6.961	2.373	−0.421	30.098	1.957	151.640
Congo DR	5.886	0.008	−1.580	24.378	3.340	6.019
Egypt	4.125	0.000	−0.884	26.568	2.411	27.196
France	1.391	0.021	1.113	28.542	1.526	99.333
Georgia	4.093	0.593	0.388	23.471	9.419	54.947
Ghana	5.214	0.329	0.033	24.692	5.636	13.516
India	6.774	0.012	−0.198	28.440	1.724	50.647
Indonesia	5.105	0.098	−0.218	27.531	2.032	38.041
Iraq	4.730	0.000	−1.460	25.908	−2.842	8.539
Japan	1.017	0.312	1.348	29.131	0.458	164.690
Kenya	4.632	0.721	−0.578	25.015	1.348	32.893
Korea Rep.	2.919	0.252	0.817	28.042	0.719	136.560
Liberia	1.280	0.017	−0.758	21.895	15.506	13.793
Mexico	2.037	0.010	−0.281	27.806	3.014	32.935
Mongolia	6.055	0.087	−0.044	23.219	3.971	55.385
Mozambique	4.916	0.003	−0.690	23.514	23.022	27.125
Nigeria	2.708	0.002	−1.071	26.898	0.684	12.396
Pakistan	4.552	0.042	−1.016	26.376	0.723	16.792
Russia	1.054	0.109	−0.678	27.965	1.626	52.567
Rwanda	6.819	0.067	−0.042	22.921	3.031	19.828
Singapore	3.494	0.057	1.598	26.489	24.335	122.500
South Africa	1.235	0.003	0.180	26.579	1.133	123.461
Tanzania	6.367	0.420	−0.487	24.644	2.539	13.215
Uganda	4.934	0.221	−0.595	24.246	2.982	13.352
United Kingdom	2.175	0.232	1.426	28.732	3.025	134.236
United States	2.378	0.188	1.221	30.553	1.841	184.492
West Bank and Gaza	3.019	0.021	−0.678	23.410	1.203	36.001
Yemen, Rep.	−6.176	0.001	−1.742	24.516	−0.835	5.637
Zambia	3.633	0.037	−0.320	23.814	4.548	16.231
Zimbabwe	1.470	0.007	−1.244	23.737	2.150	15.308
Bolivia	4.573	0.011	−0.601	24.255	1.784	60.376
Cambodia	7.131	0.080	−0.746	23.685	12.331	81.584
Costa Rica	3.275	0.024	0.625	24.793	5.160	56.152
Cote d'Ivoire	7.855	0.007	−0.614	24.613	1.221	17.467
Luxembourg	2.807	0.006	1.703	24.852	15.905	96.722
Malaysia	5.048	0.063	0.393	26.478	3.162	120.526
Morocco	3.259	0.001	−0.288	25.360	2.647	87.506
Myanmar	6.970	0.064	−1.037	24.955	4.579	22.311

(continued)

Table 6.3 (continued)

Country	GDP (%)	Fintech (%)	IQscore	Mktsize (%)	FDI (%)	Findev
Norway	1.461	0.004	1.780	26.690	0.204	139.893
Philippines	6.570	0.050	−0.298	26.516	2.282	42.261
Thailand	2.982	0.061	−0.284	26.760	1.911	145.084
Vietnam	6.457	0.068	−0.399	26.052	5.880	119.231
Total	3.759	0.171	−0.176	25.864	4.161	63.230

Notes: See Table 6.1 for acronyms description

The results obtained from panel data regression models are shown in Table 6.5. Three different specifications of Eq. (6.1) are used to check the robustness of the relationships. Model (1) contains the primary variables, whereas model (2) is based on all primary and macroeconomic control variables. Time-fixed effects on GDP growth are controlled in the model (3). There is a positive and statistical relationship found between fintech inflows and GDP growth across panels of all countries. This relationship remains significant at a 5% level after controlling for (1) other macroeconomic factors on GDP growth (model 2), and (2) year fixed effects.

IQ score does not have a direct and significant impact on GDP growth. meaning that better quality of institutions does not directly translate into higher economic growth. The result is consistent with the studies of Radulović (2020) that show that in EU countries there is no relationship between institutional quality and economic growth. In addition to the main result, we can also conjecture that market size is negatively associated with GDP growth representing a small-size effect on GDP growth.

Smaller economies tend to have higher growth rates in line with previous evidence (Kyophilavong et al., 2017), whereas foreign direct investment is positively associated with GDP growth as expected. The investments and the degree of government consumption are significantly positively and negatively related to GDP growth. This result is following that of Mohamed Sghaier (2022).

The results obtained from fixed-effect panel data regression clearly show a statistically significant and positive relationship between fintech inflows and economic development across 45 countries. However, the institutional quality score seems to have a negative but statistically insignificant impact on GDP growth.

While further testing the role of IQ score in explaining the relationship between fintech and GDP growth, we performed a 2-stage linear regression using IQ score as an instrumental variable. Table 6.6 displays the results of an Instrumental Variables Two-Stage Least Squares (IV 2SLS) regression analysis. Overall, the results show that the impact of fintech is heightened/increased after controlling for endogenous effects of institutional quality on fintech inflows. The economic impact of fintech on GDP growth increases by almost four times after controlling for the endogeneity of institutional quality score. This shows that institutional quality plays an anchoring role in determining the impact of fintech on economic development. The coefficient for market size is −0.397, and the associated p-value (0.000) indicates that the relationship is statistically significant. As the p-value is very low, we have evidence to suggest that market size is negatively associated with economic growth. The

Table 6.4 Matrix of correlations

Variables	(1)	(2)	(3)	(4)	(5)	(6)	(7)	(8)	(9)	(10)
(1) Fintech	1.000									
(2) GDP	0.154	1.000								
(3) IQscore	0.048	−0.332	1.000							
(4) Mktsize	0.218	−0.322	0.462	1.000						
(5) FDI	−0.017	0.240	−0.049	−0.262	1.000					
(6) Findev	0.254	−0.282	0.759	0.654	−0.079	1.000				
(7) Savings	0.347	0.159	0.160	0.474	−0.151	0.344	1.000			
(8) Invariate	−0.013	0.228	−0.140	−0.119	0.077	−0.105	−0.046	1.000		
(9) GovCons	−0.016	−0.408	0.348	0.121	0.067	0.349	−0.114	−0.108	1.000	
(10) Inflation	0.039	0.153	−0.356	−0.183	0.060	−0.436	−0.106	0.003	−0.464	1.000

Notes: See Table 6.1 for acronyms description

Table 6.5 Panel data regression models

Variables	Random Effect GLS		
	(1)	(2)	(3)
Fintech	0.366* (0.071)	0.436** (0.047)	0.547** (0.016)
IQscore	−0.293 (0.596)	−0.459 (0.204)	−0.453 (0.183)
Mktsize	−0.068 (0.744)	−0.351** (0.025)	−0.386*** (0.009)
FDI	0.112*** (0.000)	0.088*** (0.000)	0.086*** (0.000)
Findev		−0.001 (0.868)	0.002 (0.825)
Savings		0.062 (0.127)	0.064 (0.115)
Invariate		0.024* (0.057)	0.023** (0.046)
GovCons		−0.152*** (0.000)	−0.137*** (0.000)
Inflation		−1.709 (0.121)	−0.512 (0.694)
Constant	4.877 (0.371)	22.036*** (0.002)	17.35** (0.028)
Observations	264	222	222
Year fixed effect	NO	NO	YES
Number of groups	45	39	39
R-square	0.057	0.408	0.422

Notes: See Table 6.1 for acronyms description. *** $p < 0.01$, ** $p < 0.05$, * $p < 0.1$

Table 6.6 Instrumental variables (IV) 2SLS regression

Variables	IV-2SLS
Fintech	2.458** (0.043)
Mktsize	−0.397*** (0.000)
FDI	0.098*** (0.000)
Findev	−0.008 (0.139)
Savings	0.053* (0.086)
Invariate	0.022** (0.032)
GovCons	−0.181*** (0.000)
Inflation	−2.018** (0.050)

(continued)

Table 6.6 (continued)

Variables	IV-2SLS
Constant	25.404*** (0.000)
Chi-square	145.494
Prob > Chi2	0.000

Notes: See Table 6.1 for acronyms description

coefficient for foreign direct investment (FDI) is 0.098, and the associated p-value (0.000) indicates statistical significance. This suggests that increases in FDI are related to higher economic growth. The coefficient for government consumption is −0.181, and the associated p-value (0.000) indicates statistical significance. This suggests that higher government consumption is associated with lower levels of economic growth. The coefficient for the investment rate is 0.022, with a p-value of 0.032. This suggests a statistically significant positive relationship between investment rate and economic growth. After controlling for IQ score, inflation turns out to be another macroeconomic factor that negatively impacts economic growth across 45 countries. The coefficient for savings is 0.053, and the associated p-value (0.086) suggests a marginal level of significance. This indicates that there is a potential positive relationship between savings and fintech adoption.

In summary, the instrumental two-stage least square regression model indicates that fintech inflows, foreign direct investments, savings, and investments have a positive and statistically significant impact on GDP growth across all countries. Whereas market size, government consumption, and inflation lead to lower GDP growth. These results highlight the anchoring role of the institutional quality score of the country in determining the nexus between fintech and economic growth across countries.

6.5 Managerial Implication, Limitations, and Future Research Directions

The study results present several managerial implications. Given the clear and statistically significant positive relationship between fintech inflows and economic development, businesses, especially those in the financial and technology sectors, should consider expanding their fintech offerings. Moreover, governments should create a conducive regulatory environment to facilitate fintech adoption, thereby stimulating economic growth. The finding that the impact of fintech on GDP growth increases significantly after controlling for the endogenous effects of institutional quality suggests that improving institutional quality can be a crucial step for countries seeking to leverage fintech for economic development. The positive and statistically significant relationship between fintech inflows and GDP growth underscores the potential benefits of fintech adoption for economic development. This finding suggests that governments, financial institutions, and businesses should actively promote and invest in fintech solutions to stimulate economic growth. Managers in these sectors should explore innovative fintech applications that can enhance productivity, access to financial services, and overall economic efficiency. Managers and policymakers should focus on creating a favorable regulatory environment, strengthening property rights, and reducing corruption to attract fintech investments and ensure their positive impact on the economy.

The negative association between market size and GDP growth suggests that smaller economies tend to experience higher growth rates. Managers operating in larger markets should carefully assess their strategies for achieving sustained growth. This might involve diversifying into smaller, high-growth markets or implementing strategies that allow for agile adaptation in response to market dynamics.

The positive relationship between FDI and economic growth underscores the importance of attracting foreign investments. Policymakers and business leaders should actively seek ways to create an attractive environment for foreign investors, which can include offering incentives, ensuring political stability, and improving infrastructure.

The negative relationship between government consumption and economic growth emphasizes the need for prudent fiscal management. Policymakers should consider strategies to optimize government spending, reduce inefficiencies, and prioritize investments that have a direct positive impact on economic development.

The positive relationship between investment rate and economic growth highlights the importance of encouraging domestic and foreign investment. Businesses should assess investment opportunities that align with the country's economic policies and aim to contribute to its growth.

While the relationship between savings and fintech adoption shows marginal significance, it still indicates a potential positive connection. For financial institutions and fintech companies, this suggests an opportunity to design products and services that encourage savings through digital platforms. Strategies that promote financial literacy and incentivize savings can be beneficial.

The conclusion that institutional quality plays a significant anchoring role in the nexus between fintech and economic growth underscores that addressing governance, rule of law, and regulatory transparency is paramount. Managers and policymakers should prioritize efforts to improve institutional quality to ensure fintech investments, which translate into sustainable economic development.

The findings also provide insights for future research. The study presents an overall institutional quality analysis of six indicators, and it is recommended that future studies consider indicator-specific institutional quality analyses. Future research could include informal institutions as well.

References

Abeka, M. J., Gatsi, J. G., Appiah, M. O., & Agyemang, O. S. (2022). Trade openness and financial development in sub-Saharan Africa: The role of institutional structures. *Thunderbird International Business Review, 64*(1), 67–80. https://doi.org/10.1002/tie.22241

Aluko, O. A., & Ibrahim, M. (2020). Institutions and the financial development–economic growth nexus in sub-Saharan Africa. *Economic Notes, 49*(3), 1–16. https://doi.org/10.1111/ecno.12163

Apeti, A. E., & Edoh, E. D. (2023). Tax revenue and mobile money in developing countries. *Journal of Development Economics, 161*(April 2022), 103014. https://doi.org/10.1016/j.jdeveco.2022.103014

Aslam, F., Memon, B. A., Hunjra, A. I., & Bouri, E. (2023). The dynamics of market efficiency of major cryptocurrencies Faheem. *Global Finance Journal, 58*(100899), 1–14. https://doi.org/10.1093/rfs/hhw085

Awais, M., Afzal, A., Firdousi, S., & Hasnaoui, A. (2023). Is fintech the new path to sustainable resource utilisation and economic development? *Resources Policy, 81*(January), 103309. https://doi.org/10.1016/j.resourpol.2023.103309

Bai, C., Quayson, M., & Sarkis, J. (2021). COVID-19 pandemic digitization lessons for sustainable development of micro-and small- enterprises. *Sustainable Production and Consumption, 27*, 1989–2001. https://doi.org/10.1016/j.spc.2021.04.035

Beck, T., Chen, T., Lin, C., & Song, F. M. (2016). Financial innovation: The bright and the dark sides. *Journal of Banking and Finance, 72*, 28–51. https://doi.org/10.1016/j.jbankfin.2016.06.012

Bouchoucha, N., & Benammou, S. (2020). Does institutional quality matter foreign direct investment? Evidence from African Countries. *Journal of the Knowledge Economy, 11*(1), 390–404. https://doi.org/10.1007/s13132-018-0552-y

Bu, Y., Yu, X., & Li, H. (2022). The nonlinear impact of FinTech on the real economic growth: Evidence from China. *Economics of Innovation and New Technology., 32*. https://doi.org/10.1080/10438599.2022.2095512

Charaia, V., Chochia, A., & Lashkhi, M. (2021). Promoting fintech financing for SME in S. Caucasian and baltic states, during the COVID-19 global pandemic. *Business, Management and Economics, Engineering, 19*(2), 358–372. https://doi.org/10.3846/bmee.2021.14755

Chinoda, T., & Kapingura, F. M. (2023). Digital financial inclusion and economic growth in Sub-Saharan Africa: The role of institutions and governance. *African Journal of Economic and Management Studies., 15*. https://doi.org/10.1108/AJEMS-09-2022-0372

Cornelli, G., Frost, J., Leonardo Gambacorta, R. R., Wardrop, R., & Ziegler, T. (2020). Fintech and big tech credit: A new database. In *Bank for international settlements* (887). https://www.bis.org/publ/work887.pdf

Das, A., & Sethi, N. (2023). Modelling the environmental pollution-institutional quality nexus in low- and middle-income countries: exploring the role of financial development and educational level. *Environment, Development and Sustainability, 25*(2), 1492–1518. https://doi.org/10.1007/s10668-021-02105-5

Evans, D. S., & Pirchio, A. (2015). An empirical examination of why mobile money schemes ignite in some developing countries but flounder in most. *Review of Network Economics, 13*(4), 397–451. https://doi.org/10.1515/rne-2015-0020

Góes, C. (2015). *Institutions and growth: A GMM / IV panel VAR approach.* https://www.imf.org/en/Publications/WP/Issues/2016/12/31/Institutions-and-Growth-a-GMM-IV-Panel-VAR-Approach-43128

Gurvich, E. (2016). Institutional constraints and economic development. *Russian Journal of Economics, 2*(4), 349–374. https://doi.org/10.1016/j.ruje.2016.11.002

Hayat, A. (2019). Foreign direct investments, institutional quality, and economic growth. *Journal of International Trade and Economic Development, 28*(5), 561–579. https://doi.org/10.1080/09638199.2018.1564064

Jacolin, L., Keneck Massil, J., & Noah, A. (2021). Informal sector and mobile financial services in emerging and developing countries: Does financial innovation matter? *The World Economy, 44*(9), 2703–2737. https://doi.org/10.1111/twec.13093

Jagtiani, J., & Lemieux, C. (2018). Do fintech lenders penetrate areas that are underserved by traditional banks? *Journal of Economics and Business, 100*, 43–54. https://doi.org/10.1016/j.jeconbus.2018.03.001

Kanga, D., Oughton, C., Harris, L., & Murinde, V. (2022). The diffusion of fintech, financial inclusion and income per capita. *European Journal of Finance, 28*(1), 108–136. https://doi.org/10.1080/1351847X.2021.1945646

Khan, H., Weili, L., & Khan, I. (2022). The role of institutional quality in FDI inflows and carbon emission reduction: Evidence from the global developing and belt road initiative countries. *Environmental Science and Pollution Research, 29*(20), 30594–30621. https://doi.org/10.1007/s11356-021-17958-6

Khan, S., & Rehman, M. Z. (2022). Macroeconomic fundamentals, institutional quality and shadow economy in OIC and non-OIC countries. *Journal of Economic Studies, 49*(8), 1566–1584. https://doi.org/10.1108/JES-04-2021-0203

KPMG. (2022). *Pulse of Fintech H2'21* (Issue January). https://assets.kpmg/content/dam/kpmg/xx/pdf/2022/02/pulse-of-fintech-h2-21.pdf

Kyophilavong, P., Wong, M. C. S., Souksavath, S., & Xiong, B. (2017). Impacts of trade liberalization with China and Chinese FDI on Laos: evidence from the CGE model. *Journal of Chinese Economic and Business Studies, 15*(3), 215–228. https://doi.org/10.1080/14765284.2017.1346923

Lai, K. P. Y., & Samers, M. (2021). Towards an economic geography of FinTech. *Progress in Human Geography, 45*(4), 720–739. https://doi.org/10.1177/0309132520938461

Li, C., Razzaq, A., Ozturk, I., & Sharif, A. (2023). Natural resources, financial technologies, and digitalization: The role of institutional quality and human capital in selected OECD economies. *Resources Policy, 81*, 103362. https://doi.org/10.1016/j.resourpol.2023.103362

Mansour, H. (2022). How successful countries are in promoting digital transactions during COVID-19. *Journal of Economic Studies, 49*(3), 435–452. https://doi.org/10.1108/JES-10-2020-0489

Mehmood, W., Mohy Ul Din, S., Aman-Ullah, A., Khan, A. B., & Fareed, M. (2023). Institutional quality and economic growth: Evidence from South-Asian countries. *Journal of Public Affairs, 23*(1). https://doi.org/10.1002/pa.2824

Moe, T. M. (2005). Power and political institutions. *Perspectives on Politics, 3*(2), 215–233. https://doi.org/10.1017/S1537592705050176

Mohamed Sghaier, I. (2022). The role of institutional quality in finance-growth nexus: Evidence from North African countries. *Journal of the Knowledge Economy, 13*(4), 3472–3491. https://doi.org/10.1007/s13132-021-00850-6

Najaf, K., Schinckus, C., & Chee Yoong, L. (2020). VaR and market value of Fintech companies: An analysis and evidence from global data. *Managerial Finance, 47*(7), 915–936. https://doi.org/10.1108/MF-04-2020-0169

Olaniyi, C. O., & Oladeji, S. I. (2021). Moderating the effect of institutional quality on the finance–growth nexus: insights from West African countries. In *Economic change and restructuring* (Vol. 54, Issue 1). Springer US. https://doi.org/10.1007/s10644-020-09275-8

Pelletier, A., Khavul, S., & Estrin, S. (2020). Innovations in emerging markets: The case of mobile money. *Industrial and Corporate Change, 29*(2), 395–421. https://doi.org/10.1093/icc/dtz049

Radulović, M. (2020). The impact of institutional quality on economic growth: A comparative analysis of the EU and non-EU countries of Southeast Europe. *Economic Annals, LXV*(225), 163–182.

Shaikh, A. A., Glavee-Geo, R., Karjaluoto, H., & Hinson, R. E. (2023). Mobile money as a driver of digital financial inclusion. *Technological Forecasting and Social Change, 186*(PB), 122158. https://doi.org/10.1016/j.techfore.2022.122158

Sharma, A., Sousa, C., & Woodward, R. (2022). Determinants of innovation outcomes: The role of institutional quality. *Technovation, 118*, 102562. https://doi.org/10.1016/j.technovation.2022.102562
Shin, Y. J., & Choi, Y. (2019). Feasibility of the fintech industry as an innovation platform for sustainable economic growth in Korea. *Sustainability (Switzerland), 11*(19). https://doi.org/10.3390/su11195351
Singh, A., Jain-Chandra, S., & Mohommad, A. (2012). Inclusive growth, institutions, and the underground economy. In *Human dignity and the future of global institutions*. https://doi.org/10.5089/9781463937089.001
Tao, R., Su, C. W., Naqvi, B., & Rizvi, S. K. A. (2022). Can Fintech development pave the way for a transition towards low-carbon economy: A global perspective. *Technological Forecasting and Social Change, 174*, 121278. https://doi.org/10.1016/j.techfore.2021.121278
Tinta, A. A. (2022). Financial development, ecological transition, and economic growth in Sub-Saharan African countries: the performing role of the quality of institutions and human capital. *Environmental Science and Pollution Research, 29*(25), 37617–37632. https://doi.org/10.1007/s11356-021-18104-y
Tiwari, K. A., Abakah, A. J. E., Shao, X., Le, T., & Gyamfi, N. M. (2023). Financial technology stocks, green financial assets, and energy markets: A quantile causality and dependence analysis. *Energy Economics, 118*, 106498. https://doi.org/10.1016/j.eneco.2022.106498
Vianna, A. C., & Mollick, A. V. (2018). Institutions: Key variable for economic development in Latin America. *Journal of Economics and Business, 96*, 42–58. https://doi.org/10.1016/j.jeconbus.2017.12.002
Wang, C., Qiao, C., Ahmed, R. I., & Kirikkaleli, D. (2021). Institutional Quality, Bank Finance and Technological Innovation: A way forward for Fourth Industrial Revolution in BRICS Economies. *Technological Forecasting and Social Change, 163*, 120427. https://doi.org/10.1016/j.techfore.2020.120427
WorldBank. (2020). The global Covid-19 FinTech market rapid assessment study. *World Economic Forum*, 28–32. http://www3.weforum.org/docs/WEF_The_Global_Covid19_FinTech_Market_Rapid_Assessment_Study_2020.pdf
Xie, X., & Zhu, X. (2022). FinTech and capital allocation efficiency: Another equity-efficiency dilemma? *Global Finance Journal, 53*(May), 100741. https://doi.org/10.1016/j.gfj.2022.100741
Xu, H., Jilenga, M. T., & Deng, Y. (2019). Institutional quality, resource endowment, and economic growth: Evidence from cross-country data. *Emerging Markets Finance and Trade, 55*(8), 1754–1775. https://doi.org/10.1080/1540496X.2018.1496418
Yang, Y., Su, X., & Yao, S. (2021). Nexus between green finance, fintech, and high-quality economic development: Empirical evidence from China. *Resources Policy, 74*(September), 102445. https://doi.org/10.1016/j.resourpol.2021.102445

John Agyekum Addae is a PhD researcher at LUT University, Finland, and a Lecturer in Banking and Finance at Ghana Communication Technology University (GCTU). He holds an MSc in Microfinance and an MSc in Development Finance and is a Chartered Banker (ACIB). His research interests span FinTech, central bank digital currencies (CBDC), risk governance, banking risk-taking behavior, microfinance, development finance, digital finance, and multichannel banking systems. His scholarly work has been published in several reputable peer-reviewed journals, including Managerial Finance, International Journal of Bank Marketing, International Journal of Entrepreneurship & Innovation, and International Journal of Quality & Reliability Management, among others.

Sheraz Ahmed is an Associate Professor of Finance and the Director of the Master's Degree Program in Strategic Finance and Analytics at LUT Business School, LUT University, Finland. He earned his doctoral degree in Economics and Business Administration from the Hanken School of

Economics, Finland. His research interests encompass market microstructure, factor investing, asset pricing, portfolio performance evaluation, Fintech development and adoption under uncertainty, and corporate governance. He has published extensively in esteemed journals such as the International Review of Financial Analysis, North American Journal of Economics and Finance, The European Journal of Finance, Empirical Economics, Algorithmic Finance, and Emerging Markets Finance and Trade.

Mikael Collan is a tenured Professor of Strategic Finance at LUT University, Finland. He holds a PhD in economics and business administration from Åbo Akademi University. His research focuses on decision-making under uncertainty, investment and profitability analysis, technology adoption, application of fuzzy logic in business, and business analytics. With over 20 years of academic, consulting, and board-level experience, he has published widely and taught numerous courses on corporate finance and information systems. He is a member of the Finnish Society of Sciences and Letters.

Mara Madaleno has a Ph.D. in Economics from the University of Aveiro (UA), under the subject "Essays on Energy Derivatives Pricing and Financial Risk Management". Coordinator of the Research Unit on Governance, Competitiveness and Public Policies (GOVCOPP), and an effective member. Lectures in Finance and Economics at the undergraduate, graduate MSc, and Ph.D. levels as an Associate Professor with Habilitation at the UA DEGEIT. Author and co-author of scientific articles in peer-reviewed indexed journals, books, and book chapters in the fields of energy economics, finance, and economics. Her research interests span Financial Economics, Energy and Environmental Economics, Financial Markets, and Behavior in Finance. Collaborator in various research projects. Vice-director of the master's in Data Science for Social Sciences. Member of the Portuguese Economists Order (OE) and university and Aveiro district representative of OE, founding partner, member, and president of the Fiscal Council of APEEN (Associação Portuguesa de Economia da Energia).

Gilbert Zana Naab is an Assistant Professor of International Business and Strategy at the School of Management, Coventry University. He holds a Ph.D. in Development Economics, along with master's degrees in Development Finance and Development Administration and Planning. He is also the Co-founder and Director of Inclusive Finance at the North Centre for Development Alternatives (NCDA). Dr. Naab is an active researcher and author, with scholarly publications in peer-reviewed journals, book chapters, and policy-oriented papers. His work covers topics such as Africa-to-Africa foreign direct investment, the political economy of underdevelopment, mobile money and SME performance, and innovation ecosystems in emerging markets. His research interests include Development Economics, Financial Inclusion, Innovation in Emerging Economies, International Business Strategy, and Sustainable Finance. As an Assistant Professor, he teaches and supervises at undergraduate, postgraduate, and PhD levels. He actively supervises doctoral students and has served as an external reviewer and academic advisor across institutions. Dr. Naab is also engaged in academic and policy networks promoting inclusive growth and development in Africa.

Chapter 7
Integrating Sustainable Marketing and Innovative Financing to boost Agritourism in Western Uganda

Florence Prescah Muheebwa, Milly Kwagala, and Ahabyoona Faith Mugisha

7.1 Introduction

Agritourism is gaining recognition as a transformative tool for rural development by blending agriculture with tourism to diversify income, preserve cultural heritage, and promote environmental stewardship (Yan et al., (2020). In Uganda, particularly the Western region with its fertile landscapes, cultural richness, and biodiversity, agritourism offers substantial potential to improve rural livelihoods (Wernerfelt, 2019). However, the sector remains underexploited due to inadequate market positioning, weak brand identity, low financial literacy, and limited access to affordable and innovative financing mechanisms.

This study is anchored in the national aspirations outlined in the Uganda Vision 2040, which identifies tourism and agriculture as key pillars for transforming Uganda into a modern, prosperous nation. The Fourth National Development Plan (NDP IV) (2025/2026–2029/2030) builds on this vision by promoting sustainable industrialization, inclusive growth, agricultural commercialization, digital transformation, and increased private sector participation (National Planning Authority (NPA), 2020). Agritourism lies at the convergence of these priorities, offering pathways to expand non-farm rural employment, empower women and youth, and catalyze local economic development.

At the global level, the study aligns with several Sustainable Development Goals (SDGs), notably SDG 8 (Decent Work and Economic Growth), SDG 9 (Industry, Innovation, and Infrastructure), SDG 12 (Responsible Consumption and Production), SDG 13 (Climate Action), and SDG 17 (Partnerships for the Goals) (United Nations Development Programme (UNDP), 2019).

F. P. Muheebwa (✉) · M. Kwagala · A. F. Mugisha
Kyambogo University, Kampala, Uganda
e-mail: fmuheebwa@kyu.ac.ug; mkwagala@kyu.ac.ug; fmahabyoona@kyu.ac.ug

Y. Alhassan et al. (eds.), *Financial Innovation and Sustainable Enterprise in Developing and Emerging Economies*, Research Series on Responsible Enterprise Ecosystems, https://doi.org/10.1007/978-3-032-04500-3_7

Despite the opportunities, agritourism in Uganda continues to be constrained by fragmented marketing, weak financial infrastructure, and limited integration between the two. Most small-scale entrepreneurs rely on informal word-of-mouth promotion and personal savings, leaving them vulnerable to market shocks and growth stagnation (Sharpley & Vass, 2016).

This chapter addresses these challenges by proposing a framework that integrates sustainable marketing strategies such as experiential branding, eco-certification, and digital storytelling with innovative financing mechanisms including mobile banking, group savings, community crowd funding, and impact investing. The approach emphasizes the synergetic potential of combining market access with financial empowerment to enhance the scalability, visibility, and sustainability of agritourism enterprises.

In doing so, the study contributes to the growing body of knowledge on interdisciplinary approaches to rural enterprise development and offers practical recommendations for policymakers, financial institutions, development partners, and agritourism entrepreneurs seeking to foster inclusive and sustainable enterprise ecosystems in emerging economies.

Agritourism in Western Uganda holds significant potential as a catalyst for rural transformation, income diversification, and sustainable enterprise development (Polonsky, 2019). The region's unique combination of rich agro-ecological resources, cultural heritage, and scenic landscape positions it well for growth in this niche tourism sector However, the development and competitiveness of agritourism enterprises remain severely constrained by two interrelated challenges: limited adoption of sustainable marketing practices and restricted access to innovative financing mechanisms (Phillip et al., 2017).

Most rural agritourism entrepreneurs lack the capacity and tools to effectively promote their offerings to domestic and international markets, resulting in low tourist inflows, weak brand recognition, and underutilized local resources (Peteraf, 2023). At the same time, access to traditional financing remains elusive due to stringent collateral requirements, limited financial literacy, and geographic barriers particularly for women, youth, and informal entrepreneurs (Peattie & Crane, 2025). This dual constraint inhibits investment, market visibility, and scalability, ultimately limiting agritourism's contribution to national development goals and sustainable livelihoods.

Despite national frameworks such as the Uganda Vision 2040 and the Fourth National Development Plan (NDP IV) emphasizing tourism, innovation, and financial inclusion as strategic development priorities, there is a persistent disconnect between policy aspirations and practical support systems for rural agritourism enterprises (NPA, 2020). Moreover, the synergy between marketing and finance critical to enterprise success remains largely unexplored in both policy and academic discourse.

Addressing this gap requires a comprehensive framework that integrates sustainable marketing strategies with innovative financing models to enhance the visibility, profitability, and sustainability of agritourism ventures. Without such an approach, agritourism enterprises in Western Uganda risk remaining informal, underfunded, and marginalized in Uganda's broader tourism and rural development agenda.

7.2 Literature Review

7.2.1 Theoretical Perspective

Several theories underpin the exploration of agritourism development, sustainable marketing, and innovative financing including the Sustainable Marketing Theory. Sustainable marketing theory integrates social and environmental concerns into marketing strategies (Polonsky, 2019). However, literature shows limited application of this theory in agritourism settings within Africa, especially how such marketing influences investor confidence and access to innovative financing. Secondly is the Financial Inclusion and Innovation Theory. Innovative financing models expand access to capital in underserved markets (Demirgüç-Kunt et al., 2018). Despite recognition of mobile finance and crowdfunding's benefits, there is scarce empirical evidence on how these models directly support agritourism enterprises' marketing efforts and sustainability in rural Uganda.

The theoretical integration of these frameworks to understand the dual role of sustainable marketing and innovative financing in agritourism enterprise development remains underexplored in academic literature and practice, especially in the Ugandan context.

7.2.2 Sustainable Marketing in Agritourism

Sustainable marketing strategies such as experiential branding and eco-labeling have been shown to improve tourist engagement and loyalty (Carlsen & Butler, 2021; Machado & Rita, 2020). Digital tools facilitate market access for rural enterprises but infrastructural and knowledge barriers limit adoption in many African agritourism contexts (Adeola & Evans, 2021; Kumar et al., 2021). There is limited understanding of how sustainable marketing can be tailored and operationalized by resource-constrained agritourism enterprises in Western Uganda to enhance financial viability and investor attractiveness.

7.2.3 Innovative Financing for Rural and Agritourism Enterprises

Innovative financing mechanisms such as mobile microfinance and crowdfunding have expanded financial inclusion in East Africa (Jack & Suri, 2017; Muriithi, 2017). Yet challenges such as limited digital literacy and regulatory gaps persist (Mbiti & Weil, 2016). While studies document innovative finance adoption broadly, there is insufficient focus on how these financing methods integrate with marketing initiatives in agritourism businesses, limiting comprehensive strategies for scaling rural enterprises.

7.2.4 Intersections of Sustainable Marketing and Innovative Financing

Recent scholarship indicates that marketing signals can attract socially responsible investments, and finance can enable marketing innovations (Gordon et al., 2021; Yan et al., 2020). However, empirical studies explicitly examining the combined impact of sustainable marketing and innovative financing on agritourism growth, especially in emerging economies, are scarce (Nyaga & Were, 2017). A significant knowledge gap exists in empirical research exploring the synergies between sustainable marketing and innovative financing for agritourism enterprises, hindering integrated policy and business model development.

7.2.5 Policy and Development Frameworks

Uganda's national development frameworks (Vision 2040 and NDP IV) and the SDGs emphasize tourism, innovation, and financial inclusion (NPA, 2020; UNDP, 2019). However, practical implementation gaps remain, particularly in linking marketing and finance initiatives for rural agritourism. There is a lack of cohesive frameworks and evidence-based guidance on operationalizing integrated marketing-finance strategies that align with these policy goals at the grassroots level.

7.2.6 The Nexus Between Policy Aspirations and Practical Support Systems for Rural Agritourism Enterprises

Governments across the globe, particularly in developing economies like Uganda, have increasingly recognized agritourism as a potential tool for rural development, poverty alleviation, and cultural preservation (UNWTO, 2022; Ministry of Tourism,

Uganda, 2020). National policies such as Uganda Vision 2040, the Third and Fourth National Development Plans (NDP III & IV), and the Tourism Development Master Plan promote the expansion of tourism beyond traditional wildlife attractions, with a specific emphasis on sustainable community-based and agritourism models. These policy aspirations are often characterized by commitments to inclusive economic participation, promotion of sustainable tourism and rural livelihoods, encouragement of public-private partnerships (PPPs) as well as alignment with global development agendas, particularly SDG 8 (Decent Work and Economic Growth) and SDG 12 (Responsible Consumption and Production). However, aspirational policies often fall short in addressing the nuanced, localized needs of rural agritourism stakeholders (Kimbu & Ngoasong, 2016; Rogerson, 2016).

Practical support systems refer to the actual, operational mechanisms and institutional arrangements that enable rural entrepreneurs to succeed. These include financial support (credit, grants, subsidies), training and capacity building in marketing, hospitality, and sustainability, infrastructure development (roads, digital connectivity, water), access to markets through branding, promotion, and distribution platforms as well as institutional coordination between tourism, agriculture, and finance sectors. Studies indicate that while the policy environment may be enabling in theory, the actual implementation of supportive systems is inconsistent, underfunded, or misaligned with ground realities (Manyara & Jones, 2007; Akyeampong, 2019). In Uganda, most rural tourism initiatives lack the intersectoral coordination needed to effectively implement integrated support systems (Tumusiime, 2018).

There is a widely documented gap between what policy documents articulate and what is practically delivered at the grassroots. Key disconnects include limited decentralization of tourism development resources to local governments, lack of institutional capacity to offer technical support and training, weak monitoring and evaluation (M&E) systems to assess impact as well as inadequate stakeholder involvement in policymaking, leading to top-down approaches. Kimbu and Ngoasong (2016) argue that this gap stems from a failure to translate broad national visions into context-specific, resourced action plans. Furthermore, rural agritourism enterprises are often invisible in tourism investment frameworks dominated by wildlife and high-end hospitality projects (Rogerson, 2016).

Bridging the gap between aspirations and support systems requires collaborative governance models. Successful agritourism initiatives have emerged where local government, community groups, NGOs, and private actors collaborate to co-design and co-implement projects (George et al., 2019), capacity-building programs empower local entrepreneurs in marketing, finance, and innovation, policies are translated into implementable district-level programs with clear resource allocation. This nexus also requires feedback loops where practitioners inform policy adjustments, ensuring that evolving realities shape national strategies (UNWTO, 2022). In Uganda, agritourism has been included in policy dialogue, but practical support is still fragmented. Key challenges include lack of clear agritourism development guidelines or toolkits, minimal financial inclusion mechanisms tailored to rural tourism as well as poor integration of agritourism into mainstream tourism promotion channels. Yet, localized innovations such as mobile microfinance, experiential branding, and digital storytelling demonstrate the potential of support systems that are grounded in rural context realities (Akampumuza & Hayombe, 2017).

The literature consistently emphasizes a misalignment between policy aspirations and practical support systems in rural agritourism. While strategic policy frameworks increasingly recognize the sector's potential, the absence of coordinated, localized, and adequately resourced support systems hinders effective implementation. Bridging this nexus requires context-specific action plans, cross-sector collaboration, continuous dialogue between policymakers and grassroots actors as well as investment in rural capacity building and infrastructure. This study offers a timely and valuable contribution by critically examining this policy-practice interface and proposing a synergistic model to enhance sustainable agritourism enterprise development in Uganda.

7.2.7 The Relationship Between Marketing, Finance, and Enterprise Development

Enterprise development in rural areas particularly in the agritourism sector depends heavily on access to markets, finance, and the capacity to innovate sustainably (Barbieri & Mahoney, 2009; Rogerson, 2016). These three components marketing, finance, and enterprise development are not independent. Rather, they form a synergistic triad that underpins the viability, scalability, and resilience of rural enterprises. In the context of developing economies such as Uganda, understanding how marketing and financial mechanisms jointly contribute to agritourism enterprise development is vital for unlocking rural economic potential (Akampumuza & Hayombe, 2017). Marketing is a catalyst for enterprise growth. Marketing plays a pivotal role in connecting agritourism products with consumers by: enhancing brand visibility through destination branding and eco-labeling, driving customer engagement through experiential marketing and storytelling (George et al., 2019) as well as facilitating market access using digital platforms, especially in remote regions (Camilleri, 2018). In rural tourism, traditional marketing methods are often ineffective due to poor infrastructure and digital gaps. However, innovative tools like social media marketing, collaborative branding, and community-based storytelling have shown positive impacts on customer loyalty and enterprise performance (United Nations World Tourism Organisation (UNWTO), 2022). Finance is an enabler of marketing and innovation. Finance is critical for rural enterprise development, enabling investments in product development and innovation, marketing campaigns and digital tools as well as capacity-building and infrastructure upgrades. In the agritourism sector, financial constraints limit the ability to scale, brand, or diversify offerings (World Bank, 2020). Many rural entrepreneurs lack access to formal credit due to collateral requirements, risk perception, and financial illiteracy (International Finance Corporation (IFC), 2019). As a result, alternative financing models are gaining traction, including mobile money-based microfinance, community crowdfunding as well as impact investment targeting sustainability-focused enterprises (Munyua et al., 2021). Importantly, marketing and finance are interdependent. Effective marketing boosts revenue and investor appeal, while adequate finance enables consistent marketing and product quality (Camilleri, 2018).

Enterprise development through the integration of marketing and finance encompasses capacity building, business sustainability, innovation, and scaling. Literature suggests that enterprises that integrate marketing and finance strategies are more likely to succeed in reaching diverse customer segments, adapting to market changes as well as leveraging partnerships for growth (Rogerson, 2016; Manyara & Jones, 2007). A synergistic approach involves using marketing intelligence to guide investment decisions, aligning financial planning with brand development goals as well as leveraging digital finance to support marketing execution and distribution (Gascón, 2019). In the Ugandan rural context, integration is often hindered by policy fragmentation and a lack of inter-agency coordination. However, pilot programs such as community agritourism funds and digital marketplace platforms demonstrate the value of holistic approaches.

Empirical evidence on rural and agritourism settings from Africa, Asia, and Latin America show that agritourism enterprises with stronger marketing-finance alignment experience higher revenue diversification, better risk management as well as greater community empowerment (Lane, 1994; Kumbhar, 2012). In Uganda, few agritourism ventures have reached full enterprise maturity, in part due to siloed approaches such as finance without branding, or marketing without capital. Interventions that combine these elements such as branding grants, microfinance for promotional campaigns, or training in tourism financial planning have yielded more sustainable outcomes (Akampumuza & Hayombe, 2017).

The literature affirms a strong, interdependent relationship between marketing, finance, and enterprise development. These three pillars must function collaboratively to drive the growth of rural agritourism enterprises. Marketing increases visibility and demand; finance provides the resources to innovate and expand Together, they catalyze long-term enterprise development. Bridging gaps between them through training, policy integration, and technology adoption can significantly enhance the competitiveness and sustainability of rural tourism businesses. This study is timely in proposing frameworks that operationalize this integration, especially in contexts marked by underdeveloped markets and limited financial inclusion.

7.3 Research Methodology

This study adopted a mixed-methods research design, integrating both qualitative and quantitative approaches to gain a comprehensive understanding of how sustainable marketing and innovative financing jointly influence the growth and sustainability of agritourism enterprises in Western Uganda. The qualitative phase explored lived experiences, practices, and perceptions of agritourism stakeholders regarding marketing and financing. The quantitative phase measured relationships and trends between sustainable marketing practices, financing accessibility, and enterprise performance. This design enabled triangulation of data, offering both depth and generalizability to the findings.

The study focused on agritourism enterprises located in selected districts of Western Uganda including Bushenyi, Mbarara, Fort Portal, Kasese, which are known for agricultural production, scenic landscapes, and emerging tourism activities. The target population (N) of 1000 included included agritourism enterprise owners and managers (smallholder farm owners with tourism elements), representatives from microfinance institutions, SACCOs, and mobile money service providers, local tourism officials and district commercial officers as well as agritourism tourists (for insights on marketing effectiveness). The sample size is 200 respondents derived using Krejcie and Morgan's Table. For the qualitative research, purposive sampling was used to select 20 key informants, including agritourism operators, local government officials, and financial service providers. On the other hand, for the quantitative study, a multistage sampling technique was used to survey 180 agritourism entrepreneurs. Four (4) districts including Bushenyi, Mbarara, Fort Portal, Kasese were purposively selected based on the intense agritourism activity conducted there, followed by random sampling of enterprises from available listings or community networks.

Semi-structured interviews were conducted with key informants using the interview guide instrument to explore sustainable marketing practices in use, experiences with accessing innovative financing as well as perceived barriers and opportunities. Focus group discussions (FGDs) were also held with farmer groups or cooperative members to capture shared insights employing the Focus group discussions (FGDs) guide tool. Survey method was used to collect quantitative data. A structured questionnaire was administered to agritourism entrepreneurs. It collected data on types of marketing tools used including digital, word-of-mouth, eco-labels, access and usage of financing such as mobile loans, SACCOs, crowdfunding), enterprise performance indicators including number of visitors, revenue change, investment levels as well as challenges faced in marketing and finance. The questionnaire tool included both closed-ended Likert-scale items and some categorical variables.

Interview and FGD transcripts were analyzed using thematic analysis, guided by the theoretical frameworks (sustainable marketing and financial innovation). NVivo and manual coding helped identify patterns, themes, and emerging concepts. Statistical analysis was conducted using STATA software. Descriptive statistics (frequencies, means, standard deviations) summarized key variables. Inferential statistics like correlation and multiple regression examined the relationships between sustainable marketing strategies and enterprise performance, financing access and marketing investment as well as combined effects of marketing and finance on growth indicators.

Triangulation of qualitative and quantitative data enhanced validity. The questionnaire was pre-tested with a small sub-sample (10 respondents) to refine clarity and reliability. Cronbach's alpha was used to test internal consistency of multi-item scales in the survey.

Ethical clearance will be sought from a recognized research ethics committee. Informed consent was obtained from all participants. Data was handled with confidentiality and anonymity. Participants retained the right to withdraw at any time without penalty.

Access to reliable sampling frames for agritourism operators was limited due to informality in the sector. Self-reporting bias affected survey responses on finance and performance. Generalizability was limited to regions with similar agritourism potential.

7.4 Results and Discussion

7.4.1 Profile of Respondents

A total of 180 agritourism entrepreneurs participated in the survey, with an almost equal distribution of male (52%) and female (48%) respondents. The majority (65%) were between 30 and 50 years old, and over 70% operated mixed farming enterprises that included agro-tourism activities such as farm tours, local cuisine, and homestays. Nearly 60% had operated their agritourism business for 3–7 years.

7.4.2 Sustainable Marketing Practices

The study found that while agritourism operators acknowledged the importance of marketing, actual adoption of sustainable marketing practices was limited and informal. 65% relied on word-of-mouth marketing, especially through satisfied local tourists. Only 28% used social media platforms, mainly WhatsApp and Facebook. A mere 15% had invested in eco-labels or sustainable branding. Experiential marketing such as showcasing farm life, cultural immersion) was practiced by 40%, though without structured marketing frameworks (Table 7.1 and Fig. 7.1).

These findings echo previous studies by Tew and Barbieri (2019) and Machado and Rita (2020), which emphasized that sustainable marketing in agritourism enhances visitor loyalty and experience. However, limited skills, lack of training,

Table 7.1 Summary of sustainable marketing practices

Marketing practice	Percentage of respondents (%)
Word-of-mouth marketing	65
Use of social media	28
Eco-labeling/sustainable branding	15
Experiential marketing	40

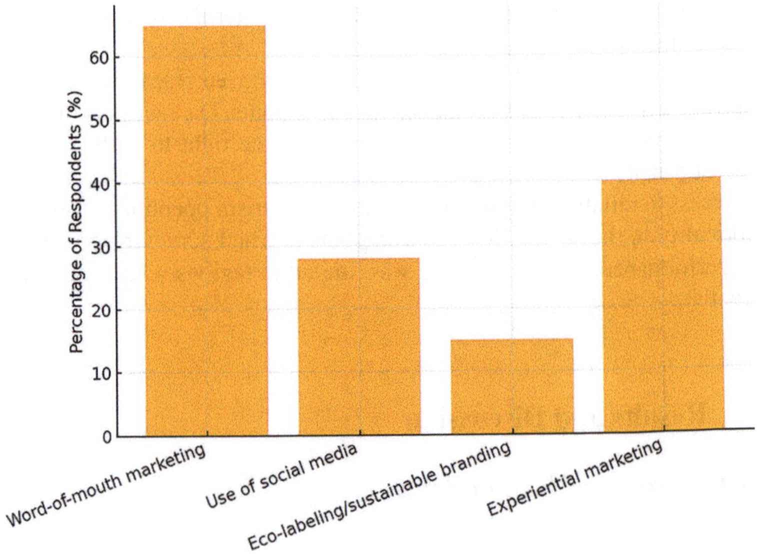

Fig. 7.1 Adoption of sustainable marketing practices

Table 7.2 Access to innovative financing mechanisms

Financing mechanism	Percentage of respondents (%)
SACCOs/village savings	48
Mobile money loans	37
Crowdfunding/project-based	8

and insufficient funding were reported as barriers to strategic marketing implementation.

The Sustainable Marketing Theory supports the argument that better communication of environmental and cultural authenticity could improve differentiation and visibility in competitive rural tourism markets.

7.4.3 *Access to Innovative Financing*

The findings revealed constrained access to traditional finance but increasing engagement with innovative financial services. 48% accessed credit through SACCOs or village savings groups. 37% used mobile money platforms (e.g., MTN MoKash, Airtel Wewole) for microloans or transactions. 8% had used crowdfunding platforms or donor-based project funding. The most cited financial challenges included high interest rates (53%), lack of collateral (46%), and short repayment periods (39%) (Table 7.2).

These results align with Muriithi (2017) and Jack and Suri (2017), who highlighted how mobile and community-based financing options have improved financial inclusion in rural East Africa. However, the low uptake of structured digital financing for enterprise investment suggests an untapped opportunity.

Through the lens of Financial Inclusion and Innovation Theory, innovative financial tools are enabling agritourism entrepreneurs to manage liquidity and small investments, but the full benefits are limited by digital literacy and awareness gaps. Moreover, women-led enterprises showed lower financing uptake, indicating a gendered dimension in financial access.

7.4.4 Relationship Between Marketing, Financing, and Enterprise Performance

A multiple regression analysis showed that both sustainable marketing and innovative financing were statistically significant predictors of agritourism enterprise performance. Sustainable marketing practices explained 31% of the variance in enterprise performance ($p < 0.01$). Access to innovative financing explained 27% of the variance ($p < 0.05$). When combined, the two variables explained 48% of the variance in business performance ($R^2 = 0.48$) (Table 7.3).

These findings empirically support the hypothesis that an integrated approach where marketing effectiveness and financial access mutually reinforce each other is vital for agritourism growth. This confirms the literature (e.g., Yan et al., 2020; Gordon et al., 2021), which shows that sustainable marketing can improve enterprise credibility, thereby attracting investment, while finance enables more robust marketing activities.

7.4.5 Challenges in Integrating Marketing and Finance

Participants cited several constraints to integrating marketing and finance including lack of training in digital marketing and branding, limited knowledge of available financing products, weak infrastructure (internet, roads) limiting access to markets as well as regulatory constraints and limited policy support.

These findings support the need for more coordinated interventions across policy, finance, and capacity-building sectors, as emphasized in Uganda's Vision 2040

Table 7.3 Regression analysis summary

Variable	Significance (p-value)	Variance explained (%)
Sustainable marketing	<0.01	31
Innovative financing	<0.05	27
Combined effect	–	48

and NDP IV, which advocate for innovation-led tourism and agricultural commercialization.

This study reinforces and extends the theoretical frameworks applied. Sustainable Marketing Theory is operationalized within low-resource settings, emphasizing the need for contextualized and community-driven strategies. Financial Innovation Theory is supported through evidence that even small-scale mobile finance can catalyze entrepreneurial activity in rural tourism.

The study revealed that sustainable marketing and innovative financing are not only individually important but collectively pivotal in determining the growth, resilience, and competitiveness of agritourism enterprises in Western Uganda. However, adoption remains fragmented and limited by capacity gaps, financial literacy, and systemic barriers.

Bridging these gaps through integrated policy frameworks, targeted financial innovations, and training in sustainable marketing is essential for unlocking agritourism's full potential as a driver of rural transformation and sustainable development.

7.4.6 Nexus Between Policy Aspirations and Practical Support Systems

7.4.6.1 Policy Awareness Vs. Implementation Gaps

Qualitative data revealed strong policy intentions supporting rural tourism and agribusiness development through documents such as Uganda Vision 2040 and NDP IV. However, most agritourism operators were unaware of these policy instruments or found them inaccessible.

> *"We always hear of government programs, but nothing reaches us. The policies are there, but no one explains them to us or gives support." (Agritourism operator, Kasese)*

7.4.6.2 Institutional Support Systems

Respondents identified district commercial offices, tourism departments, and NGOs as key actors, but support was often limited to training or sensitization workshops without follow-up. Qualitative themes highlighted limited inter-agency coordination, weak technical assistance, and lack of targeted financial support (Table 7.4).

Table 7.4 Perceived institutional support for agritourism enterprises (n = 180)

Support type	% Receiving support
Training/workshops	48
Market access facilitation	21
Financial support/subsidies	17
Branding/marketing assistance	23
Infrastructure development support	11

7.4.6.3 Alignment of Aspirations with Grassroots Needs

The majority of participants emphasized that practical support lags behind policy vision. Quantitative results showed that only 24% of respondents believed policy had directly contributed to enterprise development. FGD participants stressed the need for decentralized funding, agritourism-specific implementation frameworks, and participatory planning.

"The problem is that policies are top-down. They don't involve us in designing what would work here." FGD participant, Mbarara. Findings underscore a critical gap between national agritourism development ambitions and localized support systems. Despite strong policy rhetoric, practical engagement remains limited and fragmented. These gaps constrain the full realization of agritourism's potential as a tool for rural transformation.

7.4.7 *Relationship Between Marketing, Finance, and Enterprise Development*

7.4.7.1 Marketing Tools and Enterprise Outcomes

Survey data revealed a strong correlation between the use of digital and experiential marketing tools and improvements in visibility and visitor numbers. Enterprises using three or more marketing tools reported higher average monthly visitor numbers (Table 7.5).

7.4.7.2 Financial Access and Marketing Investment

Access to innovative financing such as mobile loans, SACCOs was positively associated with marketing investment capacity. 63% of respondents with access to finance had invested in signage, social media promotion, or branded packaging (Table 7.6).

Table 7.5 Average monthly visitors by marketing strategy used (n = 180)

Marketing strategy	Mean visitors/month
Word-of-mouth only	32
Word-of-mouth + signage	48
Digital + experiential marketing	89

Regression analysis ($R = 0.64$, $p < 0.01$) confirmed a significant positive relationship between marketing investment and enterprise performance indicators such as visitor numbers, revenue, and repeat visits

Table 7.6 Sources of finance used for marketing activities (n = 180)

Financing source	% of Respondents
Mobile-based microfinance	39
SACCO loans	28
Personal savings	59
Community crowdfunding	12

7.4.7.3 Combined Effect on Enterprise Development

Multiple regression results show that the combined effect of sustainable marketing and finance access explains 52% of the variance in enterprise growth indicators (Adjusted R^2 = 0.52, $p < 0.01$). Enterprises with both components in place showed significantly higher performance metrics.

> *"After we got a mobile loan, we hired someone to design our social media pages. Visitors doubled in two months."* (Agritourism entrepreneur, Bushenyi)

Enterprise development thrives where marketing and finance intersect. Sustainable marketing enhances demand, while innovative finance enables product and promotional investments. The co-dependency of these factors suggests that integrated strategies are essential.

7.5 Conclusion and Recommendations

7.5.1 Summary of Findings

The study revealed that sustainable marketing practices such as experiential branding, eco-labeling, and digital storytelling substantially increase consumer engagement and elevate the visibility of agritourism destinations. Concurrently, mobile-based microfinance, community crowdfunding, and impact investing were identified as vital tools for financial inclusion, enabling smallholder agritourism entrepreneurs to access capital and scale their operations. The integration of these marketing and financing strategies was found to enhance the market competitiveness, sustainability, and social impact of agritourism ventures, particularly those aligned with SDG 8 (Decent Work and Economic Growth) and SDG 12 (Responsible Consumption and Production).

The findings reveal a significant disconnect between Uganda's agritourism policy ambitions and the tangible support delivered to rural enterprises. While strategic frameworks like the National Development Plan IV and the Vision 2040, Uganda articulate inclusive goals for rural tourism development, local implementation remains fragmented and under-resourced. The study found that although institutional awareness of agritourism policies exists at the district level, practical support in the form of funding, technical assistance, branding, and infrastructure development is limited, inconsistent, and poorly aligned with grassroots realities.

A strong, statistically significant relationship was established between access to innovative finance, use of sustainable marketing strategies, and agritourism enterprise development. Enterprises that employed experiential and digital marketing, coupled with access to mobile-based microfinance or SACCO loans, demonstrated improved performance in terms of visitor numbers, revenue growth, and scalability. This indicates a clear synergistic effect: marketing enhances market access and customer visibility, while finance enables investment in quality improvement and promotions together leading to sustained enterprise growth.

7.5.2 Contributions to Knowledge

This chapter contributes to existing literature by providing an empirical and context-specific framework that synergizes sustainable marketing with innovative financing within the agritourism sector of a developing region. Unlike prior studies that often treat marketing and finance as separate pillars, this work underscores their convergence as a powerful enabler of rural enterprise development. It introduces a novel perspective on how experiential marketing and digital finance tools can work in tandem to address structural gaps in agritourism, offering a blueprint adaptable to similar regions globally.

7.5.3 Practical Recommendations

For meaningful policy impact, the study recommends to government translating national policy into local action through district-level agritourism funds, institutionalizing agritourism technical advisory units, expanding access to tailored microfinance for tourism-linked SMEs as well as scaling digital marketing literacy initiatives across rural regions. Together, these measures can bridge the aspiration-practice divide and catalyze inclusive agritourism enterprise growth in Uganda.

To enhance the marketing-finance-enterprise linkage in rural agritourism, it is recommended to develop tailored microfinance products and expand financial inclusion through mobile-based tools. Building digital and sustainable marketing capacity among agripreneurs through localized training is essential, alongside supporting cooperative marketing platforms for collective visibility. Public–private partnerships with telecoms and fintechs can strengthen access to digital financing and promotional tools. Finally, a national monitoring framework should be established to evaluate the combined impact of financial and marketing interventions on enterprise growth.

7.5.4 Limitations and Future Research Directions

While this chapter provides significant insights, it is limited by its geographical scope Western Uganda and the sample size of 150 respondents. Future studies could expand to other regions of Uganda or Sub-Saharan Africa to enhance generalizability. Moreover, longitudinal studies are recommended to track the long-term impacts of marketing-finance integration on agritourism performance. Additional research could also explore the role of public-private partnerships and digital platforms in scaling sustainable agritourism models.

References

Adeola, O., & Evans, O. (2021). Digital tourism in Africa: The role of online tourism and entrepreneurial innovation on tourism development. *Current Issues in Tourism, 24*(14), 1976–1993. https://doi.org/10.1080/13683500.2020.1829576

Akampumuza, P., & Hayombe, P. (2017). Community-based tourism enterprises in Uganda: Socio-economic benefits and challenges. *Journal of Tourism and Cultural Change, 15*(1), 61–78.

Akyeampong, O. A. (2019). Tourism and rural development in Sub-Saharan Africa: Policy issues and imperatives. Tourism Management Perspectives, 31, 331–340. https://doi.org/10.1016/j.tmp.2019.05.004

Barbieri, C., & Mahoney, E. (2009). Why is diversification an attractive farm adjustment strategy? *Journal of Rural Studies, 25*(1), 58–66.

Barney, J. B. (2021). Firm resources and sustained competitive advantage. *Journal of Management, 17*(1), 99–120. https://doi.org/10.1177/014920639101700108

Camilleri, M. A. (2018). *Travel marketing, tourism economics and the airline product: An introduction to theory and practice*. Springer.

Carlsen, J., & Butler, R. (Eds.). (2021). *Island tourism: Sustainable perspectives*. CABI.

Demirgüç-Kunt, A., Klapper, L., Singer, D., Ansar, S., & Hess, J. (2018). *The global Findex database 2017: Measuring financial inclusion and the fintech revolution*. World Bank. https://doi.org/10.1596/978-1-4648-1259-0

Gascón, J. (2019). Sustainable branding in rural tourism. *Annals of Tourism Research, 75*, 205–218.

George, R., Mair, H., & Reid, D. (2019). *Rural tourism development: Localism and cultural change*. Channel View Publications.

Gordon, R., Carrigan, M., & Hastings, G. (2021). A framework for sustainable marketing. *Marketing Theory, 11*(2), 143–163. https://doi.org/10.1177/1470593111403218

IFC. (2019). *Digital financial services in Africa: Beyond the Kenyan success story*. International Finance Corporation.

Jack, W., & Suri, T. (2017). Risk sharing and transactions costs: Evidence from Kenya's mobile money revolution. *American Economic Review, 104*(1), 183–223. https://doi.org/10.1257/aer.104.1.183

Kimbu, A. N., & Ngoasong, M. Z. (2016). Women in tourism development in Africa: Towards empowerment and inclusion. *Tourism Planning & Development, 13*(2), 105–109.

Kumbhar, V. M. (2012). Alternative finance for rural entrepreneurs: Role of self-help groups and microfinance. *Journal of Rural Development, 31*(2), 223–238.

Kumar, V., Dixit, A., Javalgi, R. R. G., Dass, M., & Dixit, A. (2021). Digital transformation of agritourism in emerging economies: Trends, prospects and future research avenues. *Journal of Business Research, 135*, 215–228. https://doi.org/10.1016/j.jbusres.2021.06.014

Lane, B. (1994). What is rural tourism? *Journal of Sustainable Tourism, 2*(1–2), 7–21.

Machado, P., & Rita, P. (2020). Sustainable tourism marketing: Understanding value co-creation in ecotourism contexts. *Sustainability, 12*(12), 4912. https://doi.org/10.3390/su12124912

Manyara, G., & Jones, E. (2007). Community-based tourism enterprises development in Kenya: An exploration of their potential as avenues of poverty reduction. *Journal of Sustainable Tourism, 15*(6), 628–644.

Mbiti, I., & Weil, D. N. (2016). *Mobile banking: The impact of M-Pesa in Kenya*. NBER Working Paper No. 17129. https://doi.org/10.3386/w17129

Ministry of Tourism, Wildlife and Antiquities. (2020). *Tourism Sector Development Plan (2020/21–2024/25).*

Munyua, A., Maina, K., & Waithaka, E. (2021). Role of mobile-based microfinance in enhancing financial inclusion. *International Journal of Development and Economic Sustainability, 9*(1), 1–15.

Muriithi, S. M. (2017). African small and medium enterprises (SMEs): Contributions, challenges and solutions. *European Journal of Research and Reflection in Management Sciences, 5*(1), 36–48.

National Planning Authority (NPA). (2020). *Uganda Vision 2040*. Republic of Uganda.

Nyaga, R., & Were, M. (2017). Innovative financing for development in Africa: The case of impact investing. *African Development Review, 29*(S1), 69–84. https://doi.org/10.1111/1467-8268.12231

Peattie, K., & Crane, A. (2025). Green marketing: Legend, myth, farce or prophesy? *Qualitative Market Research: An International Journal, 8*(4), 357–370. https://doi.org/10.1108/13522750510619733

Peteraf, M. A. (2023). The cornerstones of competitive advantage: A resource-based view. *Strategic Management Journal, 14*(3), 179–191. https://doi.org/10.1002/smj.4250140303

Phillip, S., Hunter, C., & Blackstock, K. (2017). A typology for defining agritourism. *Tourism Management, 31*(6), 754–758. https://doi.org/10.1016/j.tourman.2009.08.001

Polonsky, M. J. (2019). Transformative green marketing: Impediments and opportunities. *Journal of Business Research, 64*(12), 1311–1319. https://doi.org/10.1016/j.jbusres.2011.01.016

Rogerson, C. M. (2016). Tourism and local development in South Africa: Challenging local governments. *Development Southern Africa, 31*(1), 87–102.

Sharpley, R., & Vass, A. (2016). Tourism, farming and diversification: An attitudinal study. *Tourism Management, 27*(5), 1040–1052. https://doi.org/10.1016/j.tourman.2005.10.025

Tew, C., & Barbieri, C. (2019). The perceived benefits of agritourism: The provider's perspective. *Tourism Management, 33*(1), 215–224. https://doi.org/10.1016/j.tourman.2011.02.005

Tumusiime, D. M. (2018). Uganda's tourism policy and practice. In M. C. Hall & S. Gössling (Eds.), *Tourism and development in sub-Saharan Africa* (pp. 123–139). Routledge.

UNDP. (2019). *Sustainable development goals report 2019*. United Nations Development Programme. https://unstats.un.org/sdgs/report/2019/

UNWTO. (2022). *Tourism and rural development: A policy perspective*. World Tourism Organization.

Wernerfelt, B. (2019). A resource-based view of the firm. *Strategic Management Journal, 5*(2), 171–180. https://doi.org/10.1002/smj.4250050207

World Bank. (2020). *Digital economy for Africa initiative: Country diagnostics.*
Yan, Q., Hu, Y., Zhang, H., & Qi, X. (2020). Do green signals matter? The role of marketing innovation in sustainable entrepreneurship. *Technological Forecasting and Social Change, 161*, 120272. https://doi.org/10.1016/j.techfore.2020.120272

Florence Prescah Muheebwa, PhD, is a Lecturer, in the Department of Management and Administrative Sciences, School of Management and Entrepreneurship at Kyambogo University, Kampala, Uganda. Her academic and research interests span Sustainable Entrepreneurship, Social Entrepreneurship, and Innovation Entrepreneurship, with a particular focus on promoting inclusive, resilient, and impact-oriented business models. Dr. Muheebwa is dedicated to empowering communities through sustainable entrepreneurial education, applied research, and policy-relevant scholarship. She actively engages in projects that foster sustainability, youth empowerment, and enterprise development, and contributes to academic discourse through publications, mentorship, and collaboration with local and international institutions.

Milly Kwagala Oudi, PhD, is a dedicated academic and advocate for rural development in Uganda, with over 13 years of experience as a Lecturer and former Dean of the Faculty of Business Administration and Management at Ndejje University (2010–2023). She promotes women's entrepreneurship through innovative financing models and sustainable practices, leveraging her expertise in microfinance, business management, and the economic integration of marginalized groups. Dr. Kwagala holds a PhD in Business Management (Finance) from Nelson Mandela Metropolitan University (2012), an MBA in Accounting and Finance (2006), and a BBA in Accounting (2002). Her academic career includes roles as a Lecturer and Head of Department at Kampala International University (2024) and a Lecturer at Kyambogo University (2024–present), where she focuses on teaching, research, dissemination, and outreach in finance, accounting, and microfinance.

Faith Ahabyoona Mugisha, PhD, is an accomplished academic and finance expert with over 15 years of experience in research, teaching, and the development of financial systems, particularly in Uganda. She holds a PhD in Finance, an MBA, a Bachelor of Business Administration, and several certifications in higher education management and innovation. As a lecturer and visiting lecturer across East Africa and Europe, Dr. Ahabyoona has supervised over 100 student research projects and published more than 15 peer-reviewed journal articles. Her research focuses on financial systems, innovation, and sustainable development, with a particular emphasis on market-driven solutions for the agricultural sector. She currently serves as a Lecturer in the Department of Accounting, Finance and Micro Finance at Kyambogo University.

Part III
Sustainable Enterprise, Risk and Stocks Markets

Chapter 8
Building Sustainable Enterprises During and After Pandemics: Unearthing the Impact of COVID-19 on University Roadside Businesses

David Katamba, Tom Tamale, Maureen Basuuta, and Veronica Mukyala

8.1 Introduction

The global COVID-19 pandemic that started in Wuhan China in November 2019 (The Guardian, April 2020),[1] spread its negative effects on businesses globally, but in Uganda, these begun being felt in early March 2020. Notable effects included total lockdown of universities countrywide, for over 2 years, with no certainty of re-opening. It worth noting that business sustainability has always been at risk when confronted with pandemics (Katamba & Wickert, 2021; Katamba & Nkiko, 2016; Nkiko & Katamba, 2010; Nkiko, 2009). For example, this countrywide closure of universities automatically led to closure of over 50,000 university roadside women and men entrepreneurs whose livelihood was dependent on over 300,000 students and university operations. That is, hostels, restaurants, secretarial (photocopying and printing) bureaus, clothing boutiques, mobile money agents, groceries and food vendors, saloons, video libraries, stationery, and bookshops, among others were all closed. Lockdown as a Government of Uganda (GoU)'s measure to contain the spread of the virus, hit hard the economy. Specifically, the aforesaid roadside small businesses and enterprises serving university catchment areas faced an unprecedented economic disruption. However, the first 5th May 2020 presidential directive to ease the lockdown, combined with the most recent (20th July 2020) directives, exempted universities from re-opening. This means that much as these roadside entrepreneurs have been eased (especially by the recent, 20th July 2020

[1] https://www.theguardian.com/world/2020/apr/28/how-did-the-coronavirus-start-where-did-it-come-from-how-did-it-spread-humans-was-it-really-bats-pangolins-wuhan-animal-market

D. Katamba (✉) · T. Tamale · M. Basuuta · V. Mukyala
Makerere University, Kampala, Uganda
e-mail: dkatamba@mubs.ac.ug; ttamale@mubs.ac.ug; mbasuuta@mubs.ac.ug; vmukyala@mubs.ac.ug

Y. Alhassan et al. (eds.), *Financial Innovation and Sustainable Enterprise in Developing and Emerging Economies*, Research Series on Responsible Enterprise Ecosystems, https://doi.org/10.1007/978-3-032-04500-3_8

directives) to resume work, without re-opening the universities, their livelihoods and socio-economic life, will be greatly suffocated. Despite the COVID-19 Standard Operating Procedures (SOPs) issued by World Health Organization (WHO) and GoU's Ministry of Health,[2,3] to include operating at half capacity, social distancing, regular hand washing, using masks all the time, and sanitizing, the study is concerned that much as these roadside enterprises are opened, and even if universities re-opened, it may take another year for roadside entrepreneurs' livelihoods and socio-economic life to stabilize.

Hence, by unearthing the negative impact suffered by these roadside businesses, this research document is to inform the design of an integrated local strategy for promoting sustainable university roadside businesses and enterprises amidst the post-COVID-19 pandemic, and or even guard against other pandemic effects on local business. The research document strategically focuses on three features/aspects that reflect resilient sustainable performance of roadside entrepreneurs and businesses: *(i) Survival, (ii) Employment, and (iii) Output*. These three aspects are reflected in the in-depth views/findings and the resultant policy recommendations which are framed around these key questions:

[2] https://www.health.go.ug/covid/document/national-guidelines-for-management-of-covid-19/

[3] https://www.health.go.ug/covid/wp-content/uploads/2020/04/covid-19_case-management-guidelines_final-version-soft-copy_23april-2020.pdf

1. What was the impact of COVID-19 on roadside businesses around universities?
2. What policy measures can be taken to revive these roadside businesses and sustain them amidst the post-COVID-19 pandemic?

The uniqueness in this research work includes boosting entrepreneurship as a highlighted intervention, solution and as a useful tool to foster resilience of university roadside entrepreneurs during and after [*post*] this COVID-19 global pandemic. Empirically, the relevance of strategizing for small businesses cannot be overemphasized. Chrisman et al. (2005) for example, used data from the Small Business Development Center (SBDC) programme in Pennsylvania in 1992, 1994, and 1996 and found that there is a strong and significant relationship between what he termed as 'guided preparation' and sales and employment in firms 3–8 years after start up. Hence by using these findings to inform the design of and 'integrated local business sustainability strategy' is seen as a '*guided preparation*' to build resilience of roadside entrepreneurs amidst COVID-19 pandemic and other related pandemics. It is thus envisioned, as observed elsewhere by Chrisman et al. (2005) to contribute to increased socio-economic power among both men and female entrepreneurs around urban and sub urban universities in Uganda. The uniqueness in this strategy lies in using the John Friedmann's (Dis) empowerment model as the main framework of interpretation. Additionally, to fit into the context of women who have been most hit by the COVID-19 pandemic, we integrate gender analysis to identify the structural inequalities that may constrain the empowering impact of entrepreneurship.

8.2 Methodology for Framing the Research

Summary of the Methodology
This study findings were documented after one-on-one interviewing of 160 university roadside entrepreneurs operating all sorts of small businesses ranging from saloons, bookshops, restaurants, secretarial bureaus to hostels. We also consulted and engaged with key stakeholders, particularly from Finance Institutions, Policy Organs, and SME associations. Additionally, Focus Group Discussions (FGDs) were organized to solicit for expert opinions from leading entrepreneurs and professors. For validation of findings, preliminary findings were presented in the various forum to include Rotary meetings, conferences, and seminars. This research focuses on three impact aspects which reflect the resilient performance of university roadside businesses: (i) survival; (ii) employment, and (iii) output. We were guided by two Research Questions: (1) What has been the impact of COVID-19 on roadside businesses around universities, (2) What Policy measures can be taken to revive these roadside businesses and sustain them amidst the COVID-19 pandemic. Key stakeholders disseminated to, engaged, and consulted: Financial institutions; Entrepreneurs; Business Associations particularly for Micro, small and Medium enterprises; Rotarians; Women groups/activists; Academics; and, Policy makers and business regulators

8.2.1 Design

Scientifically, this study was informed by a cross sectional research design. To fit the study findings into the context of sustainable development (sustainability studies) and guide policy makers and business entrepreneurs, we adopted Paul. R. Smith's SOSTAC[4] (Smith, 2011) framework. That is:

- S = Situation Analysis (what is happening, where are we now?),
- O = Objectives to be achieved (where do we want to go?)
- S = Strategic focus to be pursued (Cost Leadership, Differentiation, or Niche),
- TAC = Tactics, Actions and Control measures.

8.2.2 Sample Size and Sampling Design

Initially we aimed at 100 respondents. However, after consultations and engagement with Entrepreneurship experts (see, Exhibit: FGD Zoom Meeting held on Tuesday June 30, 2020 from 11:00 am to 12:00 pm), and with roadside business stakeholder organizations notably, Federation of Small Scale and Medium Enterprises (FSME) to reinforce the dataset, an upward revised stratified sample of 160 university roadside businesses (see, Table: Business clusters), purposively informed this research/report. This was based on: (1) ownership and/or management of the business, (2) operates the business near Makerere University, MUBS, or Kyambogo university, (3) has a maximum of 10 employees. The businesses studied were clustered into 32 struts as shown in Exhibits 8.1 and 8.2.

Exhibit 8.1 Business clusters

Restaurant	Bakery	Dry cleaning	Restaurants and coffee shops
Bookshops and gifts	Honey dealers	Hardware shops	Bookshops
Photocopier and stationery	Agent Banking, mobile money. And Payment Solutions services	Computers and printers	Music, public address system and videography
Saloon	Clothes, shoes, bags, and jewelry	Career development support services	Music production
Secretarial services	Agent banking mobile money and pay way services	Flowers and decoration	Phone accessories
Electronics	Beverages	Furniture	Phones and computers
Stationery	Printing services	Internet café	Pharmacy
Fashion and tailoring	Hostels	General merchandise	Photocopier

[4] Created in the 1990s by writer and speaker PR Smith, SOSTAC was voted the third most popular model in the CIM poll on marketing models because it's easy to remember and it makes it easy to structure plans for different planning activities.

Exhibit 8.2 Selection of respondents and management of respondent selection bias

Management of respondent bias
After clustering and stratifying of business entities, the corresponding respondents were purposefully chosen based on the type of business, to cover as many types of university roadside businesses as possible. Also, different ages of the respondents and years in business were key during sampling. However, control measures to include at least 45% of women running (owning or managing) these roadside businesses were respected. To inform relevant policy, e.g., Policy on 'Skilling Uganda,' we interviewed entrepreneurship key personalities using Zoom, Policy officers from KCCA, Federation of Small and Medium Enterprises (FSME), Private Sector Foundation Uganda (PSFU) and officials from key financial institutions where these roadside entrepreneurs have been accessing finances

8.2.3 *Data Sources and Collection Procedure*

Given the current COVID-19 situations in Uganda, our research team observed the Ministry of Health (MoH) Standard Operating Procedures (SOPs) during face-to-face interactions. That is, researchers were wearing masks, carried a standby personal sanitizer, but this could largely follow if a potential respondent in our sample frame, could not be contacted through phone calls for a detailed interview.

Additionally, we used existing administrative data. Specifically, we analyzed the content appearing on Twitter pages notably @PSFU_Uganda. Private Sector Foundation Uganda (PSFU) is the apex body for the Private Sector in Uganda. We also gathered data from other twitter handles, and hashtags, notably #psfuecon2020, and #COVID-19ugrecovery. These handles were purposely sought because they contain views collected from over 5000 people in and outside Uganda during the COVID-19 e-conference of 3rd–4th May 2020, dubbed, "COVID-19 and '*The Economy: Inclusive Economic Stimulus Strategies, Opportunities, and Linkages.*"

Lastly, we collected information through phone surveys, as well as used Zoom technology to reach out to key informants (See, Exhibits 8.3 and 8.4).

Exhibit 8.3 FGD Zoom Meeting held on Tuesday June 30, 2020

Topic: Management skills for the future after the coronavirus pandemic
Zoom Meeting held on Tuesday June 30, 2020 from 11:00 am to 12:00 pm. Meeting held using the Zoom Link https://zoom.us/j/97321041217?pwd=TDloN3ZRMG5MeFRrekxkdGRtZjN0Zz09 Meeting ID: 973 2104 1217; Password: 949816.
FGD participants: Mr. Shukla Mukeshi (Owner,—Shumuk Group of Companies); Prof. Waswa Balunywa (Principal—MUBS); Mr. Sunil Inamdar (Partner,—PWC); Ms. Diana Ntamu (Director,—MUBS Entrepreneurship, Innovations, and Incubation Center); Ms. Sumaya Kagoya (PhD student); Mr. Peter Odoki; Prof. Ngoma Mohamed; Prof. Moses Muhwezi; Prof. David Katamba

Exhibit 8.4 FGD Zoom Meeting held on Wednesday August 12, 2020

Topic: Financing Business During COVID
Zoom Meeting held on Wednesday August 12, 2020 from 07:00 am to 08:00 am. Meeting held using the Zoom Link https://zoom.us/j/98828414178?pwd=ZjZjbGN4WG9zcEVXOGg3R1liOWlHdz09 Meeting ID: 988 2841 4178; Password: 099796.
FGD participants: Mr. Arthur Isiko (CEO, Bank of Africa); Prof. Waswa Balunywa (Principal—MUBS); Prof. Tomola, Researcher in Nigeria; Dr. Rachel Mindra (Head Finance, MUBS); Ms. Diana Ntamu (Director,—MUBS Entrepreneurship, Innovations, and Incubation Center); Ms. Veronica Mukyala; Ms. Maureen Basuuta; Dr. Edith Basalirwa; Mr. Peter Odoki; Prof. Ngoma Mohamed; Prof. Moses Muhwezi; Prof. David Katamba

Table 8.1 Age distribution of respondents

Mean	Median	Mode	Range	Minimum	Maximum
32	30	30	39	22	61

8.2.4 *Respondent Profile*

(a) **Age distribution**

From the above age distribution (Table 8.1), university roadside businesses are operated by all aged people right from 22 years (Minimum, 22 years) to people of over 60 years. However, on average (Mean, 32 years), these businesses are mostly (Mode, 30 years) operated by the youths. Hence, this age descriptive statistics highlight the need to review and re-align business and entrepreneurship policies in Uganda and make them responsive to benefit also the youths running university roadside businesses.

(b) **Gender distribution of respondents**

For gender responsiveness, this study attempted to balance between men and women respondents. This enabled us to fit findings into the context of women who have been the most hit by the COVID-19 pandemic. This desegregation also helped to identify the structural inequalities that may constrain the gender empowering impact of entrepreneurship. Hence, of the 160 responses, 45% (72 respondents) were female while 55% (88 respondents) were males as shown in Fig. 8.1. There were no significant differences between types of university roadside business owned by women or those own by men.

(c) **Education level of business owners**

Of the studied university roadside businesses (n = 160), the majority (39%, n = 62), were owned/started up by bachelor's degree holders, followed by O′ Level (Uganda Certificate of Education, -UCE) holders (n = 42, 26%). Higher qualifications holders (PhD, and master's holders) were found to be least involved in university roadside

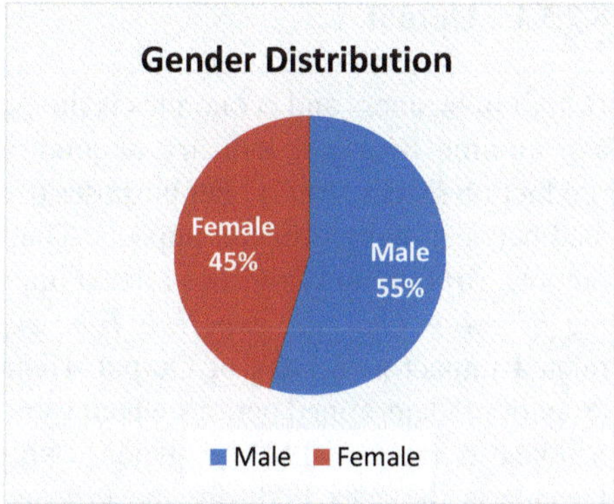

Fig. 8.1 Gender distribution

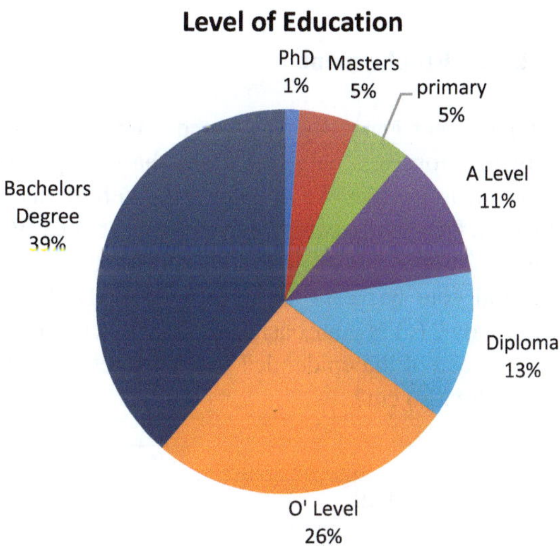

Fig. 8.2 Level of education

business. Hence, over 55% of university roadside business owners and managers, are below university level education (see Fig. 8.2). This *'education-business startup/ownership'* profile has a bearing on the 'Skilling Uganda program,' as well as on the curriculum on entrepreneurship in Uganda's education system.

8.2.5 Operationalization of Constructs

This research document resonates around three main constructs. That is: Output, Employment, and Survival. These were operationalized as described below:

8.2.5.1 Output

Output in business and economics is the "quantity of goods or services produced in a given time, by a firm, industry, or country", whether consumed or used for further production (Moss, 2007).[5] For purposes of this research/development, we differentiated between output related impacts. That is (a) Impact on key business drivers of outputs; (b) Inbound Logistics related impacts (*Inbound logistics covers the receiving of goods and raw materials from suppliers to businesses);* and (c) revenue related impact as drivers of Output. Henceforth, we subjected respondents to an array of predetermined options which were identified from the Hashtags and Twitter handles notably @PSFU_Uganda (where PSFU—Private Sector Foundation Uganda is the apex body for the Private Sector in Uganda; #psfuecon2020, and #COVID-19ugrecovery.

8.2.5.2 Employment

Employment generally means the state of having a paid job. International Labor Organization (ILO) also mentions that, *'Employment'* can also refer to the act of employing people. We adopted both definitions of Employment for this research project. Hence, an inquiry into the impact of COVID-19 on Employment created by university roadside businesses was made using these items: (a) How many employees did your business have before COVID-19, (b) How many employees do you have Now? (c) Is your business currently considering layoffs, or has it already done so because of the epidemic? (d) What percentage of staff are you expecting to (or have already) cut?

8.2.5.3 Survival

Survive can be taken to mean succeeding in keeping alive against odds, to live after or during a threatening event in this case, the event is the COVID-19 pandemic. Thus, the *'impact on survival'* could only be assessed from businesses which were active at least a month before the closure (that is, business which were active by February 10th, 2020). Survival strategies in business include diversification, access to finance/credit, and improving your bottom the bottom line (cashflow). Hence, to establish the Impact on 'Survival' of university roadside businesses, we centered investigations into aspects and parameters which could explain or destruct these strategies. These included: (a) Time needed for recovery; (b) Cash flow sustainability; and (c) Financing mechanism.

---

[5] David A. Moss is The John G. Mclean Professor Of Business Administration At Harvard Business School.

8.2.6 Reliability and Validity

Reliability and validity are all about taking measures to ensure that the information presented before any audience, is authentic and can be relied on for policy change and decision making in related or similar situations. Hence, the data which informed this research document (report) was 'triangulated' to ensure reliability and validity. Triangulation in qualitative methodology, is the equivalent of reliability testing in quantitative research (Creswell, 2007; Yin, 2008). To do this, we first undertook data source triangulation, by considering whether the data gathered from different sources (twitter handles, ≠Hashtags, Policy reviews,—of MSME policy, BUBU Policy, Youth Employment Policy, etc., Focus Groups, interviews, and content analysis) would remain unchanged in different contexts. In gathering all the above data from all these respective sources, we employed '*methodological triangulation*' by using more than one method to gather data from each source (that is, we undertook interviews, Focus Group Discussions,—FGDs, observations, and policy document reviews). Additionally, we undertook '*investigator triangulation*' where each researcher examined the same phenomenon and data independently for an independent expert opinion, where merged opinions could be considered more relevant. Lastly, we engaged in '*theory triangulation*' which involved interpreting from different entrepreneurship viewpoints (suggested by Global Entrepreneurship Monitor,—GEM report and entrepreneurship scholars/professors (Prof. Peter Rosa, Prof. Waswa Balunywa, Prof. Arthur Sserwanga) as well as Uganda's outstanding entrepreneurs and practitioners like Mr. Shukla Mukeshi (Owner,—Shumuk Group of Companies), and, Mr. Sunil Inamdar (Partner,—PWC). We termed this '*First level analysis of transcripts*' as this enabled us to extract categories and commonalities that emerged. This formed the basis for secondary analysis thus leading to themes and conclusions to emerge in our '*Data aggregation and Analysis*' as explained below.

8.2.7 Data Analysis and Aggregation

Much of the data that informed this research document (report) was qualitative in nature. This prompted use of Grounded Theory, Adaptive Theory and the generic qualitative data analysis which involves themes building and coding, was used in union with The John Friedmann's (Dis) empowerment model as the main frame of interpretation. To fit into the context of gender, this model was complemented with a gender analysis to identify the structural inequalities that may constrain the empowering impact of entrepreneurship. Specifically, we borrowed largely from Charmaz (1983)'s '*Grounded Theory.*' That is, we used arrays to display the data, created displays, tabulated the findings (as shown by various Tables and Exhibits throughout this document). We then '*ordered*' the information as guided by Miles and Huberman (1994). Thereafter, Yin's (2008) "analytical strategy" was used.

That is, "pattern-matching" (to examine the consistency of categories/themes with literature) and, "explanation building", leading us to develop a framework to finally analyze the data with respect to the characteristics that define university roadside businesses. For generalization purposes of our findings, we were guided by the "adaptive theory approach" Layder (1998). That is, *firstly (first level Analysis)*, all the data was analyzed with the purpose of identifying categories, themes, content and finally issues that could resonate with: (i) Output; (ii) Employment; and, (iii) Survival of these university roadside business. However, prior to reaching any theme, content or issue, each data source was re-cross examined. Once all the necessary information was collected, the transcripts and additional information were read to allow diversities to emerge. This process served to identify key issues and provide the opportunity to seek clarifications or additional information during FGDs (conducted using Zoom technology, see Zoom Exhibits in methodology section).

This immersion in the data was followed by writing up draft cases, which contained facts, interpretations, and links back to the literature for backing on how we could answer the research questions. Thereafter, detailed comments of key informant respondents in FGDs, incidents and repetition were extracted (see the different Tables in the Findings sections) by considering the words and documented actions and attitudes of respondents and the studied roadside businesses. At this point, we were beefing facts and cases which would allow generalizations to emerge.

8.3 Unearthing the Impact of COVID-19 on University Roadside Businesses

In this section, we answer a local entrepreneurship sustainability strategy formulation question: Where are university roadside businesses now? We answer this question by presenting the "research findings" which are a scientific validation of the Situation Analysis 1 *("Introduction")* that prompted this study as well as the designing of this strategy. We have loosely termed it, "*Situation Analysis 2*." These findings/facts presented below speak of the current situation that needs attention to 'Build Resilient University Roadside Entrepreneurs for Sustainable Socio-Economic Livelihoods,' during and after/post-COVID-19." With impact, this research (strategy formulation) focused on the negative devastation (though *'Impact'* can also be positive) that was inflicted on the university roadside business by the prevalence of COVID-19. This negative impact has been differentiated between (i) Impact on Output; (ii) Impact on Employment; and (iii) Impact on Survival as elaborated in the proceeding subsections. Below we also present a mini case that combines this impact (Exhibit 8.5).

Exhibit 8.5 Voice of a University Roadside entrepreneur in the MUBS University catchment

Case: Kitimbo Emmanuel, an entrepreneur
I am Kitimbo Emmanuel, a manager at Emma Stationers located in MUBS. I Started business in early 2011 with one machine. I worked hard and added one other machine, and subsequently, I employed some one person and with hard work we added a 3rd machine till eventually the business was expanded. Originally, I started with providing photocopying services to the MUBS community. I then elevated to other stationary services, particularly printing. Before COVID-19, the business was moving on so well that I was able to take care of family and buy some assets including land. For sure with the expansion of my business, I had never wished for formal employment because I felt I was getting enough. I have been able to partner with other businesses and the main partner being the Professional Accountancy Training Centre (PAT) an institution located at Nakawa vocational. I also partnered with Kiswa Community Nursery and Primary school located in Kiswa, partnered with some other schools in Kitintale to be providing secretarial services and supply them with stationary and also offer basic training services regarding usage and maintenance of equipment used in printing and photocopying to the upper classes in the primary school mentioned. I was sure therefore of an already market. So business was moving on so smoothly not until Covid-19 set in which led to complete closure of the business. I had employed four (4) workers on a full-time basis, but I had to lay them off and remain alone. I cut the business by almost 80% because machines are not working, I had got a loan with a money lender, this was now disaster in turbulent times because I had to sell off some of my machines to be able to pay the loan. Currently what I can only do from my business is to sell papers to an exceedingly small market. I sell these papers to those struggling to remain in similar businesses around the 'small gate' [*the originally main gateway entrance to MUBS campus, thru URA side]* who are around 8–10 people. In a week I may even sell only one realm of papers since even those who buy from me have an extremely low customer base as of now. This saw me change the way I was operating to now instead of selling a realm to an individual, I can now sell per paper. Storage of an open realm for sale is a challenge as the papers can easily get moist and the customer refuses to buy them. We are looking at the government with hope for any help more so to people like us who depend solely on schools for a customer base, like opening schools and allowing us to work under the outlined Standard Operating Procedure (SOPs). Like in my room we are not that many. I have already tried to buy sanitizers.

Source: Reproduced here with the consent of the Interviewee

8.3.1 Impact on Output

We present findings on three aspects that could reveal the impact of COVID-19 on the Output (quantity of goods and services produced). (a) Impact on key business drivers of Output; (b) Inbound Logistics related Impact on Output; and (c) Revenue related impact on Output:

(a) **Impact on key business drivers of outputs**

When asked, *"which of these, are the key problems your business is facing due to the COVID-19 pandemic?"* each respondent identified two options from these selection possibilities in Table 8.2.

We henceforth found that in combination, the key output-related effects that were faced by university roadside businesses (entrepreneurs) are (Exhibit 8.6).

Results indicate that the main impact of COVID-19 on Output of university roadside entrepreneurs was 'Reduction in orders' and 'Increased difficulty in accessing

Table 8.2 Impact on business drivers

(a) Reduction of orders	(b) Inability to deliver existing orders	(c) Increased difficulty of financing	(d) Existing loans cannot be extended	(e) Disruption of logistics	(f) Upstream and downstream chain disruptions	(g) Insufficient protective equipment (e.g., face masks)

Exhibit 8.6 Combination of the main effect on business drivers of Output due to COVID-19 epidemic

Combination of main impacts on key business drivers of outputs	Number of businesses	Percentage of businesses
1. Reduction of orders; the Increased difficulty of financing	72	45
2. Reduction of orders; Disruption of logistics	30	19
3. Reduction of orders; Inability to deliver existing orders	15	9
4. Inability to deliver existing orders; Existing loans cannot be extended	15	9
5. Increased difficulty of financing; Disruption of logistics	12	8
6. Increased difficulty of financing; Insufficient protective equipment (e.g., face masks)	12	8
7. Inability to deliver existing orders; Upstream and downstream chain disruptions	3	2

financing.' This was mainly faced by saloons, restaurants, stationery, and secretarial service businesses. While a combination of these two impacts on output affected 45% of the studies business (n = 72), 'Disruption in Logistics' and the inability to deliver existing orders were key impacts as well. These take the third and fourth positions. A combination of these four impacts on output affected over 73% of the studied roadside businesses. Businesses that had overcapitalized their investments (in infrastructure) in university catchment areas, particularly hostels and supermarkets, had their output impacted in form of Inability to deliver existing orders as well as Upstream and downstream chain disruptions. In terms of gender, there were no significant differences concerning *Impact on key business drivers of outputs* from women-owned or men-owned university roadside businesses.

(b) **Impact on Inbound Logistics**

University roadside businesses also have Inbound logistics (supplies and raw materials) which are used in the production of output. This means any change on the inflow of these logistics proportionately translates into an impact on Output levels.

What is your business's expectation in terms of *raw materials (or supplies) and total operating costs in 2020 compared to 2019?* Results indicate that the majority (30%, n = 47) businesses were unable to judge the impact of COVID-19 on their inbound logistics and the associated costs (see Exhibit 8.7). This is a strange finding

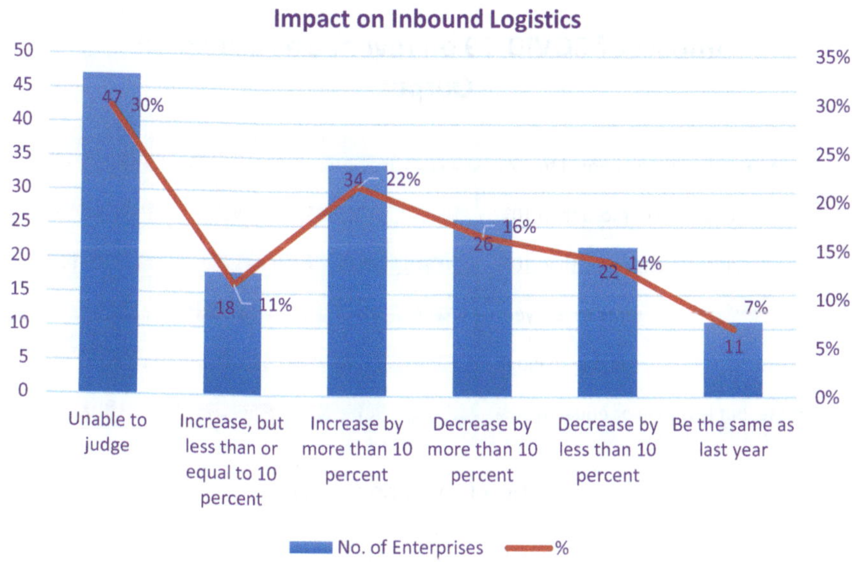

Exhibit 8.7 Inbound logistics related impact on output

considering the transport restrictions imposed by the Government during the lock down. Additionally, UBOS has found transport inflation has been a key driver of headline inflation between March–September 2020. We hence think that the respondents, underestimated the impact of these disruptions on their businesses. These businesses included saloons, restaurants, internet cafes, and general merchandise operators. It is important to note here that these businesses were registered with mainly with KCCA, but they never kept proper books of accounts/business records. This made them fail to have a clear picture of their inbound logistics needs. However, 22% (n = 34) of university roadside business expect/ project the costs of their inbound logistics to increase by more than 10%. These were mainly restaurants, and saloons, though a few photocopying bureaus were also cited here. An increase in the costs of inbound logistics means a proportionate decrease in output that would have been produced since the entrepreneur will not be able to buy those raw materials. For example, if a restaurant logistics (say, a batch of banana, or a Kilogram of rice) costs increased by 10% she/he will buy less raw materials with the same money previously used, to prepare meals. Lastly, only 7% (n = 11) businesses do not expect any change (positive or negative) in their costs of operations related to inbound logistics. These were mainly stationery and secretarial bureaus.

(c) **Impact on Revenue**

Since revenues imply demand (market), they dictate how much output should be produced. As a control and validation measure, we first investigated into total revenues registered in the previous calendar year 2019 by university roadside enterprises/businesses. Results revealed that on average, university roadside enterprises

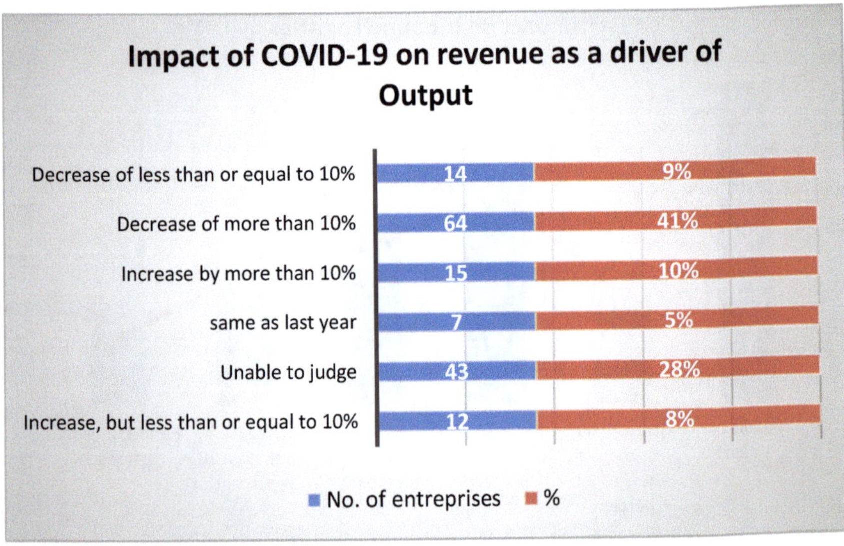

Exhibit 8.8 Revenue related impact on output

had earned revenues amounting to UGX 17,987,912 (equiv., to US$4950). However, we observed that there were enterprises that had registered over UGX 100,000,000 (equiv., US$54,800). These were mainly General merchandise stores, Dry cleaning, and Hardware stores (Exhibit 8.8).

Therefore, our probe into indications of business's total revenue expectations in 2020 compared to 2019 revealed that the majority (41%, n = 64) of university roadside enterprises will experience a decrease in the revenues by over 10%. Similarly, in this year 2020, only 10% (n = 15) will record revenues which are more than 10% compared to 2019. These were mainly: Fashion and Tailoring, Restaurants, Saloons, and Beverage shops.

8.3.2 *Impact on Employment*

(a) **Shift in employment pattern**

From the Exhibit 8.9, "*Impact on Employment,*" a total of 153 entrepreneurs revealed the impact on Employment. These could provide jobs to over 616 people (mainly youths and a few elderly men and women). However, only 74 businesses (*like restaurants serving bypasses*) could remain slightly active during the COVID-19 pandemic. Slightly active to mean that by the time of collecting this data, there was a slight ease in the lockdown, though universities were still closed. Hence, 74 enterprises could only provide 197 jobs. This means the COVID-19 pandemic created a decrease in jobs created by roadside entrepreneurs by over 60%.

Exhibit 8.9 Impact on employment

	How many employees did your business have before COVID-19?			How many employees do you have Now?		
	Number of Employees	Number of Enterprises	Total Number of people employed before COVID-19	Number of Employees	Number of Enterprises	Total Number of people employed during the COVID-19 pandemic
	0	8	8	0	12	12
	1	16	16	1	21	21
	2	31	62	2	18	36
	3	38	114	3	8	24
	4	16	64	4	6	24
	5	16	80	5	3	15
	6	10	60	6	2	12
	7	5	35	7	1	7
	8	4	32	11	1	11
	10	4	40	15	1	15
	12	2	24	20	1	20
	16	1	16			
	30	1	30			
	35	1	35			
Total		153	616		74	197

Source: Field data from university roadside businesses and entrepreneurs

Concerning the number of employees, a zero ("0") means that such a roadside business has [had] no employee, thus it is "a one-man/woman business show!' What is important to note is that after COVID-19, the number of businesses *[No. of enterprises]* of this human resource structure, had increased by 50%, that is, from 8 to 12 enterprises. This automatically means a 50% decrease in employment numbers in other categories of the Number of Employees before COVID-19. These businesses included: Mobile Money, boutiques, photographing, phones, and computer repairs. Most people employed in this business types were bachelor's degree holders. There was a balance in gender. That is, both women and men were active in this business category.

Most of the jobs (n = 114; n = 80; n = 64), that is, over 254 jobs were created before COVID-19 by university roadside enterprises *(entrepreneurs)* employing 3, 5 and 4 employees, respectively. These businesses were mainly, saloons, restaurants, stationery, and Secretarial Bureaus. The majority, over 70% of the females employed, worked in these businesses, and they were aged between 25 and 33 years. The sad news is that this business category, by the time of the survey, was employing t only63 people, indicating a decrease in employment by 75.6%, that is, from 254 jobs to 63. By this decrease, the most affected are the businesses that were employing 3 people. That is, while these enterprises were 38, and employing 114 people, they are currently 8 (which is a 79% decrease) and only employ 24.

Additionally, the three businesses that each respectively employed 16, 30, and 35 people before COVID-19, closed to date. These businesses were respectively: (i) A hostel in Kataza (part of Nakawa) operated by a male diploma holder and had started in 2005; (ii) Printing services bureau in Nakawa) operated by a male bachelor's degree holder and had started in 2015; and; (iii) a saloon and bridal center in Wandegeya (part of Kampala city centre) operated by a female master's degree graduate and had started in 2016.

Lastly, for current staff (Number of Employees now) university roadside enterprises employing 1 and 2 staff, are the majority job providers in the 'Aftermath of COVID-19.' These 39 enterprises, employ a combined pool of 57 people (men and women), disaggregated into 21 staff and 36 staff, respectively. What is unique about these enterprises, is that: (i) They have all registered with Kampala Capital City Authority (KCCA), local government authority in charge of Kampala, (ii) their entrepreneurs' education level swings most between Certificate (usually secondary school drop-outs), O′ Level, and, A' Level, while only less than 10% are degree holders. This education profile has a bearing on the skilling Uganda program and the education system with respect to entrepreneurship.

(b) **Laying off staff due to COVID-19**

Despite the impact COVID-19 inflicted on the university roadside businesses in Uganda, to include job loss, the majority (46%, n = 74) of the 160 entrepreneurs are reluctant to consider laying off their staff when asked whether they would consider laying the off (see Fig. 8.3). This means, much as businesses/entrepreneurs have

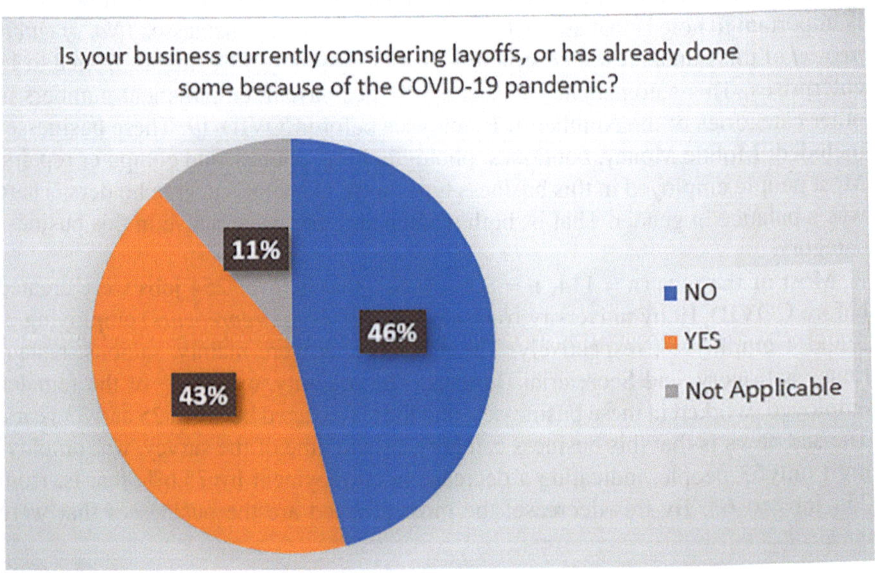

Fig. 8.3 Staff layoffs

cash flow problems due to reduced business activity resulting from Lockdown, their employees losing their jobs with them was circumstantial and not a plan from the entrepreneurs. Also, their choice was informed by the fact that most employees had lost their jobs due to travel restrictions and not necessarily because of an organized layoff. Lastly given the casual nature of the roadside jobs, during the lockdown, many employees have sought employment alternatives. The businesses that were reluctant to lay off employees include stationery, restaurants, saloons, general merchandise, medical services provider, internet cafes, and Bookshops and Stationery. Surprisingly, over 80% of the businesses that were reluctant to consider layoff, were unable to judge the time they needed to have their business re-instated to normal operations.

Similarly, 34% of the interviewed roadside business had laid off/cut over 30% of their staff (see Fig. 8.4). These belong to the 43% of the interviewed businesses who had indicated that they were already considering laying off their staff. We observed that these were highly informal and had not registered with regulative bodies. The corresponding 31% was expecting or had even cut 1–10% of their employees. These businesses were registered with KCCA and other regulatory authorities. The less number (1–10%) they were considering laying off, is justified by the tight employment laws governing them, which command compensation of staff. Given the dilemma that they don't have money to both maintain the business as well as compensate staff, the main option left was to go slow on layoff.

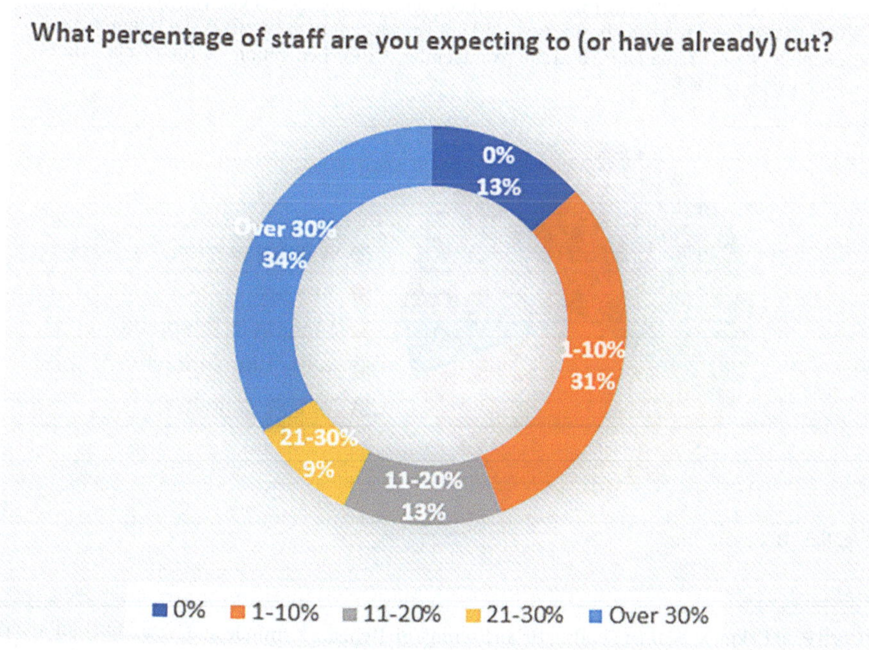

Fig. 8.4 Percentage of staff layoffs

8.3.3 *Impact on Survival*

The university institutions were closed effective 18th March 2020 (Lakuma et al., 2020). Thus, the *'impact on survival'* could only be assessed from businesses which were active atleast a month before the closure (that is, businesses which were active by February 10th, 2020).

(a) **Time needed for recovery**

The aspect of "*Time needed for recovery*" was investigated (see Fig. 8.5) because literature from Economic Policy Research Center—EPRC, May 2020[6] had indicated that during harsh economic cycles, in this case, COVID-19, informal or semi-informal business can easily fail to survive (are bound to collapse) *within just a matter of time!* Henceforth, we investigated: *"what is the expected time for university roadside businesses' recovery after re-opening of the universities?"*. We observed that the majority (over 41.3%, n = 66) could not tell when they will ever recover from the business shocks that COVID-19 imposed on them if universities re-opened. These were mainly Hostels, Restaurants, Bookshops, Boutiques, and Internet cafes. However, only 5.6% (n = 9) could recover within 2 weeks. These were 'Saloons' and 'Secretarial services providers.' Nevertheless, 26.2% of businesses indicated that they would need up to 3 months, to recover, when the universities are re-opened.

> "… I'm convinced that it may take between 2–3 years. Whereas, universities will be eventually allowed to reopen, the restrictions on how many students that can accommodate, will ensure that these roadside businesses, will not gain access to the preCOVID-19 numbers of clientele soon," remarked Mr. John Walugembe, CEO, Federation of Small and Micro Enterprises (FSME).

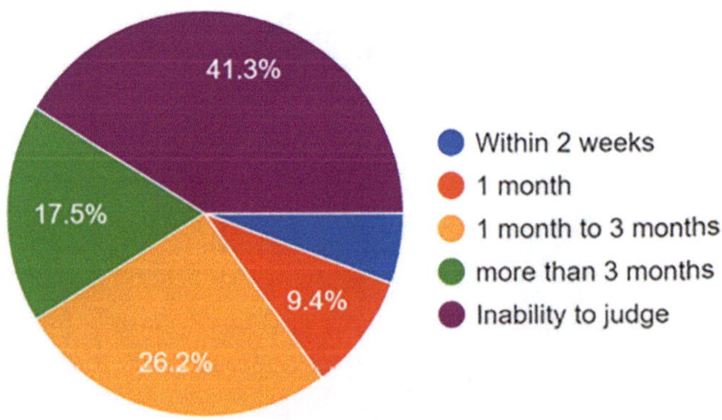

Fig. 8.5 Recovery time

[6] Corti Paul Lakuma, Nathan Sunday, Brian Sserunjogi, Rehema Kahunde and Ezra Munyambonera (2020), *The Uganda Business Climate Index, How Has The Covid-19 Pandemic Impacted Ugandan Businesses? Results From A Business Climate Survey,* EPRC, Kampala Uganda

(b) **Cash flow sustainability**

The duration for which current cashflow (cash at hand or cash in bank) could sustain the operations of a university roadside business, and thus guard it against collapse, was investigated.

At the time of data collection (June 2020), universities had closed for 3½ months. However, there was a slight ease in the lockdown. That is, Government of Uganda (GoU) had partially opened the economy and some businesses in Kampala were operating at small scale. However, universities were still closed for an indefinite time, even at the time of authoring this report. As shown in Fig. 8.6, findings indicate that over 32% (n = 50) of university roadside businesses (of which include selected stationery shops, boutiques, fashion and tailoring, some restaurants, secretarial services providers, and Music/video libraries) would no longer be in business after June 2020. This was irrespective of the gender of the entrepreneur and type of business. Surprisingly, these businesses had been in business for over 4 years on average though most of them had not been registered with any regulator, neither with any association. Hence, we may say they were still in formative stages. This loose nature of their formation, as well as their tenure in businesses, can partly explain their swift nature of collapsing/failure to withstand effects of COVID-19 in a noticeably short time. On the other hand, the majority (45%, n = 71) of businesses (which include selected Restaurants, stationery, secretarial bureaus, and mobile money agents), cannot survive beyond the third month into the Lockdown (after June 2020). Lastly, results revealed that given the indefinite period for which universities will remain closed, only 9% (n = 14) businesses have cash flows (money) which can enable them to *survive* beyond 6 months. This means should universities open in the sixth months or more from now (June 2020), only 9% will survive in business when using their already realized money, while over 90% of businesses will have to look for other financing mechanisms. These surviving businesses were all found to be registered with KCCA. They had also been in business for 8 years,

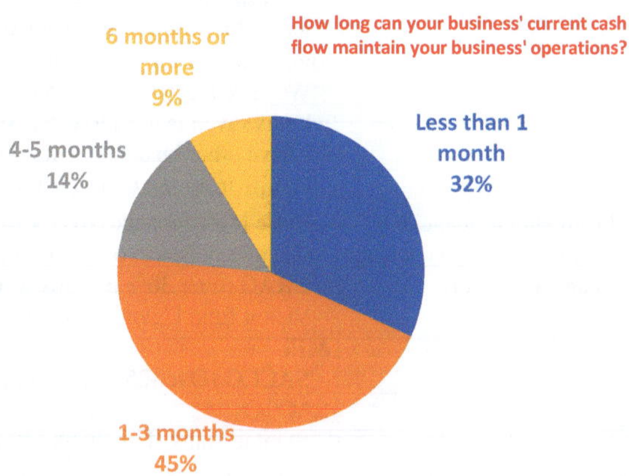

Fig. 8.6 Cash flow sustainability

on average. In fact, one business had been in the Hostel business for 16 years, while another had been in the Saloon business for 23 years, while other businesses had been dealing in General Merchandise for over 9 years. This finding means that small businesses that have been established over years, can withstand economic shock for some time. This is may be due to some accumulated cash reserves and profits made earlier compared to their grappling counterparts.

(c) **Financing mechanism**

Thus, an investigation into how the financing mechanism had been disrupted and henceforth affecting business survival, revealed the following (Exhibit 8.10):

Exhibit 8.10 Financing mechanism's impact on survival of businesses

What is your current daily expenditure level?	– On average, daily expenditure during lockdown was UGX 50,000 (approx. USD 15) for businesses that did not have loans. This expenditure was largely going towards fixed costs like provision for rent accumulation, and utilities like electricity and security. – On average UGX 150,000 (approx. USD 45) for businesses which had loans. This expenditure this was largely going towards loan servicing, in addition to provision for rent accumulation, and utilities like electricity and security.
How have you been financing your business?	– Loans (by borrowing from friends, banks, and savings), – Borrowing some materials and pay later – Profits from the sales made – Business owner capital and loans
Did you have a loan?	Yes (n = 54; 34%) No (n = 104; 66%)
If yes, how are you financing the loan?	– Requested the bank to restructure the loan to fit within other sources to finance – Paid part of it out of the savings made before covid-19 but re-negotiated the mode of payment – Per now am not financing it because my business is closed – Negotiated for reschedules as well as a grace period. Bank of Uganda has allowed each borrower 2 opportunities to request for loan restructuring within the next one year. – We have a group saving and so acts as our guarantor therefore what is saved is used to cater for the loan – I have other businesses that I do, like vegetable growing – Profits from my other business
From which financial institution are you getting financial support?	– Pride Microfinance (over 45% of borrowers mentioned this MFI)[a] – Centenary Bank (over 35% of borrowers mentioned this bank) – BRAC (over 30% of borrowers mentioned this MFI) – Vision fund Uganda (Less than 10% of borrowers mentioned this MFI – SACCO (Over 25% mentioned getting money from their group SACCOs – Stanbic Bank (Les thank 1% of borrowers mentioned this bank)

[a] In the context of this research, "Over," implies that some borrowers mentioned that they borrowed from more than one lending institution

From the table above, *'financing mechanisms,'* we observe that university roadside businesses that had loans from financial institutions (34%, n = 54), could not survive, while those without loans (66%, n = 104) had more chances of surviving during the COVID-19 lockdown. According to Mr. John Walugembe, he remarked:

> … This is interesting! Is it that that the Financial Institutions did not abide by the Bank of Uganda guidelines on loan restructuring or the university roadside entrepreneurs were not aware of this option?

We further observed that much of the financing/loans to run university roadside businesses were obtained from Microfinance institutions (MFIs), and not mainstream banks. These MFIs were mentioned as increasing on the pressure that made borrower not to survive in businesses. This finding was contrary to government of Uganda directive. Mr. Walugembe mentioned that:

> … The Uganda Microfinance Regulatory Authority also instructed MFIs to restructure their clients' loans. Strange that this did not happen!

Additionally, respondents mentioned that banks could only restructure the loans or advance grace periods, but during this term, loan interest was instead accruing. This means, financial institutions profited more from COVID-19 since they never sympathized with entrepreneurs.

Furthermore, most of the businesses which had loans, belonged to the category of 32% of businesses whose cash flow could not sustain them for more than a month. For example, much as their businesses (e.g., hostels) were closed, they had to find a daily provisional cash to pay the financing institutions. However, there were businesses (e.g., Saloons and Restaurants) which had loans, but could survive for more than 6 months of continued closure of universities. Their scenario is explained by the fact that these businesses could serve other road users as they wait to serve students when universities re-open.

Lastly, when asked *"How have you been financing your business?"* during this lockdown, those who had no loans from financial institutions, were also found to be upset with survival challenges. That is, they cited borrowing physical materials (e.g., groceries for restaurants, saloon logistics) from suppliers, or even from friends with a view to pay later. Similarly, the rent arrears and increasing tension from landlords automatically categorized them as 'borrowers.' Resultantly, those who could not settle their obligations, like rent, security, electricity, etc., could not survive in business. They were locked out of the rental premises/stalls by landlords. Hence, most university roadside entrepreneurs are already *'out of business'* because of COVID-19 disrupting the financing mechanism of their businesses.

8.4 Conclusions

To avert the negative *'survival,' 'employment,' and 'structural'* effects of the COVID-19 pandemic on university roadside entrepreneurs, urgent needs in the post-COVID-19 era include: (i) support to access loans with flexible repayments, (ii) interventions by Government of Uganda (GoU) to force lending institutions to scrap off accumulated interest on loans accruing during the six (6) months of the lockdown due to COVID-19 pandemic; (iii) GoU should subsidize landlords so that they can also relieve tenants from paying accumulated rent; (iv) a need to develop new business models and ways of delivering services and products, (v) diversify into new lines of business, and (vi) intensification of resilience skills building as part of the policy to spur SMEs growth and sustainability.

8.5 Policy Recommendations

We reviewed five key policies (including MSME policy 2015; The National Youth Policy, -NYP, 2001) and thus make these recommendations:

1. Foster entrepreneurial science-based or science-embedded activities which can spur innovation and economic growth of university and other roadside entrepreneurs. Government of Uganda (GoU) should have a policy to support and protect roadside business innovations in favor of online/remote order placing, computerized customer service, and technical skills enhancement.
2. The study found out that many roadside businesses were not registered and thus amidst the COVID-19 pandemic, these businesses could not easily get assistance. We propose that an apex body which registers all university roadside businesses is established to give a sense of belonging to these businesses. If such a body were in existence at the current times in the prevailing situation, by now the Presidential initiative of having SMEs affected by the pandemic register for assistance, would easily be done.
3. GoU should review stimulus packages *(assistive programs),* to include specific aspects that will assist university roadside (small businesses) in post COVID-19 economic recovery. Specific aspects are: (i) Outlines a simple beneficiary/application process irrespective of the academic and skills diversity of these entrepreneurs, (ii) have easier content to understand, (iii) be timely to be utilized; and (iv) indicate specific contact personnel to support these small and micro-entrepreneurs.
4. Furthermore, GoU should directly support small business associations, like Federation of Small and Micro Enterprises (FSME), Uganda Small Scale Industries Association (USSIA), UMEA, Uganda Women Entrepreneurs

Association Ltd., (UWEAL), etc., with low-cost loans which they can extend to their members, particularly roadside entrepreneurs. The loans thru Uganda Microfinance Support Center, have not been helpful to university roadside business due to politics and unclear procedures to access the funds.

5. Lastly, there has been an employment shift, and venturing into new business lines. So government should support survival of this shift in order to curb unnecessary employment swings.

References

Charmaz, K. (1983). The grounded theory method: An explication and interpretation. In R. M. Emerson (Ed.), *Contemporary field research: A collection of readings* (pp. 109–128). Little, Brown and Company.

Creswell, J. W. (2007). *Qualitative inquiry and research design: Choosing among five approaches* (2nd ed.). Sage.

Katamba, D., & Wickert, C. M. J. (2021). Corporate social responsibility in Uganda. In S. O. Idowu (Ed.), *Current global practices of corporate social responsibility. CSR, sustainability, ethics & governance*. Springer. https://doi.org/10.1007/978-3-030-68386-3_26

Katamba, D., & Nkiko, C. M. (2016). The landscape of corporate social responsibility in Uganda: Its past, present and future. In S. Vertigans, S. O. Idowu, & R. Schmidpeter (Eds.), *Corporate social responsibility in sub-Saharan Africa: Sustainable development in its embryonic form* (pp. 153–171). Springer International Publishing. http://link.springer.com/chapter/10.1007%2F978-3-319-26668-8_7

Lakuma, C. P., Sunday, N., Sserunjogi, B., Kahunde, R., & Munyambonera, E. (2020). *The Uganda business climate index, how has the covid-19 pandemic impacted Ugandan Businesses? Results from a business climate survey*. EPRC.

Miles, M. B., & Huberman, A. M. (1994). *Qualitative data analysis*. Sage.

Moss, D. A. (2007). *A concise guide to macroeconomics what managers, executives, and students need to know*. Harvard Business Review Press.

Nkiko, C. M. (2009). *Corporate social responsibility: Small medium enterprise contribution towards sustainable development in developing economies: The case of BCSDU*. unpublished DBA thesis, University of Portsmouth.

Nkiko, C. M., & Katamba, D. (2010). CSR Uganda profile. In W. Visser & N. Tolhurst (Eds.), *World guide to CSR: A country by country analysis of corporate sustainability and responsibility* (pp. 416–422). GreenLeaf Publishing.

Smith, P. R. (2011). *The SOSTAC ® Guide - to writing the perfect plan* (1st ed.). Online: www.prsmith.org

Yin, R. K. (2008). *Case study research: Design and methods: Applied social research methods*. Sage.

David Katamba, PhD, is an Associate Professor of Corporate Sustainability and Responsibility. He is an expert evaluator with Economic and Social Research Council (ESRC), a part of UK Research and Innovation (UKRI). He initiated and led the consultative process that established the United Nations (UN) Global Compact Network in Uganda, which is currently hosted by Federation of Uganda Employers (FUE). Dr Katamba is a World Bank Institute trained Corporate Sustainability and Responsibility (CSR) professional with over 16 years' experience in Higher Education quality management systems, sustainable development aspects including in youths and women entrepreneurship, Education, and Business. Currently (Jan 2023–June 2026), He is coordinating a € 1,000,000 EU Erasmus+ funded project, "Strengthening Capacity for ICT Usage and Policy Reforms for Relevant and Quality Masters Research Process Management in Uganda's Higher Education Institutions (ICT-4MRPQ, project No. 101083105). Dr Katamba is a certified CSR Consultant/Advisor and trainer for International Business Leaders Forum (IBLF), and Aga Khan Development Network (AKDN). He has won and led implementation of several international research grants including from €300,000 Netherlands' NWO WOTRO to implement AGRI-QUEST project (Project No. W 08.270.317). Dr Katamba was also part of the team that won €801,000 from EU Erasmus+ [call, EAC/A03/2016, research project No: 574218-EPP-1-2016-1-NO-EPPKA2-CBHE-JP to implement CapSEM project (2016–2019). He has supported several HEIs in and outside Uganda to strengthen their academic quality processes through coaching services, matchmaking, financial resources mobilization, and capacity building. Dr Katamba has been is a peer reviewer of proposals, grant applications, publications for several academic journals, and projects for several development organizations including for European Commission's EACEA. Additionally, he has acted as mentor, coach, and match makers for 'Start Your Business (SYB)' scheme and competitions by World Bank and Private Sector Foundation Uganda (PSFU) as well as other SME and trade and investment initiatives. Dr Katamba has delivered services and implemented projects in Netherlands, Belgium, Canada, Turkey, Italy, and East Africa. Lastly, he has helped to start the United Nations (UN) Global Compact Network in Uganda.

Tom Tamale holds a Master of Business Administration (Marketing) and a Bachelor of Science in Marketing, both from Makerere University. He is currently an Assistant Lecturer in the Department of Marketing and Media Studies at Makerere University Business School (MUBS), where he supports academic instruction and contributes to research and curriculum development. He also serves as a trainer under the MUBS Skills Development Programme and is part of the project team for the ICT-4MRPQ EU-funded Project—Strengthening Capacity for ICT Usage and Policy Reforms for Relevant and Quality Masters Research Process Management in Uganda's Higher Education Institutions (HEIs). He has over 15 years marketing experiencing working with various advertising agencies in Uganda. His academic and research interests lie in sustainable marketing, consumer behaviour, and digital marketing. Tom is passionate about bridging theory and practice to support the development of relevant, data-driven marketing strategies in emerging economies for sustainable entrepreneurship.

Maureen Basuuta is a Lecturer in the Department of Economics at Makerere University Business School (MUBS). Her Research interests are in poverty, informal sector and the energy sector particularly energy poverty and the involvement of women in the oil and gas industry. She has worked on different research projects such as the Makerere University Research and Innovations (RIF) funded projects and the NORAD—NORHED Research Grants for Capacity Building in Education and Research for Economic Governance in Uganda. She has presented several papers at different conferences and published in sustainable accounting. Maureen is also a consultant and has consulted for different organisations such as Joint Medical Store, UN Women, and the Law Development Centre in Uganda. Maureen is also a trainer for several capacity building training programmes.

Veronica Mukyala, PhD, hold a PhD in Business Management (Finance) from Moi University, Kenya, and currently serve as a Senior Lecturer at Makerere University Business School in Jinja, where she was also the Director from June 2021 to January 2025. Her responsibilities included overseeing academic and administrative matters. She is pursuing certification as a professional accountant and am a member of the Institute of Corporate Governance of Uganda, promoting principles of accountability and transparency. As a trainer in finance and leadership, she has contributed to various institutions and served on several boards, including the Mandela National Stadium Board. She has published articles on corporate governance, Reporting, and sustainability, and reviewed master's thesis at Makerere University Business School.

Chapter 9
Covid-19 and Lockdown Effects on Stock Returns

Samuel Salia, Amin Karimu, Yahaya Alhassan, and Meney Orlyne Ahochi

9.1 Introduction

The COVID-19 pandemic has reignited the debate about firm investment in cutting-edge emerging technologies (i.e. artificial intelligence (AI)) (Hogarty et al., 2019; Kakatkar et al., 2020) in order to accelerate changes in the structure of product markets. Since the outbreak, the majority of services and products have been moved online, with IT firms playing an expanded role that is being used to support the economy and provide healthcare (Faggella, 2020). At the same time, as observed in Baker et al. (2020), the pandemic has exposed the vulnerability of listed firms as government restrictions on commercial activities and voluntary social distancing have increased. This unprecedented health crisis has exerted significant shocks on firms, like the 2008 subprime mortgage lending crisis (Spatt, 2020; Chen & Yeh, 2021; Brem et al., 2020). This suggests there is the need to examine the impact of the COVID-19 health crisis on firm value.

S. Salia
Birmingham City University, Birmingham, UK
e-mail: Samuel.salia@bcu.ac.uk

A. Karimu
University of Cape Town, Cape Town, South Africa
e-mail: Amin.Karimu@uct.ac.za

Y. Alhassan (✉)
University of Sunderland in London, London, UK
e-mail: Yahaya.alhassan@sunderland.ac.uk

M. O. Ahochi
Office for National Statistics, London, UK
e-mail: ahochim@coventry.ac.uk

Y. Alhassan et al. (eds.), *Financial Innovation and Sustainable Enterprise in Developing and Emerging Economies*, Research Series on Responsible Enterprise Ecosystems, https://doi.org/10.1007/978-3-032-04500-3_9

In this study, we revisit a fundamental question in finance—what effect does COVID-19 and the public release of lockdown information into the market environment have on firm share returns in a short window around the lockdown event? In answering this important question, two additional questions emerged. If the lockdown influences firms' value, do firms react differently to the lockdown? What are the channels for the potential heterogeneous effect?

Whereas the evidence (Delcey & Thomas, 2019; Ghazani & Ebrahimi, 2019; Brown, 2020; Niroomand et al., 2020; Clapham et al., 2020; Liu et al., 2021) widely suggests that informational flow improves market efficiency, the literature theorises that where the information in relation to an asset is perceived to be positive, a correlating positive reactionary increase in the price of the asset is realized (Jiao & Yan, 2015). However, where the released information in relation to the asset is perceived to be negative, the demand for the asset is likely to diminish and cause the price to fall (Fama, 1970).

Relying on these theoretical arguments, as a motivation, prior financial studies of COVID-19 tend to focus on three areas. The first group of studies reviews the general sensitivity of stocks, currencies, mutual funds and commodity markets to the pandemic (Corbet et al., 2020; Lahmiri & Bekiros, 2020; Jackwerth, 2020; Pástor & Vorsatz, 2020). The second set of studies draws on a regional and country level analysis to understand the different impacts of the pandemic on macro-economic and micro-economic measures, respectively (Ashraf, 2020; Alber, 2020; Ma et al., 2020; Gormsen & Koijen, 2020).

The third, and closest review at the industry level, has focused on the reaction of 'essential' sectors, such as healthcare, utilities and telecoms, to the pandemic (Aravind & Manojkrishnan, 2020; Reilly, 2020). Findings from the three strands of research have concluded that, in general, there is significant securities market reaction to the Covid-19 health crisis. This evidence is consistent with our intuition that COVID-19, and related lockdowns, will lead to the stock market overreacting to good news and underreacting to bad news. Unfortunately, the extant literature, to the best of our knowledge, has not provided any evidence of the different reactions of the FTSE 100 to COVID-19 and the lockdown, and the channels to explain the potential heterogeneous reaction.

The FTSE-100 index constitutes an integral part of global investment and has reported significant gains since 2011 (Muhammad et al., 2020). However, the index posted the biggest fall by March 2020 as a results of financial markets reaction to the novel coronavirus, making it the worst quarter for the FTSE-100 index for over a decade. To tackle the effects, the London Stock Exchange intervened to limit severity of investor anxiety. These accounts provide a strong case to examine the FTSE-100 reaction within research. Thus, to contribute to this, we utilise COVID-19 and lockdown information to re-examine the reactions of FSTE-100 firms, utilising their industry specifications and easiness to move online.

To estimate the impact of COVID-19, and lockdown effects on FTSE 100 firms, we developed a fixed effect estimation model that is based on a sample of 100 firm-daily observations involving FTSE 100 constituents from Yahoo Finance over the period of April 2019–April 2020. Overall, our findings support the empirical evidence that pandemic events affect financial markets (Corbet et al., 2020; Lahmiri & Bekiros, 2020). First, the evidence from our results holds that the majority of the firms (i.e. by industry) are negatively affected by the lockdown and by extension COVID-19. Secondly, we show that the lockdown period had a significant negative effect on the FTSE 100 firm's stock return. Furthermore, different firms react differently to the lockdown; for example, pharmaceutical firms responded positively to the lockdown, whereas firms in the airline industry responded negatively; therefore, it is suggesting a heterogeneous effect of the lockdown. The findings further reveal that the heterogeneous effect of the lockdown may stem from the type of product and service that is considered essential during the lockdown and in high demand during the period rather than the easiness to move to an online channel.

This study, in the light of these findings, extends previous research in the finance field on three levels. First, it is only one of the few studies that are available that evidence the impact of COVID-19 on firm value. Secondly, by exploring the effects of COVID-19 and lockdown effects on constituents of the FTSE 100's easiness to move online, the literature is enriched with an understanding that the impact of the pandemic is indifferent to firms that find it easy to move online and to those that do not. Rather, it is the type of product and services provided by the firms that is of high demand during the pandemic that drive the firms' value. Thirdly, the study offers an understanding of the impact of the COVID-19 health crisis on firm value, which can be compared to previous events such as the effects of the 2008 subprime mortgage lending financial crisis on same.

The rest of the paper is organised as follows. The next section reviews related literature and presents the theoretical foundation of the study, while Sects. 9.3 and 9.4 present the methodology and results of the research. Section 9.5 concludes the study by presenting the summary from the findings, limitations of the study and suggestions for future research.

9.2 Related Literature

To achieve the goal of this study, we draw on three main literatures. The first critically evaluates financial market reaction to pandemics. The second reviews corporate investment in advanced technologies, notably Artificial Intelligence (AI), as a strategy to innovate and facilitate business continuity in a situation of severe pandemic disruption. The third decomposes through the lens of financial market response, the connectivity between informational flow (in the form of a Covid-19 announcement) and returns of stocks to ground the hypothesis of the study.

9.2.1 Financial Market Reaction to Pandemics

The evidence as examined (Ichev & Marinč, 2018; Hamel et al., 2019; Schell et al., 2020) has documented the reactions of global financial markets to five epidemics that were declared a Public Health Emergency of International Concern (PHEIC): The Swine Influenza (H1N1), the Poliomyelitis, the Zika virus, the Ebola virus and COVID-19. COVID-19 is highlighted as the pandemic with the strongest impact on global markets. Drawing on these prior studies, we group market reactions to the COVID-19 pandemic into three important literatures.

The first reviews the general sensitivity of stocks, currencies and commodity markets to the pandemic (Corbet et al., 2020; Lahmiri & Bekiros, 2020). This strand of literature has shown mixed results. The findings show a negative reaction of stock returns, in general, with a more considerable impact on the firms with Chinese exposure. Digital assets such as cryptocurrency are also found to be riskier during a pandemic situation. Interestingly, a stronger relationship is reported between the commodities and the stock market in their reactions to COVID-19.

The second set of studies draws on a regional and country level analysis to understand the different impacts of the pandemic on macro-economic and micro-economic measures, respectively (Ashraf, 2020; Alber, 2020; Ma et al., 2020; Okorie & Lin, 2020; Baldwin et al., 2020; Zaremba et al., 2020; Verikios, 2020). A decomposing of the literature shows a negative impact of the pandemics on GDP as well as a contagion effect between regional economies and sectors. A significant fractal contagion of COVID-19 on the stock markets and volatility is also found across the countries under review. However, the reaction and stock volatility tend to be less significant over time. Moreover, the development of a risk aversion trend is found in the stock market as the anxiety about the pandemic increases. The third, and is the closest review at the industry level, has focused on the reaction of 'essential' sectors to the pandemic (Aravind & Manojkrishnan, 2020; Reilly, 2020; Verikios, 2020). The review shows that 'essential' sectors such as Utilities, Health care and Telecom mainly benefit from the crisis.

The effects of covid-19 bring evidence that suggests a connectedness of financial markets, which is an idea shared by Ichev and Marinč (2018). Whilst these studies decompose key market sentiments in relation to COVID-19, the specific reaction of online and/or offline firms is yet to be fully explored. This is a serious omission because both the anecdotal and literature evidence (Faggella, 2020) suggests that businesses have leveraged technology to gain traction following the pandemic.

9.2.2 Artificial Intelligence in Business Innovation

According to the Financial Stability Board (2017), AI is the theory and development of computer systems to perform tasks that traditionally have required human intelligence. In parallel, our literature mainly centres on benefits and investments in the computational tools that are needed to perform a task that traditionally has required human intelligence. This is a particularly important exercise because the COVID-19 pandemic has shown that the trend may be accelerated for technology-driven changes in the structure of many product markets. To this end, the reviewed evidence shows that the perceived benefit of AI appears to explain the rising investment in the sector.

Firstly, the sector data on AI shows that companies around the world have invested between US$26 billion to US$39 billion in artificial intelligence in 2016, and that is more than three times as much as in 2013 (Mickinsey Global Institute, 2017). It is interesting to note that there is a growing trend of firm investment to enhance business operations and productivity levels, while relieving the workforce from routine tasks and activities (Cockburn et al., 2018). However, AI is at a relatively nascent and evolving phase; therefore, like any R&D project, the returns on such an investment should be viewed as a long-term prospect (e.g. see Liu & Shong, 2018; Lu et al., 2018 for discussions that propose an increase in R&D investment as the key to the development of the AI innovation system).

Secondly, the view that AI improves firm's efficiency, reduces operational cost and increases profitability is grounded in evidence (see for example; Hsu et al., 2014; Dirican, 2015; Makridakis, 2017). Artificial intelligence can do both administrative and operational tasks that consume much of the employees' time faster, better, and at a lower cost. For example, the Associate Press expanded its quarterly earnings when reporting from approximately 300 stories to 4400 with the help of AI-powered software robots (Kolbjørnsrud et al., 2016). Intuitively, this innovation is freeing up journalists to conduct more investigative and interpretive reporting. In addition, Trippi and Turban (1993) have shown strong evidence of the rapid adoption of AI for trading in securities markets, forecasting the economy and analysing credit risk (see Cortes et al., 2018; Lee et al., 2018 for insight into the current state of AI and its impact on productivity growth).

9.2.3 *Developing Hypotheses*

Drawing on the evidence from prior research (Fama, 1970; Gârleanu & Pedersen, 2018; Delcey & Thomas, 2019), we argue that financial market response can be understood through analysing impact of information on market indices (Muhammad et al., 2020); which accounts for our intuition that the COVID-19 and lockdown impacts the FTSE-100 index. Accordingly, prior studies (Tripathi & Pandey, 2021; Yarovaya et al., 2022), as examined, showed that financial markets are impacted by information (Hamel et al., 2019; Ferreira et al., 2019), and that has implications for listed firms and how they respond to market information (i.e. COVID-19 and lockdown). Like the financial crisis in 2008, where indices had plummeted, and listed firms implemented new financing strategies, technological strategies and significant on-line presences are seen amongst firms in 2020 due to the COVID-19 crisis, to keep their operations afloat (Castelblanco et al., 2022). It is within this context that our interest to test the impact of COVID-19 on stock returns finds validity. Thus, in this section, we develop testable hypotheses.

We posit that COVID-19 and the lockdown have contributed significantly to stock reactions of FTSE-100 firms. Announcements as a determinant of stock returns is espoused by Fama (1970). Informational flow, for example in the form of the lockdown, accounts for reaction of companies on the FTSE-100, as the market processes and absorbs the news (Frank & Sanati, 2018). Practically, for any relevant announcement, the market adapts to the investor reaction and sentiment. Therefore, in the context of this study, where a COVID-19 announcement in relation to an asset is perceived to be positive, a correlating positive reactionary increase in the price of the asset is realised. Contrary, when the announcement in relation to the asset is perceived to be negative, the demand for the asset is likely to reduce and the investors holding it are likely to sell at a low price. In line with this, we formulate our hypothesis as follows:

H1: COVID-19 and lockdown have a significant negative effect on the FTSE 100 firms' return.

H2: COVID-19 and lockdown have a significant positive effect on related essential firms.

The lockdown and social distance protocols limits human interactions by requiring people to either stay at home or keep a distance. In our view, the global response (lockdowns and social distancing restrictions) to contain the pandemic has meant that the businesses that have required significant human involvement to operate will be constrained. These categories of business are often unable to deliver their products and services online, and, therefore, this makes them unattractive under lockdown and social distancing restrictions. To the contrary, there is business continuity for those firms that can easily go online to deliver their products and services; hence, making them attractive during the restrictions. Thus, any significant reaction to a COVID-19 related event will be shown by the presence of significant abnormal returns for online or offline firms, depending on whether it is an event that relaxes the restrictions or increases them. In line with this, we formulate our third hypothesis as follows: Based on the literature, the following hypothesis is proposed:

H3: COVID-19 lockdown has a significant positive effect on firms that find it easy to move online.

9.3 Data and Methodology

The final sample consists of merged data from two data sources. The first set of data includes all the daily returns of stocks for the FTSE 100 listed companies captured from Yahoo Finance[1] for the period April 2019 to April 2020. Information from this database has been extensively used to examine the effects of investor attention at announcements (Lawrence et al., 2016; Topcu & Gulal, 2020). The second set of data captures information about the FSTE 100 listed companies total market capitalisation, industry and products as reported by the London Stock Exchange.[2] Furthermore, a lockdown variable (L) is created by identifying the period in the UK when lockdown came into effect. The lockdown variable takes a value 1 for all periods when the lockdown was operational in the UK and zero for non-lockdown periods. Another variable, Black Monday variable (BM) is also created to account for the 2020 stock market crash which began on Monday, March 9, when the FSTE 100 lost 7.7% due to investors panic about the likely effects of the Covid pandemic. The BM variable is also a dummy variable that takes the value 1 for March 9 and zero any other day.

Another key variable of interest is how easy a firm could move online. This variable is not in the dataset and must be created using information on the firm's product and structure of operation to determine the easiness to move online. The easy to move online variable (ES_t) is created mainly based on the products and operations of an online transaction and delivery system during the lockdown period by the companies in our dataset. Companies that have that are classified as easy to move online and those without that are classified as not able to move easily online.

This study relied on panel data regression technique. In order to address the objectives of the study, consistent with Amiram et al. (2016), we resort to the fixed effect estimation approach due to the fact that firm specific effects are by intuition likely to be correlated with some key explanatory factors on firms' value during a COVID-19 pandemic, such as the type of goods and services they produce. More importantly, there are key factors that are unobservable such as policy and taste and preference for certain products by customers that may influence a firm's value. Therefore, the fixed effect estimation can circumvent these quite well; hence, the choice of this approach as the estimation technique for the study.

The specific form of the econometric models that are utilised to help achieve the research objectives can be presented in Eqs. 9.1 to 9.3 as follows.

$$S_{it} = \beta_0 + \beta_1 L_{it} + \beta_2 BM_{it} + D_i + \varepsilon_{it} \tag{9.1}$$

---

[1] The data that support the findings of this study are openly available in [Yahoo Finance] at [https://uk.finance.yahoo.com/quote/%5EFTSE/]

[2] The data that support the findings of this study are openly available in [London Stock Exchange] at [https://www.londonstockexchange.com/indices/ftse-100]

where S_{it} denotes the stock returns of firm i at time t, L_{it} and BM_{it} are lockdown and black Monday event variables. D_i is a firm fixed effect used to capture firm specific unobservable, and the random error term is represented by ε_{it}. The model specified in Eq. (9.1) is applied to the data to address the question on the potential effect of lockdown and black Monday on firms' return (specifically FSTE 100 listed companies).

The second objective of the study is achieved via the specification that we express as

$$S_{it} = \alpha_0 + \delta \boldsymbol{P}_{it}^{'} + \gamma COVID_t + \theta \boldsymbol{P}_{it}^{'} * COVID_t + D_i + \dot{\varepsilon}_{it} \tag{9.2}$$

where $COVID_t$ denotes the period where COVID-19 cases have been reported in the UK, $\boldsymbol{P}_{it}^{'}$ is the vector of the product classification of firms that constitutes the FTSE-100 and $\boldsymbol{P}_{it}^{'} * COVID_t$ is the interaction between the vector of production classification and the COVID-19 period. S_{it}, D_i are the same as explained in Eq. (9.1), and $\dot{\varepsilon}_{it}$ is the random error term.

Furthermore, the third objective is analysed via the specification presented in Eq. (9.3), which is expressed as

$$S_{it} = \sigma_0 + \sigma_1 ES_t + \sigma_2 LD_t + \sigma_3 ES_t * LD_t + D_i + \ddot{\varepsilon}_{it} \tag{9.3}$$

In Eq. (9.3), the variable ES_t denotes an easy way to move online, and LD_t denotes the lockdown period. The dummy for easy to move online is created based on the firm's operational structure and products, where the reference dummy is difficult to move online. The interaction term is represented by $ES_t * LD_t$, where S_{it}, D_i are the same as explained in Eq. (9.1). The random error term is represented by ε_{it}.

9.4 Results and Discussions

The analysis follows three steps. First, we analyse and present the overall effect of pre-lockdown, lockdown and black Friday events on the FTSE 100 constituents, next we analyse the effect of the lockdown due to COVID-19 on the value via the stock returns of the individual category of firms based on their products and services that constitute the FTSE 100 index, and finally we analyse and present a classification into how easy or difficult a firm is able to go online during the lockdown period in order to explain the potential heterogeneous responses of firms to the lockdown.

9.4.1 The Effect of Lockdown and Black Friday on FTSE 100

To appreciate the role of the lockdown on the overall FTSE 100, we utilised a fixed effect model where we created two dummies consistent with three key events: a period before the lockdown-the reference event for the lockdown period, the lockdown period and black Monday 2020.[3] The pre-lockdown period covers the days and months before the 23 March 2020 lockdown, whereas the lockdown dummy covers the period of the lockdown, which starts from 23 March 2020 till the end of the data period (17 April 2020). The event of the 9 March that saw a significant fall in global stock returns including the FTSE 100, due in part by the misunderstanding between Russia and Saudi Arabia that led to a plunge in oil prices dubbed "black Monday", is captured with the black Monday dummy, which takes a value of 1 on the 9th of March and 0 for any other day over the sampled period.

The results from the estimated fixed effect model on the key variables (the lockdown and black Monday 2020) are presented in Fig. 9.1. The results in Fig. 9.1 should be interpreted as follows. On the x-axis we have the estimated coefficient values, and for the y-axis variables, we are interested in reporting their respective

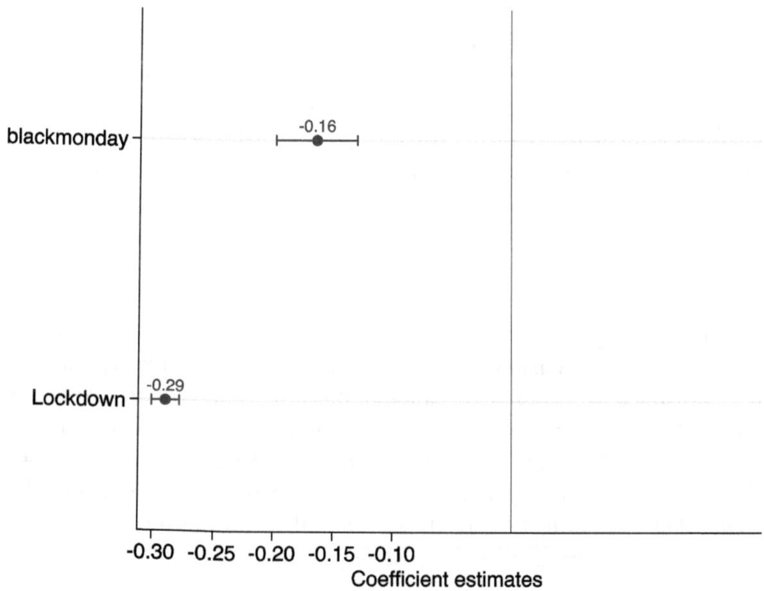

Fig. 9.1 Estimated effect of lockdown on FTSE-100 Stock returns. Note: Robust standard errors are used to correct for both potential heteroskedasticity and autocorrelation

[3] The 2020 stock market crash which began on Monday, March 9 (which some label as Black Monday 2020) occurred because investors were worried about the impact of the Covid-19 pandemic. The FTSE 100 lost 7.7%, suffering its worst drop since the 2008 financial crisis. It was also the Dow Jones worst single-day point drop (i.e. 2000 points) in U.S. market history. https://en.wikipedia.org/wiki/2020_stock_market_crash

estimates. Further, the estimated coefficient value for each variable is plotted as a point with the value written-on top of the point and a horizontal line capped at both ends, which denotes a 95% confidence interval for each point estimate. Note that the confidence intervals that do not cross both the positive and negative values indicate the statistical significance of the point estimate.

Similar to Ashraf (2020) and Alber (2020), we found that COVID-19, in general, has a significant negative effect via the lockdown on FTSE 100 stock returns relative to the pre-lockdown period and confirms our hypothesis ***H1***. The significant negative effect of the lockdown may be due to the case that some activities of some of the firms cannot easily be moved online or can be effectively worked from home. This, among other things, suggests that some of these firms may have to cut back on production, which has repercussions on the firm's value and ultimately on the stock returns. In addition, some of the firms' output may serve the international market more than the local market, such as oil and gas firms, and international airlines. Such firms may not be able to reach their customers easily via the traditional means during the lockdown period, and if they cannot easily move online, such as the airline industry, oil and gas industry, the lack of demand will cause a reduction in output and on the value of the firm as observed by Sharif et al. (2020).

Consistent with intuition and by implication the negative lockdown effect, one can conclude that, in relative terms, the pre-lockdown period has a significant positive effect on the FTSE 100 stock returns. The pre-lockdown period was characterised with the usual economic activities, whereby most countries in the world were not feeling the seriousness and the danger of COVID-19. As a result, many countries were not implementing the COVID-19 policies that are restrictive to economic activities in terms of lockdowns and social distancing protocols. These assumptions are comparatively similar to previous studies (Ma et al., 2020; Okorie & Lin, 2020; Baldwin et al., 2020; Verikios, 2020) that suggested economic laxity accounted for the negative effects.

Furthermore, the estimated black Monday effect is also significant and negative but with smaller magnitude relative to the lockdown effect. This, as indicated earlier, was caused by the tension between Russia and Saudi Arabia regarding oil output, which resulted in a significant (about a third of its biggest drop since the Gulf War) fall in the price of international oil benchmark Brent. The stock market reacted significantly to the fall in the oil price in addition to the consideration of the potential effect of the COVID-19 pandemic, which is consistent with Sharif et al. (2020) who found that parallel to COVID-19 effects, oil is leading the US market at low and high frequencies throughout the observation period.

9.4.2 Lockdown Effect on Different Categories of Firms on the FTSE 100

The previous analysis does not show how the different categories of firms that constitutes the FTSE 100 index reacted to the lockdown, and this sub-section is focused in providing such an analysis. Figure 9.2 presents the estimates of the lockdown effect on the different categories of firms in the FTSE 100 and its interpretation, as was the case for Fig. 9.1.

Out of the 16 different categories, only 4 have positive coefficient estimates, suggesting that most of the categories of firms are negatively affected by the lockdown and, by extension, COVID-19. Note that all the categories with coefficient estimates that fall within the negative range are all significant at the 5% significance level as suggested by the 95% confidence interval.

The categories that are positively impacted by the lockdown are firms that are providing catering services, hotels and motels and pharmaceuticals and manufacturing, which confirms our hypothesis ***H2***. These results are not at variance with Aravind and Manojkrishnan (2020), Reilly (2020), and Verikios (2020) who found that 'essential' sectors, such as Utilities and Health care, mainly benefited from the crisis. During the lockdown, people continued to order food to reduce the burden of cooking, or to avoid shopping at the supermarkets for food items to come home and cook. As a substitute, they relied on catering services, which, among other things, suggest the positive impact of the lockdown.

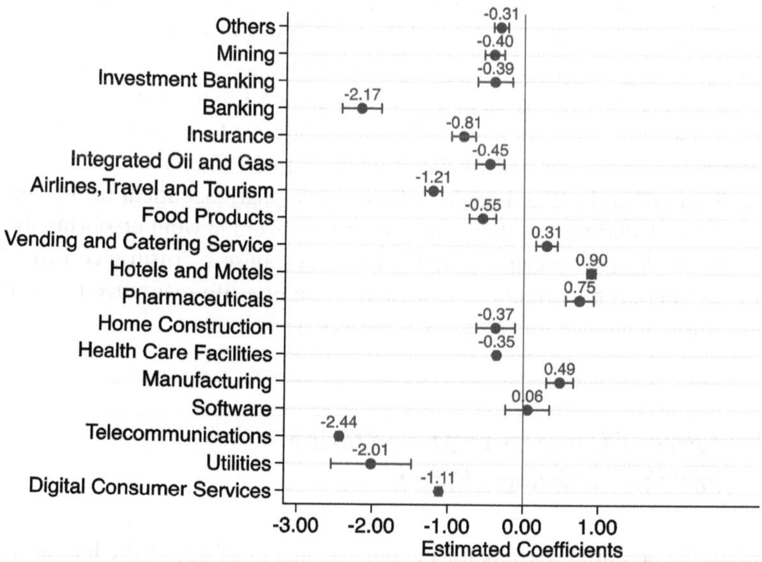

Fig. 9.2 Estimated effect of lockdown on different categories of firms in the FTSE-100. Note: Robust standard errors are used to correct for both potential heteroscedasticity and autocorrelation

Similarly, the demand for health products, such as vitamin C and other medicines that would reduce the risk of catching COVID-19, increased the value of these firms, which is captured in the stock returns. Therefore, the lockdown due to the COVID-19 pandemic rather impacted the pharmaceutical firms positively due to the essential products and role that the sector plays in the fight against COVID-19.

In the case of manufacturing, the positive effect may be due to those firms that produce the essential products required to fight COVID-19, such as ventilators, PPEs and products that will make it easy for people to adjust to the lockdown such as toiletries. Whereas, in the case of hotels and motels, the positive impact may be driven by the directive of the 14 days of quarantine that is required for the international travellers that are caught out by COVID-19. The estimated COVID-19 effect on software firms, though positive, is statistically insignificant at the 5% level.

Conversely, firm categories, such as banking, oil and gas, airlines and travel and tours, telecommunications, and utilities, among others, are negatively affected by the lockdown. It is, however, not clear why these categories of firms within the FTSE 100 were negatively impacted by the lockdown. A possible hypothesis to explain this may be that firms that cannot easily go online may find it difficult to grow during the lockdown and are more likely to be negatively impacted by the lockdown due to COVID-19, or that the products and services produced by these firms are not in high demand during lockdown, and this we will explore further under the sub-section, "Level of easiness to move online and the lockdown effect".

Furthermore, there is the fact that firms within the same category of classification may have unique differences that will cause a heterogeneous response to the lockdown. For instance, you may have two different banks that are responding differently to the lockdown due to different investment strategies in technology for the banks' operations. To reduce the masking of the effects from this categorisation, we estimate the model without the categorisations and reported firm specific effects for the lockdown period. This result is reported in table **A1** in the appendix. In general, most retail banking firms are negatively affected by the lockdown. Similarly, most airlines are negatively affected by the lockdown. Interestingly and consistent with the results based on the classification of the firms, pharmaceutical firms tend to do well during the lockdown, as their stock returns on average went up during the lockdown. The result also reveals a heterogeneous response of insurance firms to the lockdown. Whereas the effect of the lockdown on non-life insurance is positive, in the case of life insurance, the effect is generally negative.

9.4.3 Level of Easiness to Move Online and the Lockdown Effect

To explain the potential reasons for the heterogeneous effect of the lockdown, and, thus, why some of the firms experience a positive lockdown effect on their stock returns (e.g., pharmaceuticals) and others also experience a negative effect of the lockdown on their stock returns (e.g., banking, oil, and gas firms), we estimated a fixed effect model with the results reported in Table 9.1. We identify and classify the FTSE 100 firms into easy to move online and difficult to move online based on the available information on the firms' structure and products as discussed in the data section. In the analysis, we consider the difficult group as the reference group.

Results presented in Table 9.1 reveal that although the effect of the lockdown on firms that can easily move online is positive and statistically significant, it is, however, not conditional on the lockdown. Since, the estimate for the interaction term between the easy to move online dummy and the lockdown dummy is not significant at any of the conventional significance levels. This is suggesting that this may not be the reason for the heterogeneous effect of the lockdown findings from the second objective of the study.

Therefore, the tests for hypothesis ***H3,*** which assume the presence of significant abnormal returns around the lockdown window, are clearly rejected. These results are at variance with Faggella's (2020) suggestion that for businesses to ensure continuity and help overcome pandemic disruption, they have to imbed an AI related infrastructure into their products and services lines.

We also, as a further check on the results reported in Table 9.1, estimated a second model, where easy to move online is considered as the reference case, where a dummy is assigned 1 if the structure and product of the firm is such that it is difficult to move online and 0 if it is easy to move online. Results from this exercise are reported in Table 9.2. Findings suggest that firms that find it difficult to move online tend to experience a reduction in returns. This is, however, not conditional on the lockdown period since the interaction term is not significant at any of the conventional significance levels.

Taking the two findings together suggests that the level of easiness or difficulty in moving online does not appear to be the reason why some of the firms experience

Table 9.1 Fixed effect estimates on the effect of lockdown on how easy it is to go online

Variables	Stock return
	lnReturn
Easy to move online	0.363***
	(13.44)
Lockdown period	−0.309**
	(−2.29)
Easy to move online*Lockdown period	0.069
	(1.01)
Constant	7.629***
	(86.19)
R-square	0.291
F-statistic	741
Number of observations	26,743

t statistics in parentheses, * $p < 0.10$, ** $p < 0.05$, *** $p < 0.01$. Robust standard error is used to correct for both potential heteroskedasticity and autocorrelation

Table 9.2 Fixed effect estimates on the effect of lockdown on how difficult it is to go online

Variables	Stock return
	lnReturn
Difficult to move online	0.345***
	(20.17)
Lockdown period	−0.269*
	(−1.96)
Difficult to move online*Lockdown period	−0.063
	(−1.29)
Constant	7.627***
	(86.50)
R-square	0.296
F-statistic	725
Number of observations	26,743

t statistics in parentheses, * $p < 0.10$, ** $p < 0.05$, *** $p < 0.01$. Robust standard error is used to correct for both potential heteroskedasticity and autocorrelation

a positive effect of the lockdown relative to others that are experiencing a negative effect of the lockdown on their respective stock returns. However, a potential reason for this variance with prior literature in the heterogeneous effect of the lockdown is likely to be due to the nature of the product produced, and, thus, whether the products are essentials and whether they are connected to health, such as the firms that produce drugs, and the industries that manufacture the essentials that are required for survival.

9.5 Conclusion

The aim of this study was to explore the impact of COVID-19 in terms of the lockdown on the stock returns of the FTSE 100 firms in the UK and examine if the potential heterogeneous responses of the various firms that constitute the FTSE 100 can be explained by how easy their activities can move online or the nature of the product and services provided or both. Using a fixed effect approach for a panel of 100 firms that constitutes the FTSE, we explore these pertinent aspects of COVID-19 and the firms' value via the stock return reaction to the pandemic and the associated lockdown policy. This will provide evidence on the impact of COVID-19 health crisis on firm value to compare with previous crisis such as the effects of the 2008 subprime mortgage lending financial crisis on same.

Several interesting findings emerge. First, on average, the lockdown has a negative effect on the FTSE 100 stock returns, and, furthermore, black Monday 2020, which occurred on 9th March 2020, also has, on average, a negative effect on the FTSE 100 stock returns. Second, the lockdown effect is heterogeneous, with some firm's value increasing during the lockdown (pharmaceutical firms, firms providing catering services, some utilities firms such as those providing water, some manufacturing firms), whereas others experience a fall in their value (e.g., oil and gas firms, retail banking firms, life insurance firms, airlines). Thirdly, an easiness to move firms' activities online does not appear to be the reason why some firms experience an increase in value during the lockdown, but rather the nature of the product or service provided is the reason, tentatively.

These results, as a whole, mean that a firm's flexibility in adopting to or changing situations with regard to an efficient product and services delivery in response to changing demand is the key for any firm to survive unusual global changes, in general, and, in particular, the effects of pandemics. As much as the ease to move online may be a part of the process of being flexible and adapting to global economic and social changes, it may not be very useful in promoting the firms' value if the final product or service that is moved online is not consistent with what is in demand and is driven by the global economic and social change.

Conflict of Interest Statement The Authors declare that there is no conflict of interest.

References

Alber, N. (2020). The effect of coronavirus spread on stock markets: The case of the worst 6 countries. *SSRN Electronic Journal*. https://doi.org/10.2139/ssrn.3578080

Amiram, D., Owens, E., & Rozenbaum, O. (2016). Do information releases increase or decrease information asymmetry? New evidence from analyst forecast announcements. *Journal of Accounting and Economics, 62*(1), 121–138. https://doi.org/10.1016/j.jacceco.2016.06.001

Aravind, M., & Manojkrishnan, C. G. (2020). COVID 19: Effect on leading pharmaceutical stocks listed with NSE. *International Journal of Research in Pharmaceutical Sciences, 11*(Special Issue 1), 31–36. https://doi.org/10.26452/ijrps.v11iSPL1.2014

Ashraf, B. N. (2020). Stock markets' reaction to COVID-19: Cases or fatalities? *Research in International Business and Finance, 54*, 101249. https://doi.org/10.1016/j.ribaf.2020.101249

Baker, S. R., Bloom, N., Davis, S. J., Kost, K., Sammon, M., & Viratyosin, T. (2020). The unprecedented stock market reaction to COVID-19. *The Review of Asset Pricing Studies*. https://doi.org/10.1093/rapstu/raaa008

Baldwin, R., Weder, B., & Mauro, D. (2020). *What the stock market tells us about the consequences of COVID-19. Mitigating the COVID economic crisis: Act fast and do whatever it takes*. Retrieved from www.cepr.org

Brem, A., Nylund, P., & Viardot, E. (2020). The impact of the 2008 financial crisis on innovation: A dominant design perspective. *Journal of Business Research, 110*, 360–369.

Brown, S. J. (2020). The efficient market hypothesis, the financial analysts journal, and the professional status of investment management. *Financial Analysts Journal, 76*(2), 5–14. https://doi.org/10.1080/0015198X.2020.1734375

Castelblanco, G., Guevara, J., & Salazar, J. (2022). Remedies to the PPP crisis in the COVID-19 pandemic: Lessons from the 2008 global financial crisis. *Journal of Management in Engineering, 38*(3), 04022017.

Chen, H. C., & Yeh, C. W. (2021). Global financial crisis and COVID-19: Industrial reactions. *Finance Research Letters*, 101940.

Clapham, B., Haferkorn, M., & Zimmermann, K. (2020). Does speed matter? The role of high-frequency trading for order book resiliency. *Journal of Financial Research, 43*(4), 933–964.

Cockburn, I., Henderson, R., & Stern, S. (2018). *The impact of artificial intelligence on innovation*. https://doi.org/10.3386/w24449

Corbet, S., Larkin, C., & Lucey, B. (2020). The contagion effects of the COVID-19 pandemic: Evidence from gold and cryptocurrencies. *Finance Research Letters, 35*, 101554. https://doi.org/10.1016/j.frl.2020.101554

Cortes, D. G., Cortes Jofre, A. J., & Martin, L. S. (2018). Artificial intelligence based method for portfolio selection. *2018 Congreso Internacional de Innovacion y Tendencias En Ingenieria, CONIITI 2018 - Proceedings*. https://doi.org/10.1109/CONIITI.2018.8587104

D, C. (2015). The impacts of robotics, artificial intelligence on business and economics. *Procedia - Social and Behavioral Sciences, 195*, 564–573. https://doi.org/10.1016/J.SBSPRO.2015.06.134

Delcey, T., & Thomas. (2019). Samuelson vs Fama on the efficient market hypothesis: The point of view of expertise. *http://Journals.Openedition.Org/Oeconomia*, (9–1), 37–58. https://doi.org/10.4000/OECONOMIA.5300

Faggella, D. (2020). *Overcoming pandemic disruption – The AI for business continuity action*. Retrieved June 28, 2020, from https://emerj.com/report/ai-business-continuity/

Fama, E. F. (1970). Efficient capital markets: A review of theory and empirical work. *The Journal of Finance, 25*(2), 383. https://doi.org/10.2307/2325486

Ferreira, S. J., Mohlamme, S., Van Vuuren, G., & Dickason (Koekemoer), Z. (2019). The influence of corporate financial events on selected JSE-listed companies. *Cogent Economics and Finance, 7*(1), 1597665. https://doi.org/10.1080/23322039.2019.1597665

Financial Stability Board. (2017). *Artificial intelligence and machine learning in financial services: Market developments and financial stability implications*.

Frank, M. Z., & Sanati, A. (2018). How does the stock market absorb shocks? *Journal of Financial Economics, 129*(1), 136–153. https://doi.org/10.1016/j.jfineco.2018.04.002

Gârleanu, N., & Pedersen, L. H. (2018). Efficiently inefficient markets for assets and asset management. *The Journal of Finance, 73*(4), 1663–1712. https://doi.org/10.1111/jofi.12696

Ghazani, M. M., & Ebrahimi, S. B. (2019). Testing the adaptive market hypothesis as an evolutionary perspective on market efficiency: Evidence from the crude oil prices. *Finance Research Letters, 30*, 60–68. https://doi.org/10.1016/j.frl.2019.03.032

Gormsen, N. J., & Koijen, R. S. J. (2020). Coronavirus: Impact on stock prices and growth expectations. *The Review of Asset Pricing Studies*. https://doi.org/10.1093/rapstu/raaa013

Hamel, K., Tong, B., & Hofer, M. (2019). *Poverty in Africa is now falling—but not fast enough*. Retrieved October 26, 2019, from https://www.brookings.edu/blog/future-development/2019/03/28/poverty-in-africa-is-now-falling-but-not-fast-enough/

Hogarty, D. T., Mackey, D. A., & Hewitt, A. W. (2019). Current state and future prospects of artificial intelligence in ophthalmology: A review. *Clinical & Experimental Ophthalmology, 47*(1), 128–139. https://doi.org/10.1111/ceo.13381

Hsu, P.-H., Tian, X., & Xu, Y. (2014). Financial development and innovation: Cross-country evidence. *Journal of Financial Economics, 112*(1), 116–135. https://doi.org/10.1016/J.JFINECO.2013.12.002

Ichev, R., & Marinč, M. (2018). Stock prices and geographic proximity of information: Evidence from the Ebola outbreak. *International Review of Financial Analysis, 56*, 153–166. https://doi.org/10.1016/j.irfa.2017.12.004

Jackwerth, J. (2020). What do index options teach us about COVID-19? *The Review of Asset Pricing Studies*. https://doi.org/10.1093/rapstu/raaa012

Jiao, J., & Yan, A. (2015). Convertible securities and heterogeneity of investor beliefs. *Journal of Financial Research, 38*(2), 255–282.

Kakatkar, C., Bilgram, V., & Füller, J. (2020). Innovation analytics: Leveraging artificial intelligence in the innovation process. *Business Horizons, 63*(2), 171–181. https://doi.org/10.1016/j.bushor.2019.10.006

Kolbjørnsrud, V., Amico, R., & Thomas, R. J. (2016). How artificial intelligence will redefine management. *Harvard Business Review, 2.*

Lahmiri, S., & Bekiros, S. (2020). The impact of COVID-19 pandemic upon stability and sequential irregularity of equity and cryptocurrency markets. *Chaos, Solitons and Fractals, 138*, 109936. https://doi.org/10.1016/j.chaos.2020.109936

Lawrence, A., Ryans, J. P., Sun, E., & Laptev, N. (2016). Yahoo finance search and earnings announcements. *SSRN Electronic Journal*. https://doi.org/10.2139/ssrn.2804353

Lee, J., Davari, H., Singh, J., & Pandhare, V. (2018). Industrial artificial intelligence for industry 4.0-based manufacturing systems. *Manufacturing Letters, 18*, 20–23. https://doi.org/10.1016/j.mfglet.2018.09.002

Liu, L., & Shong, Y. C. (2018). Study on innovation performance of big data and artificial intelligence listed companies. *ACM International Conference Proceeding Series*, 57–62. https://doi.org/10.1145/3305275.3305287

Liu, Y., Qiu, B., & Wang, T. (2021). Debt rollover risk, credit default swap spread and stock returns: Evidence from the COVID-19 crisis. *Journal of Financial Stability*, 100855.

Lu, Y., Meng, Q., & Cai, Y. (2018). Research on the relationship between R&D investment and corporate value of "Unicorn" companies: Based on the financial flexibility of artificial intelligence company data. *Open Journal of Business and Management, 06*(04), 953–962. https://doi.org/10.4236/ojbm.2018.64070

Ma, C., Zhou, S., Rogers, J., Ericsson, N., Gao, H., Gornemann, N., Wright, J. et al (2020). Modern pandemics: Recession and recovery modern pandemics: Recession and recovery *. In *SARS*. Retrieved from https://www.researchgate.net/publication/340332593

Makridakis, S. (2017). The forthcoming Artificial Intelligence (AI) revolution: Its impact on society and firms. *Futures, 90*, 46–60. https://doi.org/10.1016/J.FUTURES.2017.03.006

Mickinsey Global Institute. (2017). *Artificial intelligence: The next digital frontier?*

Muhammad, A. S., Arcilla, F. E., & Sattar, M. F. (2020). The response of financial market indices to covid-19 pandemic. *Financial Studies*. ISSN 2066-6071, Romanian Academy, National Institute of Economic Research (INCE), "Victor Slăvescu" Centre for Financial and Monetary Research, Bucharest, 24(3) (89), 83–92.

Niroomand, F., Metghalchi, M., & Hajilee, M. (2020). Efficient market hypothesis: A ruinous implication for Portugese stock market. *Journal of Economics and Finance, 1–15*. https://doi.org/10.1007/s12197-020-09514-8

Okorie, D. I., & Lin, B. (2020). Stock markets and the COVID-19 fractal contagion effects. *Finance Research Letters, 101640*. https://doi.org/10.1016/j.frl.2020.101640

Pástor, Ľ., & Vorsatz, M. B. (2020). Mutual fund performance and flows during the COVID-19 crisis. *The Review of Asset Pricing Studies*. https://doi.org/10.1093/rapstu/raaa015

Reilly, P. (2020). The impact of the COVID-19 pandemic on the biotech industry. *Human Gene Therapy, 31*, 11–12. https://doi.org/10.1089/hum.2020.29124.pre

Schell, D., Wang, M., & Huynh, T. L. D. (2020). This time is indeed different: A study on global market reactions to public health crisis. *Journal of Behavioral and Experimental Finance, 27*, 100349. https://doi.org/10.1016/j.jbef.2020.100349

Sharif, A., Aloui, C., & Yarovaya, L. (2020). COVID-19 pandemic, oil prices, stock market, geopolitical risk and policy uncertainty nexus in the US economy: Fresh evidence from the wavelet-based approach. *International Review of Financial Analysis, 70*, 101496. https://doi.org/10.1016/j.irfa.2020.101496

Spatt, C. S. (2020). A tale of two crises: The 2008 mortgage meltdown and the 2020 COVID-19 Crisis. *The Review of Asset Pricing Studies, 10*(4), 759–790.

Topcu, M., & Gulal, O. S. (2020). The impact of COVID-19 on emerging stock markets. *Finance Research Letters, 101691*. https://doi.org/10.1016/j.frl.2020.101691

Trippi, R. R., & Turban, E. (1993). *Neural networks in finance and investing: Using artificial intelligence to improve real-world performance*. Probus Pub.
Tripathi, A., & Pandey, A. (2021). Information dissemination across global markets during the spread of COVID-19 pandemic. *International Review of Economics & Finance, 74*, 103–115.
Verikios, G. (2020). The dynamic effects of infectious disease outbreaks: The case of pandemic influenza and human coronavirus. *Socio-Economic Planning Sciences, 71*, 100898. https://doi.org/10.1016/j.seps.2020.100898
Yarovaya, L., Brzeszczyński, J., Goodell, J. W., Lucey, B., & Lau, C. K. M. (2022). Rethinking financial contagion: Information transmission mechanism during the COVID-19 pandemic. *Journal of International Financial Markets, Institutions and Money*, 101589.
Zaremba, A., Kizys, R., Aharon, D. Y., & Demir, E. (2020). Infected markets: Novel coronavirus, government interventions, and stock return volatility around the globe. *Finance Research Letters, 35*, 101597. https://doi.org/10.1016/j.frl.2020.101597

Dr Samuel Salia is an Associate Professor of Finance at Birmingham City University (UK) where he currently leads research and teaches finance. He holds a PhD in Finance from Birmingham City University. He is a member of the UK Institute of Consulting and has consulted for international organisations including the African Union and GIZ. Before joining BCU, Samuel was a Senior Lecturer in Finance and Faculty Head of Doctoral Training (Business and Law) at De Montfort University. Before this, he was a Lecturer in International Finance and Programme Director for MSc International Banking and Finance at the University of Wolverhampton. He has worked as a Management Consultant with the Ghana Ministry of Employment (MDPI) and as Managing Director of SAS Capital Money Lending Limited and has also held academic appointments abroad. He has had over eleven years of banking and consultancy experience in the SME sector, specialising in entrepreneurial finance. The findings of Samuel's research have influenced the practice of ethnic minority businesses in the UK, financial institutions, and the policy of regional bodies in Africa. For example, he recently worked on a BAL HEIF-funded project that provided training and support to Afro-Caribbean-owned businesses in the Midlands (UK) in response to COVID-19 challenges. He has also worked on projects such as evaluating the impact of services of Opportunity International Savings and Loans-Ghana, and Village Savings and Loans Associations. As a Technical Advisor, he developed a policy booklet for the African Heads of State and Governments on the AU 2021 theme of the year. He has served as a keynote speaker at national and international conferences. His focus has recently been on exploring issues of diaspora (migrant) remittance, FinTech, and investment in developing countries. Samuel has published extensively on issues relating to access to finance, green finance, SME innovation, and entrepreneurial training. His work has been published in the International Journal of Finance and Economics (ABS ranking 3*), International Journal of Entrepreneurial Behaviour and Research (ABS ranking 3*), IEEE Transactions on Engineering Management (ABS ranking 3*) Journal of Small Business and Enterprise Development (ABS ranking 2*) among others. Samuel has examined and supervised Ph.D. students, and on the strength of his research, he has received research funding totaling £26,000. He has served as a reviewer for highly ranked academic journals including the International Journal of Entrepreneurial Behaviour and Research, and the Journal of Small Business and Enterprise Development among others.

Amin Karimu, PhD, is an Associate Professor in Economics and a Senior Research Fellow at the Environmental Policy Research Unit (EPRU), University of Cape Town. His background is in Energy and Environmental Economics, He had both his master's and Ph.D. in Economics from Sweden. His research interest includes areas such as sustainable management practices in the extractive industries, Electricity market design, Renewable energy and value addition in the agricultural sector, Natural resource management and climate change, Climate change and sustainable development, Sustainable development, and its financing and Energy project evaluation and risk assessment. He has supervised more than 20 master's theses since 2016, more than 30 MBAs, external reviewer of 5 Ph.D. theses, co-supervised 3 PhDs to completion, and currently supervising 3 PhDs.

Dr. Yahaya Alhassan is the Head of Academic Operations at the University of Sunderland in London. Dr. Alhassan is responsible for leading the integration and execution of the University of Sunderland's strategic and operational priorities across all academic programmes at the London campus (UoSiL). He also oversees the development and implementation of the Academic Programme Offer, as well as the integration of the University's Research and Innovation Strategy. Alongside his leadership role, Dr. Alhassan maintains an active research profile. His current research explores investment in financial technology (FinTech) and firm growth, with several of his papers published in high-ranking ABS 3* journals. He has co-edited books, authored multiple book chapters in finance and enterprise, and frequently presents at academic conferences, contributing meaningfully to the field of finance since 2019. Dr. Alhassan has over 20 experience in teaching, academic leadership, and management, gained through his roles at the University of Sunderland in London as well as previous positions in the higher education and consultancy sectors. He holds a PhD in Business Management (Finance) from Anglia Ruskin University, an MBA in Finance and a Master of Education from the University of Sunderland, and a BA (Hons) in Business Management from Arden University. He is also a Senior Fellow of the Higher Education Academy (HEA).

Meney Orlyne Ahochi, BBA, MSc, is a Data Architect at the Office for National Statistics in the UK. She previously worked at Predictive Black as Business Data Analyst. Prior to working at Predictive Black, Meney had worked as Fintech Research Assistant at Burnmark. She holds Master's degree in Financial Technology from Coventry University London and MSc Banking and Financial Support Services from University of Wolverhampton.

Chapter 10
Managing Financial Risk in the Era of Climate Change: Strategies for Adaptation and Mitigation in the Banking Sector

Vasco Victor

10.1 Introduction

Climate change represents one of the most significant economic and financial challenges of the twenty-first century, with far-reaching implications for global financial stability and economic prosperity (Carney, 2015; IPCC, 2018). The banking sector, as a cornerstone of the global financial system, plays a critical role in managing climate-related risks and enabling the shift towards a low-carbon economy (NGFS, 2019). These climate-related risks manifest in various forms, including physical risks from severe weather events and long-term climate shifts, transition risks due to the global shift towards decarbonization and net zero emissions, and liability risks related to climate-related litigation (TCFD, 2017).

The pressing need to tackle climate change is highlighted by international agreements like the Paris Agreement, which seeks to keep global warming well below 2 °C above pre-industrial levels (UNFCCC, 2015). Achieving this ambitious target demands a substantial shift of capital towards low-carbon and climate-resilient investments, with banks playing a pivotal role in this process. However, the transition to a low-carbon economy also poses risks for banks, especially those heavily invested in carbon-intensive sectors, which could experience declining asset values or the risk of stranded assets (Caldecott et al., 2016).

While awareness of climate-related financial risks is growing within the banking sector, many institutions remain in the early stages of developing comprehensive strategies to manage these risks effectively. The complexity and long-term nature of climate change, coupled with inherent uncertainties in climate projections and policy responses, present significant obstacles to effective risk management.

V. Victor (✉)
Surrey, UK

Y. Alhassan et al. (eds.), *Financial Innovation and Sustainable Enterprise in Developing and Emerging Economies*, Research Series on Responsible Enterprise Ecosystems, https://doi.org/10.1007/978-3-032-04500-3_10

Physical risks from climate change are already becoming evident and are projected to intensify. These include acute events like hurricanes, floods, and wildfires, as well as chronic changes such as rising sea levels and long-term shifts in temperature and precipitation patterns. Such events can cause direct losses for banks through damage to physical assets held as collateral, and indirect losses by affecting borrowers' ability to repay loans (Batten et al., 2016). The growing frequency and severity of these events challenge traditional risk assessment models, which often rely on historical data that may not accurately predict future climate conditions (Chenet et al., 2019).

Transition risks emerge from the shift towards a low-carbon economy, driven by changes in policy, regulations, technological advancements, and evolving market sentiment (TCFD, 2017). For banks, these risks can result in stranded assets within loan portfolios, shifts in borrower creditworthiness, and reputational damage from financing environmentally harmful activities (Campiglio et al., 2018). Liability risks, an increasingly relevant issue, stem from potential climate-related legal claims and actions against financial institutions for their role in financing activities that contribute to climate change (Nachmany et al., 2017). With the rise in climate litigation globally, banks are facing heightened scrutiny over their lending decisions and their responsibility in assessing and managing climate-related risks.

This research aims to analyse climate risk management practices in the banking sector, focusing on the adaptation and mitigation strategies adopted by global systemically important banks (G-SIBs). The research seeks to evaluate how banks currently measure and assess climate-related financial risks, examine their adaptation strategies, explore how banks contribute to climate change mitigation through financial activities, and identify key challenges and opportunities in climate risk management within the banking sector.

10.2 Literature Review

This literature review aims to examine the current state of research on climate risk management in the banking sector. It focuses on how banks are assessing, measuring, and mitigating climate-related financial risks, as well as the regulatory frameworks and policy initiatives shaping these practices. The review covers literature from 2015 to 2021, encompassing the period following the Paris Agreement, which marked a significant shift in global climate policy.

10.2.1 Understanding Climate-Related Financial Risks

Carney's (2015) seminal work laid the groundwork for understanding climate-related financial risks in the banking sector. His categorisation of risks into physical, transition, and liability has been widely adopted and forms the basis for much of the subsequent research and policy development. Dietz et al. (2016) conducted a quantitative assessment of physical risks and determined that, in a business-as-usual emissions scenario, the "climate value at risk" (climate VaR) of global financial assets would be 1.8% with a 1% possibility of a $24 trillion loss. Although this analysis highlights the extent of climate threats to the financial system, it may mask sector-specific or geographical variations because it is based on aggregated worldwide data.

Transition risks have been extensively explored by Campiglio et al. (2018), who provide a comprehensive overview of these risks, including policy changes, technological disruptions, and shifts in market sentiment. They argue that abrupt implementation of climate policies could lead to a "carbon bubble" and significant asset stranding. However, their analysis relies heavily on theoretical models and scenario analysis, highlighting the need for more empirical research in this area.

Although they haven't been examined as much, liability issues are getting more attention. According to Nachmany et al. (2017), there were over 1000 cases filed in 24 countries as of 2017, indicating the surge in climate-related litigation worldwide. A revised analysis by Setzer and Byrnes (2020) noted a rise in lawsuits against financial institutions for their part in funding high-emission ventures.

10.2.2 Regulatory and Policy Frameworks

The 2015 Paris Agreement (UNFCCC, 2015) set a global framework for addressing climate change, spurring numerous regulatory initiatives targeting the financial sector. The Task Force on Climate-related Financial Disclosures (TCFD, 2017) has been particularly influential, providing recommendations for voluntary climate-related financial disclosures. Carney (2019) argues that such disclosures are crucial for pricing climate risks and supporting the transition to a low-carbon economy.

At the international level, the Network for Greening the Financial System (NGFS, 2019) provides guidelines on incorporating climate risks into microprudential supervision, financial stability monitoring, and monetary policy. Bolton et al. (2020) argue for a more proactive role for central banks in promoting the low-carbon transition, terming this approach the "green swan." However, this view is not universally accepted, with some arguing that such actions could compromise central bank independence (Cochrane, 2020).

At the national and regional levels, various initiatives have emerged. The European Union's Action Plan on Sustainable Finance includes measures such as a taxonomy for sustainable activities and disclosure requirements for investors (European Commission, 2018). In the UK, the Prudential Regulation Authority (PRA) has issued supervisory expectations for banks and insurers on managing climate-related financial risks (Bank of England, 2019).

10.2.3 Risk Assessment and Measurement

Scenario analysis and stress testing have emerged as important methodologies for assessing climate-related financial risks. The NGFS (2020) has developed a set of climate scenarios for forward-looking risk assessment, which have been widely adopted by financial institutions and regulators. Vermeulen et al. (2019) applied a climate stress test to the Dutch financial sector, finding that losses in severe transition scenarios could exceed 10% of the system's total assets. Their methodology combines macroeconomic modelling with detailed sector-level analysis, providing a more nuanced view of potential impacts.

Allen et al. (2020) further developed stress-testing methodologies, incorporating both physical and transition risks. They argue for the importance of considering how these risks interact and potentially amplify each other. While their approach offers a more comprehensive view of climate risks, it also highlights the challenges of data availability and the need for sophisticated modelling capabilities.

Carbon footprint analysis has emerged as another important tool for assessing transition risks in bank portfolios. Ehlers et al. (2020) propose a measure of carbon risk exposure based on the carbon intensity of bank loan portfolios. They find significant variation in exposure across banks and countries, suggesting that some institutions may be more vulnerable to transition risks than others. Climate Value-at-Risk (Climate VaR) models represent an attempt to quantify the financial impact of climate change on portfolios. Dietz et al. (2016) developed a Climate VaR framework that incorporates both physical and transition risks. Jung et al. (2018) propose an extension using adaptive market theory, arguing that traditional VaR models may underestimate climate risks due to the nonlinear and potentially abrupt nature of climate impacts.

10.2.4 Adaptation Strategies

Banks are adopting various strategies to manage and mitigate climate-related risks. A key area of focus has been the integration of climate considerations into governance and risk management frameworks, as guided by the TCFD (2017) recommendations. Eccles and Krzus (2018) analysed TCFD-aligned disclosures across multiple sectors, including banking. They found significant variation in the quality and depth of climate risk governance disclosures, suggesting that many banks are still in the early stages of developing comprehensive climate risk management approaches.

Portfolio diversification and reallocation strategies have also been explored. Battiston et al. (2017) argue that banks could reduce their exposure to climate policy risks by divesting from carbon-intensive industries. However, Schoenmaker and Schramade (2019) advocate for a more nuanced approach, suggesting that banks should evaluate companies' transition plans within high-carbon sectors rather than pursuing blanket exclusion strategies.

The development of new financial products to enhance climate resilience is another area of adaptation. Tanner and Surminski (2016) highlight the potential role of parametric insurance and catastrophe bonds in managing climate risks, particularly in developing countries. Martínez-Díaz et al. (2019) emphasize the importance of banks in financing climate adaptation projects, such as resilient infrastructure and water management systems.

10.2.5 Mitigation and Sustainable Finance

Mitigation strategies and sustainable finance initiatives are increasingly important for banks. Green lending and investment have seen significant growth, with the Climate Bonds Initiative (2020) reporting global green bond issuance reaching $258.9 billion in 2019. Scholtens and van't Klooster (2019) find a positive link between banks' environmental performance and financial performance, suggesting that sustainable finance strategies could improve both sustainability outcomes and profitability. Banks are also increasingly engaging with clients to promote climate mitigation. Ceres (2018) documents various approaches taken by banks to support their clients' transition to low-carbon business models. However, Rainforest Action Network et al. (2020) argue that many banks continue to finance fossil fuel expansion, highlighting contradictions in their climate strategies.

Internal carbon pricing has emerged as another tool for banks to manage climate risks and align their portfolios with climate goals. Ahluwalia (2017) examines the adoption of internal carbon pricing by financial institutions, finding that it can help in risk assessment and decision-making.

10.3 Methodology

This study employs a comprehensive mixed-methods approach to investigate how global systemically important banks (G-SIBs) are managing financial risks associated with climate change, focusing on adaptation and mitigation strategies. The complexity of climate-related financial risks necessitates a multifaceted research design that can capture both quantitative trends and qualitative insights.

10.3.1 Research Design

This study adopts a pragmatic research philosophy, allowing for the integration of various perspectives and methods to address the complexity of climate-related financial risks (Creswell & Creswell, 2018). This approach recognizes that there is no single, universal solution for managing climate risks in banking; instead, a range of strategies may be effective depending on the context. Building on this pragmatic foundation, the study employs an abductive approach, iteratively moving between theory and data to combine existing theories on climate risk management with new insights from data collection and analysis (Saunders et al., 2019). This method allows for refining theoretical understanding based on empirical evidence while using theoretical frameworks to guide data collection and analysis.

The research design follows a sequential explanatory mixed methods approach, as outlined by Creswell and Plano Clark (2017). This design consists of two key phases: a quantitative phase followed by a qualitative phase. In the quantitative phase, numerical data on banks' climate risk exposure, financial performance, and risk management practices are collected and analysed. The subsequent qualitative phase involves an in-depth analysis of bank disclosures and case studies, offering context and explanation for the quantitative findings.

10.3.2 Data Collection

The sample for this study consists of eight global systemically important banks (G-SIBs) as identified by the Financial Stability Board. These banks were selected due to their significant role in the global financial system and their potential impact on climate risk management practices across the industry. The focus on G-SIBs is consistent with previous research on climate risk in banking, such as the work by Battiston et al. (2017) and Ehlers et al. (2020).

Data collection for the quantitative phase draws from multiple sources to ensure a comprehensive and reliable dataset. These sources include:

1. Annual reports
2. Sustainability reports (ESG)
3. Financial databases (e.g., YAHOO Finance)

Yin (2018) suggests using various data sources for case study research since this technique allows for triangulation and helps eliminate potential biases or inconsistencies in any one data source.

The key variables examined include:

1.

$$\text{Return on Equity}\left(\text{ROE}\right): \frac{Net\,Income}{Shareholders\,Equity}$$

2. Carbon Intensity (measured in tonnes of CO_2 per FTE (Full Time Employees))
3.

$$\text{Debt to Equity Ratio calculated} : \frac{\textit{Total Liabilities}}{\textit{Total Shareholders Equity}} \times 100$$

This approach to variable selection is consistent with previous studies on bank performance and environmental risk, such as those by Scholtens and van't Klooster (2019) and Delis et al. (2019). The data collection process involves a systematic review of each bank's public disclosures over the 5 years from 2016 to 2020. This timeframe is chosen to capture recent developments in climate risk management practices as well as the information preceding the Paris Climate Agreement that was signed in 2016 while providing sufficient historical data for trend analysis. For the qualitative phase, a content analysis framework is developed based on the Task Force on Climate-related Financial Disclosures (TCFD) recommendations (TCFD, 2017). This framework guides the systematic analysis of banks' climate-related disclosures.

10.3.3 Data Analysis

The quantitative analysis employs several statistical techniques:

1. Descriptive Statistics: Calculating measures of central tendency (mean, median) and dispersion (standard deviation, range) for all key variables.
2. Trend Analysis: Examining the evolution of key metrics over the study period (2016–2020).
3. Correlation Analysis: Constructing a correlation matrix to examine bivariate relationships between key variables.
4. Panel Data Regression: Using fixed-effects panel data regression models to examine the relationship between carbon intensity and financial performance while controlling for other relevant factors. The basic model is specified as:

$$\text{ROE}\_\{\text{it}\} = \alpha + \beta_1 \text{CI}\_\{\text{it}\} + \beta_2 \text{DE}\_\{\text{it}\} + \gamma\_\{\text{i}\} + \delta\_\{\text{t}\} + \varepsilon\_\{\text{it}\}$$

where;

- ROE_{it} is the dependent variable Return on Equity for bank i at time t
- CI_{it} is the carbon intensity,
- DE_{it} is the debt-to-equity ratio,
- γ_{i} represents bank fixed effects,
- δ_{t} represents time-fixed effects,
- ε_{it} is the error term.

5. Dynamic Panel Model: To account for potential persistence in ROE and address potential endogeneity concerns, a dynamic panel model using the Arellano-Bond GMM estimator is employed (Arellano & Bond, 1991). The model specification is:

$$\text{ROE}\_\{\text{it}\} = \alpha + \rho\text{ROE}\_\{\text{i,t}-1\} + \beta_1\text{CI}\_\{\text{it}\} + \beta_2\text{DE}\_\{\text{it}\} + \gamma\_\{\text{i}\}$$
$$+\delta\_\{\text{t}\} + \varepsilon\_\{\text{it}\}$$

where;

- ROE_{i,t-1} represents the lagged dependent variable
- CI_{it} is the carbon intensity
- DE_{it} is the debt-to-equity ratio
- γ_{i} represents bank fixed effects
- δ_{t} represents time-fixed effects
- ε_{it} is the error term

6. Scenario Analysis: Using scenarios developed by the Network for Greening the Financial System (NGFS, 2020) to assess the potential impact of different climate pathways on banks' ROE.

For the qualitative phase, a content analysis of banks' climate-related disclosures is conducted, followed by in-depth case studies of selected banks. The content analysis involves the examination of disclosures based on the developed framework.

10.3.4 Data Interpretation

The interpretation of quantitative results is guided by existing literature on climate risk in banking and financial performance. The qualitative data is interpreted through a thematic analysis approach, identifying key themes and patterns in banks' climate risk management practices.

10.4 Results

The quantitative analysis of our dataset, which comprises financial and environmental performance metrics for eight global systemically important banks (G-SIBs) over the period 2016–2020, reveals several interesting patterns and relationships. We begin with a descriptive overview of the key variables: Return on Equity (ROE), Debt to Equity Ratio, and Carbon Intensity.

10.4.1 *Quantitative Analysis*

10.4.1.1 Descriptive Statistics

We begin our analysis by examining the descriptive statistics of our key variables: Return on Assets (ROA), Carbon Intensity, and Momentum across all banks in the sample period 2016–2020 (Table 10.1).

The descriptive statistics provide an initial overview of our key variables across the sample period. The mean ROE for our sample is 9.97% (SD = 4.14%), indicating generally positive profitability across the banks, though with considerable variation. The average Debt-to-Equity Ratio is 14.51 (SD = 4.86), suggesting that these banks are typically highly leveraged, which is common in the banking sector. The mean Carbon Intensity is 2.37 (SD = 1.78), measured in tonnes of CO_2 equivalent per number of full-time employees (FTE). This relatively high standard deviation in Carbon Intensity indicates significant variation in the banks' exposure to carbon-intensive assets or operations.

10.4.1.2 Trend Analysis

To understand how our key variables have evolved over the study period, we conducted a trend analysis (Fig. 10.1).

The trend analysis reveals several interesting patterns. ROE shows some fluctuation over the period, with a peak in 2019 (11.40%) followed by a sharp decrease in 2020 (8.48%). This decline in 2020 can likely be attributed to the economic impact of the COVID-19 pandemic, which affected bank profitability globally (Demirgüç-Kunt et al., 2021).

The Debt-to-Equity Ratio shows a gradual increase over the study period, from 14.22 in 2016 to 15.68 in 2020. This trend suggests that the banks in our sample have been increasing their leverage over time, potentially to boost returns in a low-interest-rate environment. However, this also indicates an increase in financial risk, which is particularly noteworthy given the growing awareness of climate-related risks during this period.

Most strikingly, there is a clear downward trend in Carbon Intensity over the study period, with the mean decreasing from 3.40 in 2016 to 1.11 in 2020. This

Table 10.1 Descriptive statistic of key variables

Statistic	ROE (%)	Carbon intensity	Debt-to-equity ratio
Mean	9.97	2.37	14.51
Median	10.43	1.82	11.32
Std dev	4.14	1.78	4.86
Min	2.07	0.11	8.81
Max	17.87	12.27	23.73
N	40	40	40

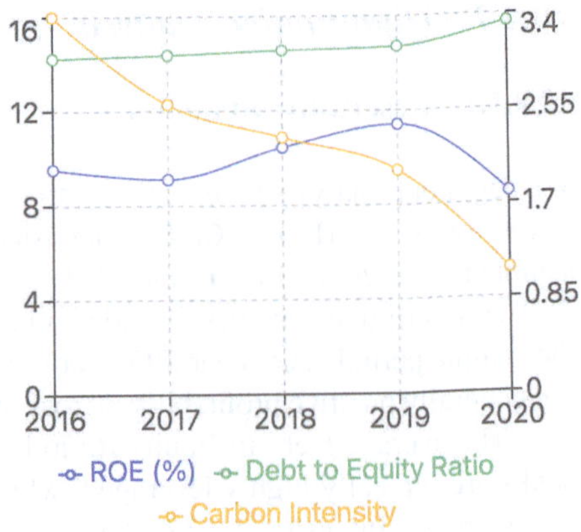

Fig. 10.1 Trend analysis of key variables

Table 10.2 Correlation matrix

Variable	ROE	Debt to equity ratio	Carbon intensity
ROE	1.00	−0.15	−0.28
Debt to equity ratio	−0.15	1.00	−0.22
Carbon intensity	−0.28	−0.22	1.00

substantial reduction suggests that banks have been making significant efforts to reduce their exposure to carbon-intensive sectors, possibly in response to increasing regulatory pressure and growing awareness of climate-related financial risks (Ehlers et al., 2020).

10.4.1.3 Correlation Analysis

Before proceeding with regression analysis, we examine the correlation between our key variables (Table 10.2).

Where;

$$\text{Return on Equity}\left(\text{ROE}\right) = \frac{\textit{Net Income}}{\textit{Shareholders Equity}}$$

$$\text{Carbon Intensity}\left(\text{tonne}\,\text{CO}^2\,/\,\text{FTE}\right) = \frac{\textit{Total Emissions}}{\textit{Full Time Employees}}$$

$$\text{Debt to Equity Ratio} = \frac{\textit{Total Liabilities}}{\textit{Total Equity}} \times 100$$

The correlation matrix reveals several important relationships. ROE shows a weak negative correlation with the Debt-to-Equity Ratio (−0.15), suggesting that higher leverage is associated with slightly lower profitability in our sample. This finding is somewhat counterintuitive, as increased leverage is often associated with higher ROE. However, it may reflect the complexities of bank capital structure and the potential risks of excessive leverage (Berger & Bouwman, 2013).

More notably, Carbon Intensity shows a negative correlation with both ROE (−0.28) and the Debt-to-Equity Ratio (−0.22). The negative correlation with ROE suggests that banks with lower carbon intensity tend to have slightly higher profitability. This aligns with the findings of Scholtens and van't Klooster (2019), who found a positive link between banks' environmental performance and financial performance. The negative correlation between Carbon Intensity and the Debt-to-Equity ratio might indicate that banks with lower carbon intensity have slightly lower leverage, possibly reflecting a more conservative risk management approach.

10.4.1.4 Panel Data Regression Analysis

To examine the relationship between carbon intensity and financial performance while controlling for other relevant factors, we used fixed-effects panel data regression models. The basic model is:

$$\mathbf{ROE}\_\{\mathbf{it}\} = \alpha + \beta_1\mathbf{CI}\_\{\mathbf{it}\} + \beta_2\mathbf{DE}\_\{\mathbf{it}\} + \gamma\_\{\mathbf{i}\} + \delta\_\{\mathbf{t}\} + \varepsilon\_\{\mathbf{it}\}$$

where;

- ROE_{it} is the dependent variable Return on Equity for bank i at time t
- CI_{it} is the carbon intensity
- DE_{it} is the debt-to-equity ratio
- γ_{i} represents bank fixed effects
- δ_{t} represents time fixed effects
- ε_{it} is the error term

The panel data regression results indicate a significant negative relationship between Carbon Intensity and ROE. Specifically, a one-unit increase in Carbon Intensity is associated with a 0.582 percentage point decrease in ROE, holding other factors constant. This relationship is statistically significant ($p = 0.009$), providing strong evidence that banks with lower carbon intensity tend to have higher profitability. This finding aligns with the growing body of literature suggesting that environmental performance can positively impact financial performance in the banking sector (Scholtens & van't Klooster, 2019) (Table 10.3).

The Debt-to-Equity ratio also shows a significant negative relationship with ROE (coefficient = −0.195, $p = 0.030$). This suggests that contrary to traditional financial theory, higher leverage is associated with lower profitability in our sample of banks. This could reflect the increased costs and risks associated with high leverage in the banking sector, particularly in the context of evolving regulatory requirements and

Table 10.3 Panel data regression results dependent variable ROE

Variable	Coefficient	Std. error	t-statistic	p-value
Carbon intensity	−0.582	0.214	−2.720	0.009
Debt to equity ratio	−0.195	0.087	−2.241	0.030
R-squared: 0.653 Adjusted R-squared: 0.589				

Table 10.4 Panel data regression results dependent variable D/E ratio

Variable	Coefficient	Std. error	t-statistic	p-value
Carbon intensity	−0.437	0.196	−2.229	0.0031
R-squared: 0.581 Adjusted R-squared: 0.589				

growing awareness of climate-related risks. Alternatively, it could be an implication of excessive leverage in the banking industry due to mismanagement.

We also ran a regression with the Debt-to-Equity ratio as the dependent variable to further explore its relationship with Carbon Intensity:

$$\mathrm{DE}\_\{\mathrm{it}\} = \alpha + \beta_1 \mathrm{CI}\_\{\mathrm{it}\} + \gamma\_\{\mathrm{i}\} + \delta\_\{\mathrm{t}\} + \varepsilon\_\{\mathrm{it}\}$$

where; DE_{it} is the dependent variable Return on Equity for bank i at time t (Table 10.4).

This regression reveals a significant negative relationship between Carbon Intensity and the Debt-to-Equity Ratio. A one-unit increase in Carbon Intensity is associated with a 0.437 unit decrease in the Debt-to-Equity Ratio, holding other factors constant. This relationship is statistically significant ($p = 0.031$), suggesting that banks with lower carbon intensity tend to have lower leverage.

10.4.1.5 Dynamic Panel Model

To account for potential persistence in ROE and address potential endogeneity concerns, we also estimated a dynamic panel model using the Arellano-Bond GMM estimator.

The model specification with ROE as the dependent variable is:

$$\mathrm{ROE}\_\{\mathrm{it}\} = \alpha + \rho \mathrm{ROE}\_\{\mathrm{i,t}-1\} + \beta_1 \mathrm{CI}\_\{\mathrm{it}\} + \beta_2 \mathrm{DE}\_\{\mathrm{it}\} + \gamma\_\{\mathrm{i}\} + \delta\_\{\mathrm{t}\} + \varepsilon\_\{\mathrm{it}\}$$

where:

- ROE_{i,t-1} represents the lagged dependent variable.
- ROE_{it} is the dependent variable (ROE, ROA, or Stock Return) for bank i at time t
- α is the intercept term ·

- ρ is the coefficient for the lagged dependent variable
- CI_{it} is the carbon intensity for bank i at time t
- β_1 is the coefficient for carbon intensity
- X_{it} is a vector of control variables (such as bank size and leverage) for bank i at time t
- β_2 is a vector of coefficients for the control variables
- γ_{i} represents bank-specific fixed effects
- δ_{t} represents time-specific fixed effects
- ε_{it} is the error term (Table 10.5)

The dynamic panel model results confirm the negative relationship between Carbon Intensity and ROE, even after accounting for persistence in ROE. The coefficient for Carbon Intensity (−0.431) remains statistically significant ($p = 0.023$), although slightly smaller in magnitude compared to the fixed-effects model. This suggests that the relationship is robust to different model specifications and helps address potential endogeneity concerns.

The model specification with D/E Ratio as the dependent variable is:

$$\mathrm{DE\_\{it\}} = \alpha + \rho DE\_\{\mathrm{i,t}-1\} + \beta_1 \mathrm{CI\_\{it\}} + \gamma\_\{\mathrm{i}\} + \delta\_\{\mathrm{t}\} + \varepsilon\_\{\mathrm{it}\}$$

where;

DE_{it} represents the Debt-to-Equity Ratio (Table 10.6)

This regression reveals a significant negative relationship between Carbon Intensity and the debt-equity ratio. A one-unit increase in Carbon Intensity is associated with a 0.437 unit decrease in the Debt-to-Equity Ratio, holding other factors constant. This relationship is statistically significant ($p = 0.031$), suggesting that banks with lower carbon intensity tend to have lower leverage.

10.4.1.6 Scenario Analysis

To further explore the implications of these results, we conducted a scenario analysis to assess the potential impact of different climate pathways on banks' ROE. We used scenarios developed by the Network for Greening the Financial System

Table 10.5 Dynamic panel model regression results with ROE as dependent variable

Variable	Coefficient	Std. error	z-statistic	p-value
Lagged ROE	0.342	0.103	3.320	0.001
Carbon intensity	−0.431	0.189	−2.280	0.023
Debt to equity ratio	−0.176	0.079	−2.228	0.026

Table 10.6 Dynamic panel model results with D/E ratio as dependent variable

Variable	Coefficient	Std. error	z-statistic	p-value
Debt to equity ratio	−0.437	0.196	−2.229	0.031

(NGFS, 2020), including an orderly transition, a disorderly transition, and a hot-house world scenario.

Figure 10.2 illustrates the estimated impact on ROE under each scenario. The orderly transition scenario shows the highest potential improvement in ROE at 1.8%, while the disorderly transition scenario indicates a more modest improvement of 0.7%. In contrast, the hot house world scenario suggests a potential decrease in ROE of 1.2%.

To provide more context to these projections, we estimated the potential changes in carbon intensity associated with each scenario and their corresponding impacts on ROE, based on our regression results and expert judgments regarding the likely pace of change.

Figure 10.3 presents a more detailed breakdown of each scenario, showing both the estimated change in carbon intensity and the corresponding impact on ROE. These estimates suggest that banks could potentially improve their ROE by reducing their carbon intensity through a transition to a low-carbon economy. Key observations include:

Fig. 10.2 Scenario analysis impact on ROE

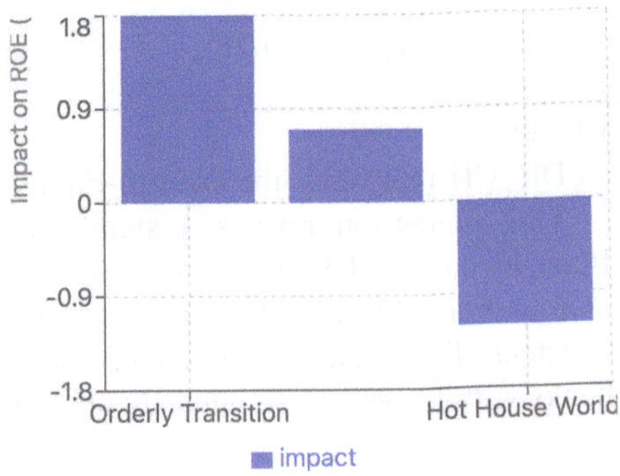

Fig. 10.3 Climate scenario analysis

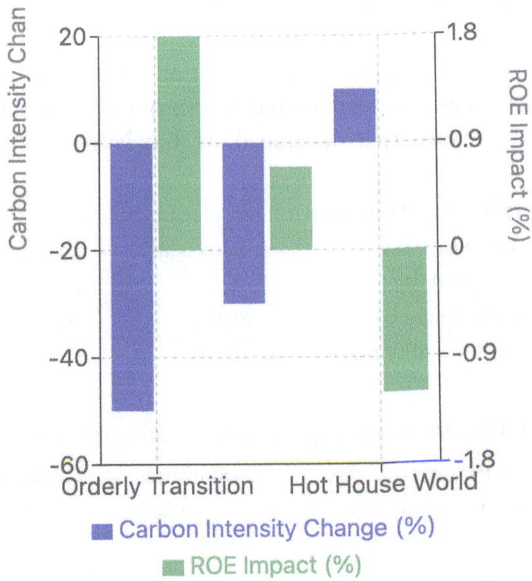

I. Orderly Transition: This scenario offers the highest potential improvement in ROE. The gradual nature of the transition allows banks to adjust their portfolios and strategies over time, minimizing disruption and maximizing benefits. We estimate a 50% reduction in carbon intensity in this scenario, corresponding to a 1.8% improvement in ROE.
II. Disorderly Transition: While still beneficial, the delayed and abrupt nature of this transition results in lower ROE improvements compared to the orderly scenario. We project a 30% reduction in carbon intensity, leading to a 0.7% improvement in ROE. This underscores the importance of early and planned action in climate risk management.
III. Hot House World: This scenario leads to a decrease in ROE, as banks face increased physical risks and potential stranded assets in their portfolios. We estimate a 10% increase in carbon intensity in this scenario, corresponding to a 1.2% decrease in ROE.

To illustrate the potential long-term impacts of these scenarios, we projected the cumulative changes in ROE over 5 years under each scenario:

Figure 10.4 illustrates the potential cumulative changes in ROE over a 5-year period under each scenario. The orderly transition scenario shows a steady increase in ROE, reaching a cumulative improvement of 10% by year 5. The disorderly transition scenario also shows improvement, but at a slower rate, reaching a 3.5% cumulative increase. In contrast, the hot house world scenario depicts a continual decline in ROE, accumulating to a 7% decrease over the 5-year period.

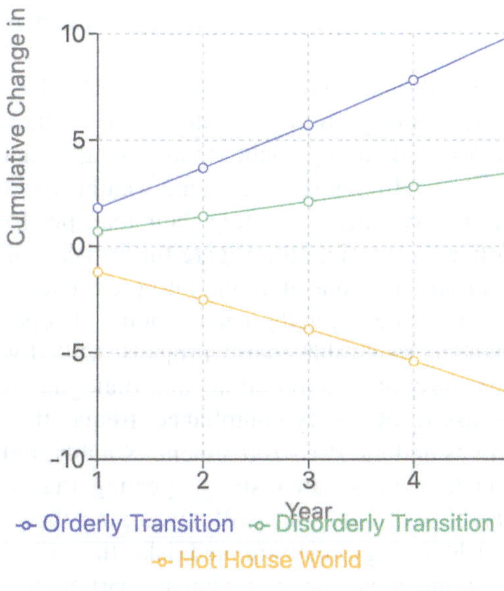

Fig. 10.4 Projected cumulative changes in ROE under different climate scenarios

This analysis highlights the potential financial benefits of proactive climate risk management and the risks of inaction. The significant divergence in outcomes between the transition scenarios and the hot house world scenario underscores the importance of effective climate risk management strategies in the banking sector.

However, it's important to note that these are simplified projections and actual outcomes may vary based on numerous factors, including policy changes, technological advancements, and individual bank strategies. The scenario analysis should be viewed as a tool for strategic planning and risk assessment rather than a precise forecast of future performance.

In conclusion, this scenario analysis provides valuable insights into the potential financial implications of different climate pathways for banks. It suggests that proactive management of climate-related risks and opportunities, particularly in the context of an orderly transition to a low-carbon economy, could yield significant financial benefits for banks. Conversely, failure to adequately prepare for and respond to climate change could result in substantial financial losses. These findings underscore the importance of integrating climate considerations into banks' risk management frameworks and strategic planning processes.

10.4.2 Qualitative Analysis

10.4.2.1 Content Analysis of Bank Disclosures

We conducted a detailed content analysis of the climate-related disclosures of the eight banks in our sample, focusing on their annual reports, sustainability reports, and CDP responses. This analysis aimed to identify key themes in banks' approaches to climate risk management and their alignment with best practices such as the TCFD recommendations (Fig. 10.5).

Key findings from the content analysis show that all eight banks in the sample addressed their approaches to assessing climate-related risks, typically focusing on physical risks (e.g., extreme weather) and transition risks (e.g., policy and technology shifts) affecting their loan portfolios and operations. Seven banks outlined strategies to mitigate these risks, such as setting targets for reducing financed emissions and integrating climate factors into credit risk assessments. Six banks highlighted green financing efforts, including issuing green bonds and financing renewable energy projects, while five emphasized stakeholder engagement through collaborations and dialogues on climate issues. All eight banks discussed regulatory compliance, frequently referencing the TCFD recommendations and the Paris Agreement. Notably, only four banks reported conducting climate scenario analysis, suggesting that scenario analysis remains an area where many banks are still developing their capabilities. Overall, while banks are addressing climate-related risks, the variation in the depth of their approaches highlights areas for improvement, particularly in scenario analysis.

THEME	FREQUENCY (OUT OF 8 BANKS)
Risk Assessment	8
Mitigation Strategies	7
Green Financing Initiatives	6
Stakeholder Engagement	5
Regulatory Compliance	8
Scenario Analysis	4

Fig. 10.5 Frequency of key themes in bank disclosures

10.5 Discussion

The quantitative analysis revealed several key findings. Firstly, there is a significant negative relationship between carbon intensity and Return on Equity (ROE) across our sample of G-SIBs. This relationship persists in both our panel data regression and dynamic panel models, suggesting a robust association between lower carbon intensity and higher profitability. Secondly, we observed a general decrease in carbon intensity across the sample from 2016 to 2020, indicating growing efforts by banks to reduce exposure to carbon-intensive sectors. Thirdly, our analysis revealed an unexpected negative relationship between carbon intensity and the Debt-to-Equity ratio, suggesting that banks with lower carbon intensity tend to have higher leverage.

The qualitative analysis of bank disclosures and case studies complemented these quantitative findings. We found that all sampled banks are addressing climate-related risks in their reporting, focusing on both physical and transition risks. However, there is considerable variation in the depth and quality of these disclosures. The case studies highlighted innovative approaches such as proprietary tools for assessing clients' transition readiness and integration of climate risk into traditional risk categories.

These findings align with and extend several key themes identified in our literature review. The negative relationship between carbon intensity and ROE supports the "doing well by doing good" hypothesis proposed by Scholtens and van't Klooster (2019). This provides empirical evidence for the argument that effective climate risk management can yield financial benefits for banks, contributing to the growing body of literature on the relationship between environmental and financial performance in the banking sector (Dell'Atti et al., 2017).

The observed decrease in carbon intensity across our sample from 2016 to 2020 aligns with the findings of Ehlers et al. (2020), who noted a growing awareness among banks of the need to manage their carbon risk exposure. This trend suggests that banks are responding to the increasing regulatory and stakeholder pressure for improved climate risk management, as highlighted by Carney (2019) and the TCFD (2017) recommendations.

The unexpected negative relationship between carbon intensity and the Debt-to-Equity ratio adds a new dimension to our understanding of how climate risk management relates to bank capital structure. These finding challenges traditional assumptions about the relationship between environmental performance and leverage in the banking sector. It suggests that banks with lower carbon intensity may be able to maintain higher leverage, possibly due to lower perceived risk or better access to capital markets. This relationship warrants further investigation and may have implications for how we understand the interaction between climate risk and financial stability in the banking sector.

The variation in the depth and quality of climate-related disclosures observed in our content analysis is consistent with the findings of Eccles and Krzus (2018), who noted significant differences in the quality of climate risk governance disclosures across financial institutions. This underscores the ongoing challenges in implementing comprehensive climate risk management approaches, as discussed by Chenet et al. (2019).

Our scenario analysis results support the arguments of Carney (2015) regarding the "tragedy of the horizon" in climate risk management. The finding that an orderly transition scenario offers the highest potential improvement in ROE underscores the importance of early and planned action, aligning with the recommendations of the NGFS (2020) for forward-looking risk assessment.

The case studies reveal practices that align with recommendations from researchers such as Caldecott et al. (2018) for more sophisticated assessments of potential stranded assets, and Giglio et al. (2021) for a holistic approach to risk management that considers the interconnected nature of climate risks.

The negative relationship between carbon intensity and ROE can be interpreted as evidence that banks are beginning to effectively manage climate-related risks and capitalize on associated opportunities. This relationship suggests that reducing exposure to carbon-intensive sectors and investing in low-carbon activities may lead to improved financial performance. It's important to note, however, that this relationship may be influenced by various factors, including the overall financial health of the bank, macroeconomic conditions, and regulatory environment.

The decreasing trend in carbon intensity across the sample indicates a growing recognition among banks of the importance of managing climate-related risks. This trend may be driven by a combination of factors, including regulatory pressure, stakeholder expectations, and an increasing awareness of the potential financial impacts of climate change. The variation in the rate of decrease across institutions suggests that some banks are more advanced in their climate risk management practices than others.

The negative relationship between carbon intensity and the Debt-to-Equity ratio is particularly intriguing. This finding suggests that banks with lower carbon intensity tend to have higher leverage. There are several possible interpretations of this relationship:

Risk perception: Banks with lower carbon intensity may be perceived as less risky by creditors and investors, allowing them to maintain higher leverage ratios without facing higher borrowing costs or regulatory scrutiny.

Strategic positioning: Banks that are more advanced in their climate risk management may be better positioned to take advantage of opportunities in the growing sustainable finance market, potentially allowing them to expand their balance sheets more aggressively.

Regulatory influence: The evolving regulatory landscape around climate risk may be influencing banks' capital structure decisions, with those banks that are more proactive in managing climate risks potentially facing less pressure to deleverage.

This relationship challenges conventional wisdom about the link between environmental performance and financial risk and merits further investigation. It may have implications for how regulators and investors assess the stability and resilience of banks in the context of climate change.

The variation in the depth and quality of climate-related disclosures observed in our content analysis suggests that while all sampled banks recognize the importance of addressing climate risks, there is still significant room for improvement in terms of comprehensive and consistent reporting. This variation may reflect differences in institutional capacity, regulatory environments, or strategic priorities.

The results of our scenario analysis underscore the potential financial benefits of proactive climate risk management, and the risks associated with inaction or delayed action. The finding that an orderly transition scenario offers the highest potential improvement in ROE highlights the importance of early and planned action in addressing climate-related risks.

These results have several important implications for the banking sector, regulators, and policymakers:

For banks, the findings suggest that investing in comprehensive climate risk management strategies, including reducing carbon intensity and developing innovative sustainable finance products, could yield financial benefits. This implies a need for banks to integrate climate considerations more fully into their risk management frameworks and strategic planning processes. The relationship between carbon intensity and leverage also suggests that effective climate risk management could potentially allow banks to optimize their capital structure.

For regulators, the variation in climate risk management practices across banks highlights the need for more standardized and potentially mandatory reporting requirements to ensure consistency and comparability across the sector. The potential for climate risks to create systemic vulnerabilities, as suggested by our scenario analysis results, underscores the importance of incorporating climate considerations into financial stability assessments and stress testing exercises. The relationship between carbon intensity and leverage may also have implications for how regulators assess bank stability and set capital requirements in the context of climate risk.

For policymakers, the results emphasize the importance of creating a policy environment that supports an orderly transition to a low-carbon economy. This could include measures to incentivize sustainable finance and disincentivize high-carbon activities. The findings also suggest that policies aimed at improving banks' climate risk management could have positive spillover effects on financial stability.

The findings have implications for investors and other stakeholders, suggesting that a bank's approach to climate risk management could be an important factor in assessing its long-term financial prospects and risk profile.

More broadly, the results underscore the growing importance of climate risk management in the banking sector and its potential implications for financial performance, capital structure, and the transition to a low-carbon economy.

In conclusion, this study provides empirical evidence of the growing importance of climate risk management in the banking sector and its potential implications for financial performance, capital structure, and sustainability. The findings suggest that banks are making progress in assessing and managing climate-related risks, but significant challenges remain. These include methodological difficulties in assessing long-term, non-linear risks, challenges in integrating climate considerations into existing risk management frameworks, and tensions between short-term profitability and long-term sustainability goals.

The negative relationships between carbon intensity and both ROE and the Debt-to-Equity ratio suggest that effective climate risk management could yield financial benefits for banks and potentially allow for more efficient capital structures. However, the complexity and uncertainty associated with climate change necessitate ongoing research and innovation in risk assessment methodologies, scenario analysis techniques, and sustainable finance products.

As climate change continues to reshape the global economic landscape, banks will play a crucial role in managing climate-related financial risks and supporting the transition to a low-carbon economy. Realizing this potential will require continued efforts to overcome existing barriers, develop new methodologies and tools, align incentives with long-term sustainability goals, and navigate the complex trade-offs inherent in balancing financial performance with environmental and social responsibilities.

The banking sector's approach to climate risk management will have far-reaching implications not only for the financial industry but for the global economy as a whole. As such, it is crucial that researchers, practitioners, and policymakers continue to work together to develop and implement effective strategies for managing climate-related financial risks and promoting sustainable economic development.

10.6 Conclusion

This study explored the critical issue of managing financial risk in the era of climate change, with a specific focus on adaptation and mitigation strategies within the banking sector. Through a comprehensive analysis of eight global systemically important banks (G-SIBs) over the period 2016–2020, this study has provided empirical evidence of the growing importance of climate risk management in the banking sector and its potential implications for financial performance and sustainability. The findings suggest that banks are making progress in assessing and managing climate-related risks, but significant challenges remain. These include methodological difficulties in assessing long-term, non-linear risks, challenges in integrating climate considerations into existing risk management frameworks, and tensions between short-term profitability and long-term sustainability goals.

The negative relationships between carbon intensity and both ROE and the Debt-to-Equity ratio suggest that effective climate risk management could yield financial benefits for banks and potentially allow for more efficient capital structures. However, the complexity and uncertainty associated with climate change necessitate ongoing research and innovation in risk assessment methodologies, scenario analysis techniques, and sustainable finance products.

As climate change continues to reshape the global economic landscape, banks will play a crucial role in managing climate-related financial risks and supporting the transition to a low-carbon economy. Realizing this potential will require continued efforts to overcome existing barriers, develop new methodologies and tools, align incentives with long-term sustainability goals, and navigate the complex trade-offs inherent in balancing financial performance with environmental and social responsibilities.

The banking sector's approach to climate risk management will have far-reaching implications not only for the financial industry but for the global economy as a whole. As such, researchers, practitioners, and policymakers must continue to work together to develop and implement effective strategies for managing climate-related financial risks and promoting sustainable economic development.

By addressing the limitations identified in this study and pursuing the suggested avenues for future research, we can continue to advance our understanding of climate risk management in the banking sector. This ongoing effort is essential for building a more resilient, sustainable, and equitable financial system capable of supporting the transition to a low-carbon economy while maintaining stability and promoting prosperity for all.

References

Ahluwalia, M. B. (2017). *The business of pricing carbon: How companies are pricing carbon to mitigate risks and prepare for a low-carbon future*. Center for Climate and Energy Solutions.

Allen, T., Dees, S., Boissinot, J., Caicedo Graciano, C. M., Chouard, V., Clerc, L., de Gaye, A., Devulder, A., Diot, S., Lisack, N., & Pegoraro, F. (2020). *Climate-related scenarios for financial stability assessment: An application to France*. Working Paper Series No 774. Banque de France.

Arellano, M. & Bond, S., 1991. Some tests of specification for panel data: Monte Carlo evidence and an application to employment equations. The Review of Economic Studies, 58(2), pp.277–297.

Bank of England. (2019). *Enhancing banks' and insurers' approaches to managing the financial risks from climate change*. Supervisory Statement SS3/19.

Batten, S., Sowerbutts, R., & Tanaka, M. (2016). *Let's talk about the weather: The impact of climate change on central banks*. Bank of England Staff Working Paper No. 603.

Battiston, S., Mandel, A., Monasterolo, I., Schütze, F., & Visentin, G. (2017). A climate stress-test of the financial system. *Nature Climate Change, 7*(4), 283–288.

Berger, A. N., & Bouwman, C. H. (2013). How does capital affect bank performance during financial crises? *Journal of Financial Economics, 109*(1), 146–176.

Bolton, P., Despres, M., Pereira da Silva, L. A., Samama, F., & Svartzman, R. (2020). *The green swan: Central banking and financial stability in the age of climate change*. Bank for International Settlements.

Caldecott, B., Harnett, E., Cojoianu, T., Kok, I., & Pfeiffer, A. (2016). *Stranded assets: A climate risk challenge*. Inter-American Development Bank.

Caldecott, B., Dericks, G., & Mitchell, J. (2018). *Stranded assets: Environmental drivers, societal challenges, and supervisory responses*. Springer.

Campiglio, E., Dafermos, Y., Monnin, P., Ryan-Collins, J., Schotten, G., & Tanaka, M. (2018). Climate change challenges for central banks and financial regulators. *Nature Climate Change, 8*(6), 462–468.

Carney, M. (2015). Breaking the tragedy of the horizon–climate change and financial stability. *Speech given at Lloyd's of London, 29*, 220–230.

Carney, M. (2019). *A new horizon*. Speech given at the European Commission Conference: A global approach to sustainable finance, Brussels, 21.

Ceres. (2018). *Turning up the heat: The need for urgent action by banks in adopting climate-smart practices*. Ceres.

Chenet, H., Ryan-Collins, J., & van Lerven, F. (2019). *Climate-related financial policy in a world of radical uncertainty: Towards a precautionary approach*. UCL Institute for Innovation and Public Purpose Working Paper Series (IIPP WP 2019-13).

Climate Bonds Initiative. (2020). *2019 green bond market summary*. Climate Bonds Initiative.

Cochrane, J. H. (2020). *Challenges for central banks*. Economics Working Paper, 2011.

Creswell, J. W., & Creswell, J. D. (2018). *Research design: Qualitative, quantitative, and mixed methods approaches*. Sage.

Creswell, J. W., & Plano Clark, V. L. (2017). *Designing and conducting mixed methods research*. Sage.

Dell'Atti, S., Trotta, A., Iannuzzi, A. P., & Demaria, F. (2017). Corporate social responsibility engagement as a determinant of bank reputation: An empirical analysis. *Corporate Social Responsibility and Environmental Management, 24*(6), 589–605.

Demirgüç-Kunt, A., Pedraza, A., & Ruiz-Ortega, C. (2021). Banking sector performance during the COVID-19 crisis. *Journal of Banking & Finance, 133*, 106305.

Delis, M. D., De Greiff, K., & Ongena, S. (2019). *Being stranded with fossil fuel reserves? Climate policy risk and the pricing of bank loans*. EBRD Working Paper No. 231.

Dietz, S., Bowen, A., Dixon, C., & Gradwell, P. (2016). 'Climate value at risk' of global financial assets. *Nature Climate Change, 6*(7), 676–679.

Eccles, R. G., & Krzus, M. P. (2018). Why companies should report financial risks from climate change. *MIT Sloan Management Review, 59*(3), 1–6.

Ehlers, T., Mojon, B., & Packer, F. (2020, September). Green bonds and carbon emissions: Exploring the case for a rating system at the firm level. *BIS Quarterly Review*.

European Commission. (2018). *Action plan: Financing sustainable growth*. COM(2018) 97 final.

Giglio, S., Kelly, B., & Stroebel, J. (2021). Climate finance. *Annual Review of Financial Economics, 13*, 15–36.

IPCC. (2018). *Global Warming of 1.5°C. An IPCC Special Report on the impacts of global warming of 1.5°C above pre-industrial levels and related global greenhouse gas emission pathways, in the context of strengthening the global response to the threat of climate change, sustainable development, and efforts to eradicate poverty*.

Jung, J., Herbohn, K., & Clarkson, P. (2018). Carbon risk, carbon risk awareness and the cost of debt financing. *Journal of Business Ethics, 150*(4), 1151–1171.

Martínez-Díaz, L., Sidner, L., & McClamrock, J. (2019). *The future of disaster risk pooling for developing countries: Where do we go from here?* World Resources Institute Working Paper.

Nachmany, M., Fankhauser, S., Setzer, J., & Averchenkova, A. (2017). *Global trends in climate change legislation and litigation: 2017 update*. Grantham Research Institute on Climate Change and the Environment.

NGFS. (2019). *A call for action: Climate change as a source of financial risk*. Network for Greening the Financial System.

NGFS. (2020). *Guide to climate scenario analysis for central banks and supervisors*. Network for Greening the Financial System.

Rainforest Action Network, BankTrack, Indigenous Environmental Network, Oil Change International, Reclaim Finance and Sierra Club. (2020). *Banking on Climate Change: Fossil Fuel Finance Report 2020*.

Saunders, M. N., Lewis, P., & Thornhill, A. (2019). *Research methods for business students*. Pearson Education.

Schoenmaker, D., & Schramade, W. (2019). *Principles of sustainable finance*. Oxford University Press.

Scholtens, B., & van't Klooster, S. (2019). Sustainability and bank risk. *Palgrave Communications, 5*(1), 1–8.

Setzer, J., & Byrnes, R. (2020). *Global trends in climate change litigation: 2020 snapshot*. Grantham Research Institute on Climate Change and the Environment and Centre for Climate Change Economics and Policy, London School of Economics and Political Science.

Tanner, T., & Surminski, S. (2016). *Realising the 'triple dividend of resilience': A new business case for disaster risk management*. Springer.

TCFD. (2017). *Recommendations of the task force on climate-related financial disclosures*. Task Force on Climate-related Financial Disclosures.

UNFCCC. (2015). *Paris Agreement*. United Nations Framework Convention on Climate Change.

Vermeulen, R., Schets, E., Lohuis, M., Kölbl, B., Jansen, D. J., & Heeringa, W. (2019). *The heat is on: A framework for measuring financial stress under disruptive energy transition scenarios*. DNB Working Paper No. 625.

Yin, R. K. (2018). *Case study research and applications*. Sage.

Vasco Victor, BEng, MSc, is a dynamic professional with a multidisciplinary background in petroleum engineering and finance. A graduate of the University of Sunderland in London, he holds a Master of Science in Finance and Management, where his research focused on financial risk management in the context of climate change. Vasco also earned a Bachelor of Engineering in Chemical and Petroleum Engineering from the University of Surrey, completing a final year project on desulphurization using ChemCad. He has practical experience in both engineering and finance, having worked as an intern at the National Petroleum Corporation of Namibia, where he ensured fuel quality and infrastructure safety at a 70-million-liter petroleum storage facility. He later served as a Finance Assistant at Sakhiwo Health Solutions, where he developed capital planning models, streamlined financial operations, and supported compliance with healthcare finance regulations. Vasco is currently pursuing the CFA charter and brings strong analytical, multilingual, and cross-functional collaboration skills to every role. His professional interests lie at the intersection of finance, sustainability, and infrastructure development.

Index

A

B

C

D

E

Y. Alhassan et al. (eds.), *Financial Innovation and Sustainable Enterprise in Developing and Emerging Economies*, Research Series on Responsible Enterprise Ecosystems, https://doi.org/10.1007/978-3-032-04500-3

MIX
Papier aus verantwortungsvollen Quellen
Paper from responsible sources
FSC® C105338

If you have any concerns about our products,
you can contact us on
ProductSafety@springernature.com

In case Publisher is established outside the EU,
the EU authorized representative is:
Springer Nature Customer Service Center GmbH
Europaplatz 3, 69115 Heidelberg, Germany

Printed by Libri Plureos GmbH
in Hamburg, Germany